Encounter of Two Worlds:
The Mexican Experience

Enrique René Ramírez
Texas College

KENDALL/HUNT PUBLISHING COMPANY
2460 Kerper Boulevard P.O. Box 539 Dubuque, Iowa 52004-0539

This edition has been printed directly from camera-ready copy.

Copyright © 1992 by Enrique René Ramírez

ISBN 0-8403-7559-X

Printed in the United States of America
10 9 8 7 6 5 4 3 2 1

To my wife Lydia, with love.

CONTENTS

Preface

The world of the Ancient Mexicans has always fascinated the Western mind. For most Americans, Mexico is a place of mystery, enigma, and intrigue. As the editors of *Venture* magazine wrote in 1967: "No people have ever suffered so much agonizing analysis as the Mexicans. They have been admired, envied, dammed, imitated, satirized and serenaded. What, one asks, is so compelling about these people? The answer, perhaps, is in their history."

The celebration of the 500th anniversary's of the discovery of America is a magnificent time to reevaluate the ancient Mexican civilization and its impact on our modern world.

The Aztec society that emerged in the central valley of Mexico half a millennium ago was a microcosm of ancient America. These Indians were the dominant force in Mesoamerica when Hernan Cortes arrived on the shores of Mexico. Their empire represented a compendium of thousands of years of earlier native accomplishments.

Since their discovery, there have been many misconceptions about the role that they played in Mexican history. Ignorance of their traditions and customs resulted in poor judgments. Were they uncivilized people who piled the skulls of sacrificial victims near their religious temples? Were the Spaniards mesmerized by the sight of blood and death when they entered the Aztec cities? Did nightmare visions of the grotesque, the fantastic and the terrifying abound in the Aztec culture?

Often the imagination of the early Spanish writers who wrote about these Indians ran ahead of their common sense. The "father of Aztec chronology," the respectable Spanish Friar Bernardino de Sahagun, even joined the feast of allegorical descriptions. He described the ritual to the rain-god Tlaloc with an intensity that only those who specialize in writing melodramas can fully understand.

Now that the people of the Old and the New Worlds are reevaluating the extraordinary "encounter" that took place five hundred years ago, the story of the Aztec Nation must be reassessed under the light of recent discoveries.

"The Encounter of Two Worlds: The Mexican Experience," explores the world of the past in a general way. It combines historical and archaeological data with "just plain common sense" to narrate an interesting story.

To understand Mexico and its people, it is essential that we study their values, their heritage, and their traditions. By understanding their past we may be able to evaluate their present and their future, and their hopes for a better society. Mexico plays an important role in our national economic activities, especially now that thousands of Mexican immigrants have been accepted by our nation and will become American citizens in the future.

In spite of the great gulf that separates pre-Columbian thought from our own, the culture and traditions that the Aztecs established hundreds of years ago shines down to our day. Its message is still meaningful for those who will take the time to study their civilization and the essence of their way.

Acknowledgments

I would like to thank my friends at the Legal & Historical Research Company of Kansas City, Missouri, for giving me the idea to write this book. They coordinated the publication, prepared the index and served as dedicated advisors. I am also indebted to the staff of Kendall/Hunt Publishing Company, for their patience, interest and constant advice during the manuscript preparation. The magnificent drawings of Hector Ramirez and his concern for accuracy and perfection made the artistic presentation a reality. The research, typing and stylistic improvements made by Roxanna Hall and Blanca Garcia helped substantially the organization of the book and prevented a number of errors.

Grateful acknowledgment is made to Kevin Schmidt and Bruce Burnham for their computer programming assistance, and to Robert Kudrick and Herman Hubbard for their excellent photographic work and high quality standards. Other notable contributors who helped during the research phase were Francisco Santos Beltrán y Emilio B. Sánchez, Biblioteca Nacional, Madrid; Gloria Muñiz Romero, Archivo General de Indias, Seville; Anne Jordan, Rare Books Librarian, LAC, University of Texas; and the staffs of the Museo Nacional de Antropología e Historia, Mexico City, and Museo Regional de Antropología, Mérida, Yucatán. Their belief in the success of the research was even more vital than the facts they provided.

I can do little than bow down in gratitude before the person to whom I dedicate the book - my wife. She worked exceedingly long hours to help in the preparation of the book. Her constant enthusiasm, caring and commitment to the project helped the completion of the work.

Finally, a word of thanks to the community of scholars and researchers whose writings make the study of the Aztec nation possible.

The Sun Stone, also known as the Calendar Stone.

Figure 1   **El Castillo, or Temple of Kulkulcan, Chichen Itzá, Yucatán.**

The Discovery of New Worlds

The Columbian Enterprise

Christopher Columbus discovered America on October 12, 1492. Fifty years ago the great naval historian Samuel Eliot Morrison called the ordeal an "accident." But more recently, professor James Riley has noted that the event "was neither an accident nor a shockingly bold venture into the unknown" (29-30). It was a well-planned voyage that sought to enrich the sponsors and find a new commercial route to East Asia. Columbus also hoped to discover new territories, expand Christianity, and aggrandize the glory of Spain.

While Columbus did not find the western route to Asia that he sought, his achievement was greater. Historians have called it perhaps the most important event in recorded history. His accomplishment increased significantly the size of the known world and changed considerably the history of humanity. It brought western civilization and Christianity to the New World and, as researcher Robert Royal points out, it launched a process that brought the world's people together (46).

Television executive producer Zvi Dor-Ner and author William Scheller have written "that Christopher Columbus changed the world." The forces he set in motion transformed Europe, Africa and America, and removed the Western Hemisphere from the realm of unknown territory. The discovery of America enriched European civilization and resulted in a migration of thousands of people that continues even to this day (Dor-Ner 1).

It also created an ecological disaster in the New

Figure 2   **Pyramid of the Sun, Teotihuacan.**

World, exterminated millions of people, and extended the institution of African slavery to the Western Hemisphere. The undertaking brought colonialism, the plunder of a pristine land, and the destruction of ancient societies and magnificent cities the world had never seen.

Columbus organized his enterprise very carefully. He studied the scientific and geographical records of the times and the results of the Portuguese western African explorations. He also used his experience as a seasoned navigator for the planning of his voyage of discovery.

When he left the port of Palos in Southern Spain Friday morning, August 3, 1492, amid the tears and lamentations of those who bid the adventurers a farewell, he was sure of success. His personal diary expresses a sense of satisfaction and divine calling. He saw a need to Christianize the "princes, lands, and towns of the Orient" for the glory of God and of the Royal Highness that had entrusted him with the historic mission. (Colón 28).

His personal motives were never questioned when his ships sailed to the unknown impulsed by the dry wind of the Sahara desert. While the Portuguese had debated the distance involved on purely practical reasons, "the venture was considered risky but not insane" (Riley 35). What is more important, before Columbus sail to the New World no one analyzed the possible outcome of his enterprise with the emphasis and interest that modern generations are doing it.

Some Important Considerations

Sailing under an agreement with the Spanish Crown, the Genoese sailor attempted to reach the continent of Asia by sailing to the West. Unaware of the existence of a large land mass in the midst of his route, Columbus never considered the possibility of a setback or the eventual failure of his plan. Since he believed the circumference of the earth to be about half its actual size, he was confident of fulfilling his goal in a reasonable time. Columbus expected to arrive at his final destination after sailing westward for about 3,500 miles.

While the discoverer of the Western Hemisphere had not considered finding North America during his journey, he anticipated the discovery of new islands between Europe and Asia. Since these lands were probably uninhabited, one of the principal problems of the expedition was to carry aboard the ships enough provisions for a return trip (Riley 35).

On the other hand, to overload the vessels with supplies would have reduced their sailing capabilities and might have given the impression that the trip was going to take longer than expected. After careful consideration, Columbus decided to take sufficient food and water for a year. His small ships were vulnerable and "should be viewed as akin to space vessels, in that they carried all the supplies necessary for the crew. When the water and food were consumed, there were nowhere to turn and death by starvation or dehydration was inevitable." (Riley, 31, 34).

A shrewd businessman, Columbus represented the traditional Italian mercantilist philosophy of controlling wealth by state monopoly. To carry out that doctrine, and to secure his long time aspiration, he demanded from the Spanish monarchs the title of Admiral for himself and his descendants. He also requested the governorship of new territories and the receipt of ten percent of the wealth he encountered during his journey.

The Spanish Crown rejected initially Columbus demands and almost undid the enterprise before it had begun. The Spanish monarchs could not agree initially to something so uncertain and dangerous as sailing to the uncharted waters of the West. As historian J. H. Parry writes: "Much ink and erudition has been expended on the problem of what Columbus hoped to find, and probably the exact answer will never be known. He was a secretive man, who kept the details of the `enterprise of the Indies' to himself" (42).

The Spanish monarchs finally allowed Columbus to sail according to a set of rules known as the *Capitulaciones de Santa Fe* (Stipulations of Santa Fe). The government of Spain did not invest any capital on the venture because the recent wars against the Muslim had exhausted the royal treasury. The story that Queen Isabella sold her jewels to pay for the expedition fall within the realm of fantasy.

The financial records of the diocese of Badajoz in Spain show that the Queen's adviser Luis de Santángel, a member of a distinguished Jewish family, persuaded the *Santa Cruzada* (Holy Crusade) to lend the expedition $19,800. Columbus also gave an additional $32,500 for the enterprise. Merchants from Seville and Palos provided the remaining balance for the operation, which cost about $151, 780 in modern financial terms (Riley 39, Dor-Ner 119).

When Columbus left Spain and set sail for the west his purpose was to find a new trade route to Eastern Asia. The establishment of a commercial linkage with that region had been for many years one of the main objectives of both Portuguese and Spanish explorations. The success of a commercial enterprise and not the spirit of adventure, therefore, impulsed Columbus to travel to the west in search of the East.

Tales of Mystery and Wonder

The story of the discovery of America starts with the Crusades (1095-1291). These military expeditions were organized by the Christian monarchs of Europe to recover the Holy Land from the Muslim. Though the purpose of these religious wars failed, the ordeal of the Crusaders rekindled western interest in Asia and the Middle East.

The sensational tales of the European soldiers who went to Palestine during the Crusades amazed those who lived in the despair and misery of the Middle Ages. The travelers talked about the luxury and comfort of the Muslim society and the beauty and simplicity of their life style. They described the lore of oriental art, the literature and the strange remedies and medications used in the Middle East.

During the wars, Venetian and Genoese merchants were very active carrying men and materials to Palestine. On their return trip, they brought back silk, species and luxury goods for sale to the Europeans. The success of these activities and the stories of the returning soldier increased western knowledge of the Middle East and spurred interest in foreign travel.

European merchants and missionaries traveled to the regions beyond the Black Sea under relative security. The Italian traders built colonies in the cities of Constantinople, Kaffa, and Tana, and expanded their business activities to central Asia. Their financial, trading and commercial houses became very wealthy. For over one hundred years these merchants pioneered a profitable commercial trade with the Eastern World.

Slave Trade in the Medieval World

There was also a profitable trade in oriental slaves. Geographer Henry H. Hart notes that most of the traffic was in the hands of the Italians. According to him, Venetian merchants sold about two thousand women and eunuchs in Alexandria every year. The Egyptian used the female slaves as courtesans, servants and entertainers. They also purchased human beings for their armies. In Italy, merchants bought and sold human beings by the thousands during the thirteenth century. "One wonders," writes Hart, "at those who argue for the purity of blood of any European nation" (10-11).

The trade was not just limited to the Middle East and the Mediterranean. Hart provides very impressive information about the sale of slaves to the nobility and to the rich landlords of northern Europe. Most of those who bought slaves used them to replace their paid servants. The author mentions that "a law of Florence of 1364 . . .permitted the importation of slaves for resale or gift. In 1364 there were so many slaves in Genoa and Venice that their presence threatened the stability of the state." Even March Polo owned a slave who he called "Peter the Tartar" (Hart 10-11).

Spices and Mercantilism

During this time, the spice trade also flourished and made the Italian businessmen very rich. Parry notes that the shortages of winter feed for cattle forced the Europeans to slaughter most of their herds every autumn. The beef was salted, smoked or pickled for winter consumption. To prevent spoilage, the farmers used great quantities of spices as condiments and preservatives (Parry 32).

Between 1250 and 1300, several Venetian merchants went to China to see the magnificent wealth and wonders of that nation. Nicolo and Matteo Polo journeyed to the Far East in 1260. On the return visit Niccolo brought his son Marco, and the three remained in China for twenty-one years. In 1275 they visited the capital of the Mongolian emperor Kublai Khan. For the next seventeen years young Marco Polo served the Chinese ruler in various official positions. The occupation provided him with the opportunity to visit most of the empire and study oriental customs. In 1295 the Polos returned to Italy, where Marco published his experiences after being imprisoned for a short time.

The Description of the World of Marco Polo became the most important source of knowledge about the Far East until the Portuguese reached India in the sixteenth century. It expanded the accounts of the Franciscan missionaries, merchants and soldiers who had visited the region. While Marco Polo's story was not widely accepted initially, and many of his contemporaries did not believe the account, the tale amazed many influential Europeans.

Merchants and businessmen from northern Europe developed a special interest in the people who lived in faraway and mysterious lands. Afterward, many of them visited the Court of the Great Khan, but little is known today about their journeys. A copy of Marco Polo's book accompanied Columbus during his first trip to America.

The Short Glory of the Italian Trade

During the fourteenth century Genoa and Venice expanded considerably their commercial contacts with the Middle East and Asia. Hundreds of merchant ships traveled to Asia Minor, Egypt, Syria, and the Black Sea to bring spices, porcelain, silk, perfumes, cotton cloth and jewels. The Italian cities became the principal trading centers of the Mediterranean and the richest in Europe. China, Japan, India, Arabia and Persia became famous for their precious stones, jade, fabrics, species, luxuriant goods and fabulous wealth.

In May 29, 1453, the Ottoman Turks interrupted the European trade when the armies of the Sultan Mehemmed II captured the city of Constantinople. The invaders swept from Asia Minor the Christian outposts and the Italian commercial enclaves. Trade with central and eastern Asia came to a standstill by the aggressive activities of the Turks. To the South, the trading posts of Palestine and Arabia also fell victims to the onslaught of Islamic raiding parties.

The Muslim merchants who controlled the remaining trading routes began to demand heavy tolls from the Europeans. Religious differences, the Plague and criminal recklessness also contributed to the end of eastern commerce (Hart 262).

With the expansion of the Ottoman Empire, Muslim

competition, and the decrease of trade the political and economic importance of the Italian cities declined. The end of their commercial supremacy saw the emergence of Portuguese and Spanish seaports as new centers of trade. Those with access to the mid Atlantic were to keep a substantial control of European commerce for the next two hundred years.

Bruun and Commager summarize these events as follows: "The Mediterranean ceased to be `the middle sea' as it had been since classical times. First Lisbon and Cadiz, then Amsterdam and London, usurped the lead as center of maritime commerce, while the Italian ports sank into `the slow white death that waits for privilege in defeat" (43).

The Portuguese Challenge

While the capture of Constantinople by the Turks in 1453 has been traditionally held responsible for the shift of sea trade to the Atlantic, two other historical factors should be considered. First, the Renaissance technical innovations enabled Iberian merchants and sailors to venture out beyond the sight of land and voyage to unknown seas. Second, the support that the government gave to sea ventures increased interest in exploration. With the extension of business operations to northern Europe, the merchants had the necessary incentives to make the Atlantic the center of their commercial activities.

The application of geography and astronomy to navigation and the development of better shipbuilding techniques made the nature of exploring the Atlantic much easier. The invention of new tools such as the mariner's compass, the astrolabe and the triangular sail also improved the sailing of ships. The use of firearms and better navigation charts expanded the expansion of voyages of exploration to remote areas of western Africa.

Since the beginning of the thirteenth century Castilian and Portuguese sailors had been exploring the coasts of Africa. By 1460 Portuguese navigators had made significant progress in establishing profitable trading outposts in that region. The accumulation of wealth that resulted from their commercial ventures increased Portugal's financial reserves and provided capital for subsequent undertakings. Portuguese monarchs, associated with bankers and traders, financed most of the new explorations and set the standards of leadership required for the expansion of the maritime operations.

The Portuguese took the lead in the exploration of West Africa as result of the need for grain, fish and slave workers for the sugar plantations of Madeira. Other motives were the need to expand the country's wealth with gold from Africa, investigate the extent of Moorish power and discover new profitable trade routes.

The Exploration of West Africa

Under the leadership of Prince Henry the Navigator, the Portuguese began to explore the coasts of Africa in 1415. Merchants, sea captains and bankers supported the Prince's efforts to increase the nation's prestige and power. He established a navigation school and an observatory to study navigation, improve sailing techniques and design better ships.

The first Portuguese explorers did not know the size and shape of the African continent. They made no attempts to find initially a new route to the Indies. As Parry suggests, it was not until the death of Prince Henry that the Portuguese considered the possibility of traveling to India by way of South Africa (Parry 29).

By 1436 Prince Henry's ships were sailing pass Cape Bojador and Western Sahara. Portuguese sailors reached Senegal and Cape Verde in 1446 and in the subsequent forty years they established outposts in the African coast from Ghana to Angola. In 1475 Portuguese vessels crossed the Equator, and in 1488 Bartolomeu Dias reached the Cape of Good Hope.

During the third quarter of the fifteenth century, Andalusian and Castilian sailors developed a special interest in West Africa and often contested the Portuguese hegemony in the area. An outbreak of hostilities between Portugal and Spain in 1474 resulted in the Treaty of Alcacovas that granted Spain the Canary Islands in return for Portuguese's monopoly of the African trade and exploration.

Slavery and Colonial Wealth

The discovery made by Bartolomeu Dias fulfilled the

Portuguese dream of finding a southern passage to the Indies. Ten years later Vasco Da Gama sailed to the Kenyan enclave of Malindi in his way to Calicut, India. To commemorate the occasion, the Portuguese built there a monument that is still standing today.

By the end of the fifteenth century, Portugal's African territories were producing more than 1600 pounds of gold a year. Products from the tropical areas were reaching the European markets in increasing number. The Portuguese also gained access to thousands of African slaves who they sold or used in the sugar plantations. They established a profitable commercial monopoly of the slave trade and maintained it for many years.

With the discovery and settlement of Brazil and the establishment of Spanish plantations in the New World, the slave trade augmented considerably and so the profits of the Portuguese merchants. In the last seventy years of the sixteenth century the Portuguese shipped between 500,000 and 800,000 slaves to the Western Hemisphere, according to Professor James Duffy of Brandeis University (36).

The Spanish Response

In Spain, the formation of a unified centralized government accounted for the success of its commercial expansion. The War of Reconquista that the feudal Christian kingdoms waged against the Moslems for many years helped to unify the country. During the struggle, a sentiment of solidarity that culminated with the union of the kingdoms of Castille and Aragon in 1479 emerged among the royal families that ruled the Spanish feudal states.

While the kingdom of Castille was fighting the Muslim, the Crowns of Aragon and Cataluna were extending their political control to the central and eastern Mediterranean. In the subsequent one-hundredth years, their rulers seized the Baleares Islands, Sardinia, Sicily, southern Italy and the Duchy of Athens in the Aegean Sea. The kingdom of Aragon fortified by the commercial wealth of the Spanish merchants expanded trade throughout the Mediterranean.

The Spanish historian Claudio Sánchez Albornoz wrote in 1929 that the Reconquista "created a war superexcitement that took Aragon to Italy and pushed

Portugal to explore the African coast and the Atlantic, increased the religious spirit of the people and the influence of the Church" (3).

During the fourteenth century, Portuguese and Spanish merchants did a substantial amount of business in England and the Baltic region. Their ships used the Strait of Gibraltar and the Atlantic coast for most of the business activities. "Once the Oceanic Age opened," note Geoffrey Bruun and Henry Steele Commager, "the states that faced the Atlantic were the favorites of fortune, and the Mediterranean cities lost the commercial primacy they had long enjoyed." Other historians have suggested that the farsightedness of the Iberian monarchs, the end of the Reconquista and the development of better technology contributed to the commercial expansion of Portugal and Spain (43).

The Age of Explorations

Columbus discovered America six years before Vasco Da Gama found the new route to India. The Italian sailor never realized that he had reached a world that had been isolated for thousands of years. There are many claims concerning earlier maritime travel to the American continent. Of these tales, the one that has more validity is the story of the Vikings' journeys to North America.

In 1838 the Royal Society of Copenhagen submitted evidence of Norse voyages to the New World during the tenth and eleventh centuries. Recent archaeological evidence supports the claim that Viking sailors may have visited Labrador, Newfoundland, Nova Scotia and parts of northeastern United States during that time.

According to the Norwegian sagas of the thirteenth century, Eric the Red traveled to Greenland in 982 A.D. and established there a settlement that survived until the fifteenth century. About 1000 A.D., his son Leif Erickson explored the coasts of North America and settled Vinland in the northeastern part of Canada. The settlers abandoned it fifteen years later because of increasing Indian attacks. The exact location of this settlement has never been found. The Norse discoveries had little impact on the history of North America or on the development of world civilization.

Christopher Columbus

The life of Columbus has been a challenge to historians. The hidden character of his personal activities has made the task of investigation difficult. The misinformation created by his son Ferdinand, who wanted to hide from the Spanish society his plebeian origin, has not helped either. Columbus birthplace has always been in question and there have been doubts about his true origins.

He was born in Genoa, Italy, in 1451. No much is known about his youth, except that he had little education, was trained as a weaver and preferred the life of a sailor since an early age. For many years he lived in Portugal where he became an accomplished map maker. It is possible that he conceived his plan for a new route to the Indies while preparing geographical navigation charts in Lisbon.

In 1474 he exchanged information with the Florentine scholar Paolo Toscanelli concerning the possibility of sailing west toward the Indies. While in Portugal, Columbus realized that the undertaking required men, supplies and money and that he had to persuade others to support the expedition if it was to become a reality.

There are no means of ascertaining if Columbus presented his plan to other nations of Europe. He visited Ireland, the Portuguese enclaves in West Africa, and perhaps Iceland, but his writings show very little information about his professional activities outside Portugal.

In 1484 Columbus presented his "Enterprise of the Indies" to the Portuguese court, but King John II of Portugal rejected his proposal. Bartolomeu Dias had recently rounded the Cape of Good Hope and found a sea route to India. The Portuguese monarch preferred to continue the exploration of the African coast than to begin a different project.

In 1485 Columbus went to Spain to propose his plan to the Spanish Crown. After waiting for seven years for a decision, he finally received the required support. In 1492 Ferdinand and Isabella, representing the union of the kingdoms of Aragon and Castille, accepted Columbus proposition.

Figure 3   **Christopher Columbus**

The Italian sailor left Spain with two caravels and a nao after he made the necessary preparations for the journey. His crew consisted of 87 men, most of them seasoned sailors from Palos. Only one of them had a serious criminal record. The three ships were well-suited for the purpose since they could be controlled by a small crew. They were sleek, fast vessels that could withstand the storms of the mid-Atlantic with little effort.

Columbus personal ambitions apparently determined the selection of the nao Santa María. According to the Italian professor Pietro Barozzi, since the navigator's destination was the land of the Grand Khan, he assumed that upon arrival he would see a local potentate. To arrive in a foreign court in less than an imposing ship would have been unfavorable to his mission and to the respect owed to the king and queen of Spain.

The Discovery of America

The Columbian fleet stopped in the Canaries Islands for about a month to repair the rudder of "La Pinta." The ships then proceeded west on a predetermined course along the 28 degrees parallel that followed the prevailing northeastern trade winds of the Mid Atlantic Ocean. After thirty-three days at sea, where he had to deal with the threat of mutiny, the uncertainty of the trip, and several navigation errors, Columbus discovered America.

Columbus landfall was a small island in the Bahamas that its inhabitants called Guanahani and he renamed San Salvador. There is some uncertainty today about the location of that landing place. No reliable records of the original log of Columbus exist except a copy made by the priest Bartolome Las Casas. The original record of the visit "has not been seen since it was dispatched to Queen Isabela on the Admiral's return to Spain" (Judge 568).

After a detailed study of the first Columbian voyage to the New World, geographer Joseph Judge has concluded that Columbus landed at Samana Cay in the Bahamas, not in Watling Island as has been commonly accepted. After the initial landing, the Spaniards exchanged presents with the local Arawak inhabitants (568).

The Spaniards stayed in the Bahamas for several days and then left for the northeast where they discovered

Cuba. In December, Columbus sailed south toward Hispaniola to search for other territories. He reached the coast of Haiti at Christmas time, where he lost near Cape Haitien the Santa Maria, the biggest of the three Spanish ships.

Martin Alonzo Pinzón, the captain of La Pinta, also left the expedition then to search for gold and glory. After almost five months in the Caribbean, Columbus returned to Spain on March 15, 1493. He was disappointed for not having discovered the riches of the East Indies, but highly satisfied with the results of his maritime adventure.

The monarchs of Spain received Columbus with great honor. They awarded him the title of grandee of Spain, a member of the nobility. They also promoted Columbus to the rank of Admiral of the Ocean Sea and appointed him Viceroy of the new discovered territories. After that, Columbus returned to the Western Hemisphere three more times to discover other islands and the coasts of South and Central America.

Columbus himself established the first Spanish settlement in the West Indies. He built a small fort in Haiti with timbers from the Santa Maria. He named it La Navidad and left behind thirty-nine members of the surviving crew of the Santa Maria. After his departure, the settlers turned quickly to pillage and the kidnapping of native women. The Indians reacted by killing them and destroying the fort.

During his second voyage Columbus founded Isabela, about seventy miles to the east of the first settlement. In 1498 the Spaniards, exhausted by illness, dissension, and Indian attacks abandoned the colony and moved to Santo Domingo, the site of the present capital of the Dominican Republic. The subjugation of the native population of Hispaniola did not take long. By 1502 the colony had attained peace. After that year, it became the center of operations for the conquest of the Antilles and for the launching of new expeditions to the mainland.

The First Settlements

Columbus was a poor administrator and could not handle the responsibilities of governor. He tried to govern the colony honestly but failed. In the process he created many powerful enemies. Some of them returned to Spain with complaints about him. The Crown sent Francisco de Bobadilla to the colony as a royal commissioner to investigate the accusations. He arrested Columbus and sent him back to Spain to face charges of dereliction of duty. Columbus was found innocent but could not return to his previous position. Nicolas de Ovando succeeded him as governor of the colony in 1502. The new official promptly enslaved the surviving Indians to satisfy Columbus detractors and force them to work in the colonial mines.

Nicolas de Ocampo explored the island of Cuba in 1508. Three years later Diego Velasquez organized the first settlement on that island. Later, the Spaniards founded additional colonial towns in Cuba to expand their political control and suppress growing influence of the Indians. In 1509 Juan de Esquivel conquered Jamaica after a long struggle with the natives of that island.

Juan Ponce de Leon founded a colony in the northern part of Puerto Rico in 1508. The following year the government named Diego Colon, the son of Columbus, as the official governor of the West Indies.

Colonization and Exploration

The Spanish exploration and colonization of America followed initially a mercantilist scheme of mining exploitation instead of a program of agricultural development. Columbus himself could be blamed for this policy. Bruun and Commager have observed that "the vivid phrases in which he described his discoveries fired the zeal and cupidity of restless men."

Columbus insisted that the Antilles had many spices, and great mines of gold and other metals. The aborigines were marvelously timorous with no other arms than weapons made of canes. According to Bruum and Commager "this inviting prospect of a gentle people who possessed `gold incalculable' and were `so guileless and so generous with all they possess' had an irresistible attraction. It is small wonder that when Columbus set out on his second voyage 200 stowaways hid themselves aboard his ships" (47).

Columbus believed that the new land could be exploited at a very low cost. After the discovery he wrote to the Spanish monarchs saying that the Indians made good servants. "Your Highness may, whenever you so wish, have them all sent to Castille or keep them all captives in

Figure 4   Façade of La Iglesia, Chichen Itza, Yucatán.

Figure 5   Serpent head, Temple of the Warriors,
Chichen Itza, Yucatán.

the island, for with fifty armed men you will keep them all under your sway and will make them do all you may desire" (Achenbach 11).

The Spanish government, considering the amount of gold that was to be mined followed the Castilian commercial criteria of paying the employees who were involved in the exploration and settlement of the colonies. The government did not allow them initially to share the wealth. This system of government control of the mineral resources created discontent among the earlier settlers who were told to look for a gold that they could not keep. The government changed the system eventually.

The Final Outcome

The Spanish explorations of the West Indies gave the Spaniards a new outlook at life. Their relative isolation broken by an age of discovery, they thrust themselves into an orgy of false hopes and exaggerated expectations. Hundreds of Spanish adventurers went to the Caribbean to enrich themselves with the gold and silver of the Indies. They expected to make substantial fortunes overnight and to return as wealthy men to the Old World.

Spain, too, envisioned streams of gold and silver filling their coffers. The government prepared itself to control the richness of the New World by promulgating thousands of laws of doubtful substance. As the excitement and drama increased, the Spanish enslaved the Indians of the West Indies to work in an unprofitable mining economy.

The West Indies were not the proper setting for the type of colonization envisioned by the first Europeans who came to America. The native populations of those islands were small and still living in the stone age. The resources of the land were limited and agriculture was unreliable. The settlers could not find sufficient gold to pay for their expenses. They "had expected to find the treasures of fabled Cathay and the Orient -- not and endless strings of islands and dark tropical coastline peopled by half-naked Indians" (Wood 19).

The enslavement of the Arawaks and the killing or wholesale shipment abroad of the Caribs reduced the available labor force. Thousands of Indians also died as result of European diseases since they lacked natural immunity. In Hispaniola " by 1514 only 26,000 of the island's original half a million natives would survive; by 1517, only 11,000. Smallpox would strike the last stragglers in 1518. Within fifty years of their first contact with Europeans, the Arawaks would be dead from disease and over work," writes Dor-Ner (218).The same pattern of human misery and destruction was repeated throughout the rest of the Caribbean islands.

By 1515 Spain's New World empire was collapsing. The limited treasure found, the considerable amount of expenses required to maintain the settlements, and the extermination of the native populations caused a serious setback to the colonial plans. Many colonists consider abandoning the islands and returning to Spain. Others were demoralized and afraid since they, too, were dying from unknown fevers, modorra (drowsiness) and "the pestilence of the tropics."

Two important developments saved the Spanish empire during this critical time. In Hispaniola, Nicolas de Ovando realized that the true wealth of the new settlements lay in the production of sugar and tobacco, not in gold mining. Frustrated with the Indian labor force, he began to import black slaves from West Africa to work in the sugar plantations and tobacco fields. The cultivation of these products on a commercial scale saved the colonies from a possible extinction.

The other event, which really rekindled the old dying dream of glory and wealth, was the discovery of the Aztec Empire. Within three years of the conquest of Mexico, the Spaniards had overrun most of the native civilizations of the Western Hemisphere and overwhelmed the entire continents of North and South America searching for gold. Historian Wood writes: "In the first century of conquest the weight of gold from South America alone mounted to something on the order of 10.5 million troy ounces, or 750,000 pounds -- more than a third of all the gold produced in the entire world during those years." But not only gold increased the richness of Spain and its citizens. The colonists also found "two mountains of silver at Potosí on the Andean plateau and Guanajuato in Mexico" (Wood 19).

They promptly extracted the new wealth with the sweat and toil of the Indians.

2

The Messengers of Death

La Villa Rica de la Vera Cruz

At noontime, on Holy Thursday, April 21, 1519, Hernan Cortes anchored his small fleet on the eastern coast of Mexico and prepared to land. The following day, on Good Friday, he went ashore with 508 soldiers, 110 sailors, 200 Cuban Indians, two Mayan interpreters, several Black servants, 16 horses, 14 cannons and a handful of dogs.

Cortes began, in that way, the conquest of one of the most powerful empires off the world, a country he had never seen before and of which he knew very little. His only sources of knowledge of the Aztec empire had been the reports of few Indians and the tall stories of those who had survived two previous expeditions into the area. Among Cortes' soldiers were 32 archers and 13 musketeers, a military force that proved to be a very valuable asset to the conqueror.

Within months, the Spaniards founded La Villa Rica de la Vera Cruz near the Totonac town of Quiahuiztlan. Six years later, they moved the settlement to a new location called La Antigua. By the end of the century the colony had been relocated to its original site. For over two hundred years that settlement became the principal seaport of the Gulf Coast and the major link between colonial Mexico and Spain.

The First Spanish Expeditions

The Spaniards had begun their incursions into the

Mexican territory many years before the arrival of Cortes. In 1502, during his fourth voyage to the New World, Columbus visited the island of Guanaja on the coast of Honduras. He saw there a large Indian merchant canoe with men, women and children. The occupants carried weapons, provisions, cacao beans, garments and many other articles; and apparently, they were passengers and traders. Columbus retained one of the Indians as an interpreter, and renamed him Juan Perez (Morison 595).

The natives told Columbus that they were "from a province called Maian." The Spaniards probably saw then one of the trading canoes of the Chontal Maya. These native merchants sold or bartered Mexican goods with the natives of the Gulf coast and Central America. Their trading vessels traveled regularly from Yucatan to Honduras and Nicaragua.

The historian Samuel Eliot Morison wrote that Columbus noticed on these Indians "wealth, culture, and industry" and "that he was tempted to change course and follow them." If Columbus had done so, the Indians "would undoubtedly have conducted him to the Gulf of Honduras" (596).

If, on the other hand, Columbus had turned north instead of south after the encounter, he probably would have discovered the splendors of the ancient Mayan civilization of Yucatán. That event could have given him the success and fame that he had been searching for so many years in the New World.

The Cordoba's Enterprise

In January 1517, a wealthy landowner from Cuba named Francisco Hernandez de Córdoba, organized an expedition to discover new territories on the mainland. On February 8 he embarked for the Mexican coast with three ships and 110 men with orders to coast along the continent and barter with the natives. He followed a westerly direction until a storm redirected his destination. Twenty-one days later the Spaniards discovered the Yucatan peninsula and the Maya civilization.

In March, Córdoba and his men visited Cape Catoche, where the sailors saw a beautiful Indian city they called "Gran Cairo." When the explorers went ashore, they had a violent and dangerous confrontation with the local natives that wounded fifteen soldiers. They reembarked,

Figure 6   Hernán Cortes

and for the next fifteen days Cordoba continued to explore the Mexican coast, sailing during the daytime and anchoring at night.

A lack of water forced the expedition to land in Campeche on the Gulf Coast, where the Indians threatened them again. They left the area and sailed along the coast toward the village of Champoton, south of Campeche. Another violent confrontation with the Maya that killed fifty Spanish soldiers and wounded many others ended the journey. Cordoba and his men returned to Cuba disappointed and suffering from thirst and hunger. He died few days later from wounds he had received in the skirmish with the Indians.

In spite of Cordoba's disaster, the tales of gold, silver, and rich Indians cities, told and retold by the survivors, continued to impress the Spaniards. The sailors gave astonishing accounts of massive temples and towns where people dressed with rich and costly garments, almost like Europeans. The report that they gave to the governor of Cuba mentions Indians living in masonry houses with rich cultivated maize fields and possessing large amounts of gold and other treasures.

The Grijalva Expedition

These accounts developed so much interest that the governor of Cuba Diego Velazquez decided to send another expedition to the Mexican coast the following year. Two hundred forty men, under the command of Juan de Grijalva, sailed in four ships for the mainland on April 8, 1518. One month later, the expedition discovered the island of Consumel in southeastern Mexico.

Grijalva explored the Mexican coast as far as present-day Veracruz, trading and gathering information. In Campeche he battled the Maya, as Cordoba had done before. But, for the remaining of the trip, the Indians received the Spaniards peacefully and even provided food and water to them.

On the Banderas river, Grijalva received messengers and presents from Moctezuma II, the Aztec ruler. After exploring the region for several more days,? Grijalva returned to Cuba on September 21, 1518. While he had explored most of the southern and eastern coasts of Mexico, the governor of Cuba considered the expedition a failure. Velazquez believed that Grijalva should have taken the opportunity offered by the peaceful Indian contacts to establish a permanent settlement on the mainland (Solis 36-40).

The governor worried that someone else might attempt to send an expedition to the Mexican coast after the rumors of the discoveries by Córdoba and Grijalva had begun to circulate in the colonies. To prevent this development, the governor decided to outfit another expedition for the exploration of the Mexican coast. He named Hernan Cortes to command the new venture, with specific instructions to explore the region and return to Cuba (Díaz del Castillo 31-32).

Hernan Cortes

Cortés was a rash, thirty-four years old, landowner who was looking for fame, glory, and the opportunity to make a fortune. The son of a military officer, he grew up in the town of Medellín on the Spanish region of Extremadura. There are few details about his life, but we know that he attended the University of Salamanca where he studied law for two years. Uncertain about his future and impelled by enthusiasm, in 1504 he left Spain for the New World. In the Caribbean he participated in the conquest of Hispaniola and Cuba and helped found the city of Santiago in 1511.

Cortés became a business man and a landowner in Cuba, after working briefly as a notary public. He was arrested and condemned once for his political views. Velazquez, however, rehabilitated the soldier and even appointed him as mayor of Santiago. After living fifteen years in the colonies, where he gained abundant experience, Cortés was a logical choice for the command of the expedition.

While in Cuba, he learned of the misfortunes of the two expeditions that had visited the Mexican coast, and readily accepted the command of the third one when the governor offered it to him. With the official commission secured, Cortés made plans for the journey using his funds and several loans from his friends.

Cortés enlisted many men for the venture, especially those who had previously sailed for the mainland and had experience. He also recruited many survivors of the two previous expeditions, and purchased large quantities of supplies and equipment for the voyage. Slowly, the

Spaniard adventurer organized a fleet of eleven vessels for the journey and made preparations to depart from Cuba on February 1519.

Apparently, the pace of Cortes' activities made Velazquez apprehensive and jealous. The governor changed his mind even before the preparations were completed, but did not relieve Cortes from his responsibility. The future conqueror of Mexico disobeyed the governor's instructions to appear before him and sailed to the West on February 18, 1519. He had to smuggle himself aboard his vessel to prevent being arrested by the local authorities.

The Search for Glory

The expedition crossed the Yucatan Channel and arrived to Consumel island few days later. The Spaniards rested there and reviewed their small army. Cortes followed the route of the two previous expeditions, and on his way, he rescued Jeronimo de Aguilar, a Spanish sailor that the Indians had captured before.

Aguilar had lived in Yucatan for many years as a slave of the Indians and spoke several of their dialects. After his rescue, he served as an interpreter and became one of the expedition's best and most dedicated soldiers. His knowledge of the Indian customs and traditions served the Spaniards very well, especially during their march to the Aztec capital.

The expedition continued its course along the coast of Yucatan and Campeche. The Spaniards made several attempts to disembark and explore the lowlands of Yucatan, but had no success. Finally, in March 1519, they landed at Centla on the Tabasco coast, where the Chontal Maya also gave them a violent reception.

The Spaniards defeated the Indians, and their chief gave Cortes twenty young women as a present. One of them, Malintzin, was a handsome and intelligent woman who became Cortes' interpreter and mistress. A priest baptized her later as Dona Marina, but she became better known as Malinche by the Spaniards who accompanied Cortes across the land.

The Indian maiden told Cortes about the Aztec empire and of the political conditions that prevailed there. This information enabled him to prepare adequate plans for the subjection of the Mexican nation.

The Beginning of the End

On April 21, 1519, Cortés arrived at the site where Grijalva had traded with the Indians. The Spaniards landed without any opposition. Two Indian chiefs, one of them the local governor and the other an Aztec officer, came with more than four thousand unarmed soldiers to greet them. The Indians and the Spaniards exchanged presents and provisions and Cortés asked them if he could see their ruler.

To insure that there were no doubts about the Spanish intentions, Cortés ordered a display of military might. It included the firings of several cannons and a cavalry charge. Impressed by the performance, the Indians sent messengers to the Aztec emperor with pictographic sketches of the Spaniards. Cortés added a statement to the governor's message that said he was the envoy of a great king and the bearer of a commission to the Aztec emperor.

Moctezuma, who already had been informed of Cortés' arrival to the Mexican coast, could not decide about the reception to be given to the strangers. The Aztec leader was a man deeply influenced by the past and superstitious beliefs clouded his judgment during this critical and important period.

Meanwhile, the Indians built for the Spaniards more than one thousand huts, and brought them ample supplies of food. Seven or eight days later, the Indian Chief Teudilli returned with many presents and Moctezuma's reply. The delicacy and workmanship of the bounty astonished the Spaniards. Among the gifts were gold necklaces and ornaments, a turquoise mask, rich mantles and garments of white and colored textiles, blankets, many colored feathers, exotic birds, and many jewels and objects of gold and silver.

Among the finest of the Aztec presents were two disks, one of them made of pure silver that weighted more than twenty-six pounds and represented the moon. The other one of hammered gold and weighting more that fifty pounds represented the sun. According to the chronicler Francisco López de Gómara, the Aztecs had prepared these gifts for the members of the Grijalva expedition, if they ever returned to the Mexican coast (41-43, 61-62).

Moctezuma's ambassadors told Cortés that the emperor

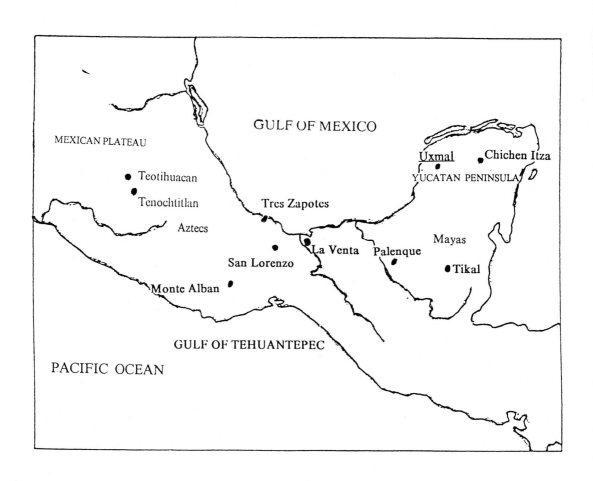

Figure 7 **MESOAMERICA**

rejoiced with the news of their arrival. That he wanted to provide the Spaniards with everything that they may need, but he could not meet with them because he was ill and could not travel to the coast. As for Cortes going to his capital, he said the journey was very dangerous and difficult. The high mountains, the arid deserts and other uncounted hardships would have made the journey to central Mexico very hard.

The Journey Begins

The gifts did not calm the expectations of the Spaniards and they continued to make preparations for their journey to the Aztec capital. Cortés searched for allies among the local Indians and found the Totonacs willing to help him, despite the Spanish destruction of many of their idols and religious symbols. The Aztecs had recently conquered them and they were still unhappy with their presence in the region. Cortés offered them an alliance and the opportunity to fight for their freedom and the Totonacs accepted it.

The members of the expedition were divided about the objectives of the journey. The followers of Velazquez wanted to return to Cuba. To decide the issue and unify the small force, Cortés founded the town of La Villa Rica de la Veracruz near their landing place. His followers set up a civilian council and named him Captain General, Chief Justice, and Commander of the Army. Since Cortés had founded the colonial settlement without proper authority, the appointments made him directly responsible to the Emperor Charles V instead of the governor of Cuba.

On July 16 Cortés dispatched his best ship, under the command of Anton de Alaminos, to carry to the king of Spain the Indian presents, news about the journey, and a detailed description of their activities. He also requested in his message to the king the governorship of the new discovered territory and a royal recognition for his followers.

To prevent possible desertions from those who had protested his authority, he enforced many disciplinary measures. He condemned two dissenters to death and ordered the flogging of many others. He also dismantled the remaining ships and scuttled or beached them so no one could escape.

Figure 8 Tlaxcaltecan warrior with
heron emblem (Lienzo de Tlaxcala)

In August Cortés began to march inland with about 400 soldiers, an equal number of Totonac warriors, and few Indian servants from Cuba. He left the rest of his army behind to protect the new settlement.

As he marched on, Cortés learned that there was considerable anxiety and dissatisfaction in the territories dominated by the Aztecs. The people of the provinces yearned for the day when they could remove their influence. Taking advantage of this development, he promptly persuaded other Indian groups to join him in the subversion of the Aztec empire. In a magnificent display of psychological warfare he convinced the natives to revolt against their rulers.

Cortés used diplomacy wherever possible and this tactic brought him the support of the Indian tribes who despised their Aztec overlords. On their way to the Valley of Mexico, the army crossed the tall Sierra Madre mountains near Jalapa and reached the Anahuac plateau later in October. The Totonacs suggested that Cortés seek the friendship of the Tlaxcalans since they, too, hated the Aztecs.

The Tlaxcalan Experience

The Tlaxcalans, however, could not be immediately convinced of the Spanish motives for entering their territory. Their leaders, disregarding all suggestions, confronted Cortés in open battle. With an estimated 40,000 warriors and under the leadership of their Chief Xicotencatl, the Tlaxcalans fought four major engagements before Cortés finally defeated them. Afterward, and with the help of Dona Marina, the Tlaxcalans agreed to follow the Spaniards during their march to the capital of the Aztec empire (Solis 109-118, Muñoz Camargo 207).

At Cholula, Cortés learned of an Aztec ploy to destroy his forces. To prevent the conspiracy from taking place, he invited the local Indian warriors to a meeting without arousing suspicion. At dawn the Indians began to arrive to a plaza in the center of the town. Before they had the opportunity to defend themselves, the Spaniards and their allies attacked them. By midday more than 3,000 Indians laid death on the ground. Cortés later wrote that the slaughter took less than two hours (Wilkerson 454)

Critics have argued that the massacre was unnecessary

Figure 9   Mixtec king "8 Deer-Jaguar Claw." (Codex Nuttall.

since the Indian warriors were there for religious ceremonies at the temple of Quetzalcoatl. The fact remains, wrote S. Jeffrey K. Wilkerson, that " after this display of Spanish ferocity, Cortés encountered no further armed resistance as he moved through the high mountains barriers toward the great city of Tenochtitlan" (454).

Few days later, another group of Aztec ambassadors arrived at the Spanish camp to deny Aztec participation in the affair. They blamed the members of the local military garrisons for the incident. As a sign of friendship, they gave Cortés more presents, including gold plates, cotton cloth, turkeys, bread cacao and wine. They assured the Conqueror that Montezuma meant well, that he was their friend, and that he was expecting their arrival to his city.

The slaughter at Cholula had impressed and frightened Moctezuma. According to Aztec chroniclers he said, "These are the people that our god told us will come to rule and dominate this land." Then he went to a temple and shut himself up to fast and pray for eight days. He also ordered the sacrifice of several victims to appease the gods, according to Aztec religious practices.

Moctezuma consulted with his officers and priests about the Spanish demand to enter Tenochtitlán. The impact that the strangers had made on his subjects and on the enemies of the empire also concerned him. He feared an uprising among the Otomí and the Tlaxcalans, and of those who had sided with Cortés. So, he decided to let the strangers enter Tenochtitlán without any opposition under the false belief that he had an upper hand in the affair.

Tenochtitlán

On November 8, 1519, Cortés entered Tenochtitlán, the Aztec bastion and capital of the empire, after traveling for 83 days and more that 400 miles. The 400 Spaniards and over 6,000 Indian allies that entered the city marched with great difficulty because the roads and causeways were full of people who came out to see them.

Moctezuma, walking under a pallium of gold and green feathers, and accompanied by the princes Cuitlahuac and Cacama, personally received Cortés. Two hundred Indian lords wearing rich clothing followed the royal

Figure 10 Tlaxcaltecan warrior with
sword and shield (Lienzo de Tlaxcala)

procession, accompanied by priests, soldiers and servants.

Cortes dismounted and attempted to embrace the monarch but could not do so because it was prohibited to touch Moctezuma. Both leaders greeted each other and exchanged presents. They walked toward a large courtyard in the center of the city and entered the palace of the lord Axayacatl, the site of today's National Pawnshop. The Aztecs lodged the Spaniards in small rooms and provided food to them.

The following day Cortes visited Moctezuma in his palace. According to the Spanish soldier and chronicler Bernal Diaz del Castillo, Cortes spoke to the Indian hosts about the reasons for being there, of God and the Holy Trinity, of the martyrdom of Christ, of evil and the meaning of eternal damnation.

The speech about theological matters could not be understood by the Indians, in spite of the efforts of Dona Marina and Aguilar, who served as interpreters. The statements made by Cortes represented the attitude of fifteenth century Spain where religion was a serious matter. The years of war with the Moslems and the Reconquista had increased the religious fervor of the Spaniards and the ties between Spanish royalty and the Church. Moctezuma replied with tact and gravity that "we also have many gods who have been kind to us. There is no doubt that your god has been also kind to you" (Diaz del Castillo 164-165).

The success of Cortes daring action had been possible because the Aztecs believed that the Spaniards were divine emissaries from heaven, representatives from the god Quetzalcoatl. The peculiar position of that god in Mesoamerican religion needs some explanation to understand properly the limited Aztec military opposition to Cortes forces during their journey across the highlands.

The god Quetzalcoatl was the patron of the arts, agriculture and sciences, the bearded god of learning and priesthood, and widely venerated as the father of creation. The "feathered serpent" was honored from the Maya lowlands to the highlands of central Mexico.

An Indian prophesy said that Quetzalcoatl was going to return to the Valley of Mexico in the year Ce Acatl, which corresponded to 1519, to reclaim his empire. Tradition also described the god as light-skinned, bearded, and returning from the East. The coincidences of the event and the physical description of the Spaniards predisposed the Aztecs to believe that Cortes was either Quetzalcoatl himself or his personal ambassador. Moctezuma's mother had told him the story often and the Aztec leader believed it to be true.

The arrival of Cortes to the Mexican coast bewildered Moctezuma. The insistence of the Spaniards on coming to Tenochtitlan in spite of Moctezuma protestations also forced the emperor to adopt a vacillating policy. During Cortes long and arduous march across the Sierra Madre mountains of eastern Mexico, some of them more than 12,000 feet tall, Moctezuma could have overwhelmed the small body of Spaniards with his well-disciplined forces. He did not dare to do so because he was not sure of whom the visitors really were, or if they had arrived under divine guidance from heaven. The prophecy enabled Cortes to reach Tenochtitlan unopposed.

Hernan Cortes and the Spaniards spent six days visiting the Aztec capital and studying its defenses. As they understood better their position inside the Indian stronghold and saw the size and number of the Aztec army, they realized that they could be killed at any moment. An escape from the city would have been impossible during a popular uprising. The need for supplies and outside help made any defense meaningless.

Concerned with his military situation and to avoid any danger, the Spaniards decided to arrest Moctezuma. Since Cortes also suspected that the Aztec emperor planned to kill the invaders, he decided to act as soon as possible. The opportunity arose when Cortes received several letters concerning the killing of seven Spanish soldiers by armed Indians in Villa Rica.

Cortes demanded to know why the Aztec chief had ordered the taking of arms against the Spaniards. He also requested that Moctezuma go with him to the Spanish quarters and remained there under house arrest. The weak emperor refused initially the request, but when he was threatened by Cortes' captains, he acceded to the demand, becoming a hostage and a puppet of the Spanish soldiers.

Moctezuma accepted his fate without any struggle. He informed the people and his principal military chieftains that there was no danger to his life, that he had joined the visitors voluntarily. Moctezuma never permitted a rescue nor allowed the people to revolt. The ruler never

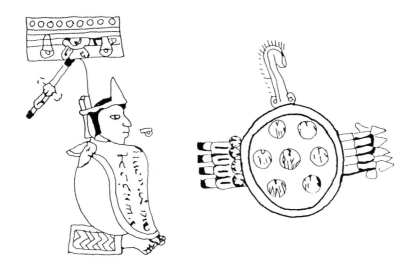

Figure 11 Emperor Moctezuma with arrow piercing the sky. The glyph depicts his second name (Codex Mendocino)

questioned the repeated Spanish demands for treasure, nor the purpose of their activities in the Aztec capital. He even permitted Cortes to condemn to death the Aztec captains who had slaughtered the Spanish soldiers at Villa Rica.

The Aztec Rebellion

Cortes learned from Moctezuma's couriers that more Spanish soldiers had landed in Veracruz. These forces had been sent by governor Velazquez to arrest and punish Cortes for being disloyal to him. Leaving a token force of soldiers and Indian helpers in the Aztec capital, under the command of Pedro de Alvarado, Cortes returned to the coast to face the new danger.

With his Indian allies, he attacked Velazquez's troops one rainy night and defeated them. He then persuaded the survivors to join him on his return to the Aztec capital with promises of plunder and wealth. The new force increased significantly the Spanish army. Among the new arrivals was a soldier with the smallpox virus. He later became Cortes' most deadly weapon in his struggle with the Aztecs.

While Cortes was fighting his enemies on the coast, the people of Tenochtitlan celebrated a religious ceremony. Alvarado permitted the Aztecs to gather and celebrate the festival, but prohibited any human sacrifices. According to the Aztec religion, the ritual was an essential part of the celebration, so the Indians ignored the Spanish orders. When the Aztecs began their sacrificial ceremony, Alvarado entered the main temple with his soldiers and slaughtered 200 of the unarmed participants.

The Aztecs rose in anger and fought the Spaniards and their companions, forcing Alvarado and his followers to take refuge in the center of the city. The prompt arrival of Cortes forces saved Alvarado's forces from slaughter. The Aztecs, however, had lost their fear of the visitors and were ready to expel them from Tenochtitlan.

Historians have noted that if the Aztecs had revolted much earlier the history of the conquest of Mexico may have been different. The Aztec forces were sufficiently strong to overrun the Spaniards that had remained in the city, and with adequate preparations they could have stopped the return of Cortes' army. Why then, there was no

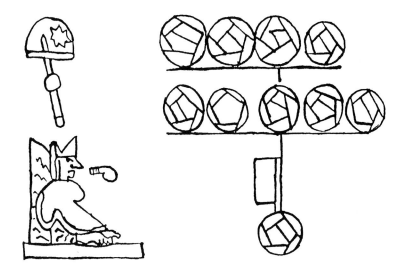

Figure 12 Chronological hieroghyphic
depicting Moctezuma's reign

rebellion until it was too late? Perhaps the psychological impact of the Conquest, or the dissatisfaction with the Aztec rule that existed among the Indian themselves contributed to a slow reaction. But, when their religious practices were challenged, their anger could not be contained and they rose against the Spaniards with hate and vengeance.

La Noche Triste

The Aztecs continued to fight after the return of Cortes. To prevent any further bloodshed Cortes persuaded Moctezuma to appeal for calm, but his cousin Cuauhtemoc defied the emperor's suggestion and accused him of treason and cowardice The people angered by the emperor's appeasement stoned him to death. Cuitlahuac, an Aztec noble, was chosen as the next Aztec emperor.

Under the leadership of Moctezuma's nephew Cuitlahuac and the 20-years old warrior Cuauhtemoc, the Aztecs attacked the Spanish soldiers at night. They cut the elevated causeways, plunging many Spaniards to their death. Outnumbered, the defenders fought a retreating action, losing many of their men during the attack. Fighting constantly and at close quarters along the western causeway that linked the island-city to the mainland, the Spaniards retreated slowly and with great difficulty. They had many losses because they packed the causeway during the retreat and could not move fast enough, while the Aztecs attacked them constantly from all sides.

Many Spanish soldiers died under the weight of their plunder when they fell into the water. Others threw their treasure into the lake in desperation. While there are no exact figures about the total losses, it is known that more than eight hundred Spaniards, thousands of Indians, and eighty horses perished during that night. The Spaniards later called it *La Noche Triste*, or the "Night of Sorrows." Most of the survivors that reached the mainland were suffering from wounds received during the battle.

The Spaniards lost their plunder, their weapons and most of their equipment. Cortes wept under a now famous tree at Popotla when he saw the remnants of his defeated army. The charred stump of the tree is all that remain today of the fateful night of July 1, 1520, when his

Figure 13 Emperor Moctezuma II
(Codex Mendocino)

badly beaten army fled disorganized after the successful Aztec uprising. Those unfortunate soldiers that could not escape on time were promptly sacrificed to the Aztecs' religious deities.

The Aztecs continued to pursue their enemies as far as Ozumba, thirty-five miles south of Mexico City. There, another desperate battle took place on July 7. A combined army of Aztecs, Texcocans and their allies, numbering perhaps 20,000, attacked the Spaniards during their retreat. The Indians were defeating Cortes when he remembered that they normally abandoned the battlefield when a leader was killed. He instructed his men to kill the Aztec chiefs at any cost.

As Cortes expected, the Aztecs left the battlefield when one of their leaders was slain. The attempt of the Indians to capture as many prisoners as possible also saved many Spaniards from being killed. Spanish weapons and tactics provided a significant advantage, since the Europeans were trained soldiers who acted as a unit, while the Aztecs had difficulty operating without a chief. Cortes quick thinking during the battle of Ozumba probably saved his remaining forces from total disaster.

The Return of the Invaders

The Spaniards returned to Tlaxcala, where they were received well although thousands of Tlaxcalans also had died during the rebellion. There, the Spaniards rested and reorganized their forces. Cortes revived his army with more Indian allies and from July 2 until December 20 prepared his soldiers to conquer Tenochtitlan.

It has been suggested that without the help of Tlaxcala Cortes would never have subdued the Aztec empire. The Tlaxcalans provided him with warriors, weapons, food, supplies and a place to rest after the defeat. They also helped the Spaniards built boats to fight the Aztecs in the canals. They helped the Europeans because they hated the Aztecs and wanted their total destruction. If, on the other hand, these Indians had allied themselves with their enemies instead of doing it with the Spaniards, Cortes would probably have failed to conquer Mexico.

After the Indian victory, a terrible plague devastated Tenochtitlan. Smallpox, which the Spaniards had unwittingly brought from home, devastated the city and killed thousands of its residents, including the best soldiers of the Aztec army who had been in close contact with the Spaniards.

The Aztec society had been isolated from the rest of the world for several centuries. This isolation had weakened the Indians' resistance and protection to the major diseases of mankind. As a result, the spread of the disease, brought by one of the soldiers who had joined Cortes on the coast, could not be stopped nor could it be cured. The disease did little harm to the Spaniards, but killed the Indians by the thousands. Among those who died was the new emperor Cuitlahuac who had succeeded Moctezuma after his death.

The End of the Aztec Empire

Cuauhtemoc became the last Aztec emperor. The terrible death toll inside the city weakened the Indian resolve and resulted in a significant reduction of Indian attacks. The delay gave Cortes time to prepare a new expedition.

He built a new and larger army with Indians from Tlaxcala, Chalco, Texcoco and Xochimilco to attack the Aztec stronghold. With thirteen small vessels, 6,000 canoes, 16 pieces of artillery and 60 horses, the Spaniards laid siege to Tenochtitlan.

The people of Chalco, who were bitter enemies of the Aztecs, declared war on the few towns that were loyal to Tenochtitlan and forced them to submit to the Spaniards (Gomara 277, 293).

The Aztecs fought with great valor and courage and often forced the Spaniards to retreat; but, Cortes' superiority in number and use of the brigantines decided the outcome of the battle. The terrible Indian losses caused by the epidemic and the war, their inability to receive reinforcements from the rest of the empire, and the lack of food forced them to capitulate seventy-three days after the final attack. On August 13, 1521, the Aztec empire and Tenochtitlan fell to the Spanish invaders.

The next day the Spaniards moved in on a city completely obliterated by war, ravaged by fire, infested by smallpox and littered with hundreds of death bodies. Cortes' secretary Francisco Lopez de Gomara wrote: "In

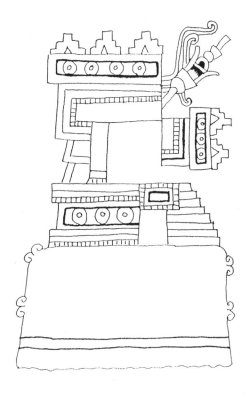

Figure 14 Temple with burning spear,
a symbol of destruction (Codex Nuttall)

the three months of siege the enemy lost more than 100,000 men not including those who died of hunger and pestilence . . . . The people suffered from hunger and had to drink salt water; they slept among the death and walked among the perpetual stench. They ate twig and bark and drank salt water . . . but they never sued for peace" (293).

The writer Zvi Dor-Ner, quoting Bernal Diaz del Castillo, writes that Cortes soldiers ". . . could not walk without treading on the bodies and heads of dead Indians . . . the dry land and the stockades were piled with corpses. Indeed, the stench was so bad that no one could endure it . . . even Cortes was ill from the odors which assailed his nostrils . . . "(Dor-Ner 230).

The pestilence and the dead of Tenochtitlan had been caused by the fighting and the smallpox epidemic that the Indians could not prevent. " More than three centuries were to pass before the American continent could again boast a city so vast and magnificent as the city wantonly destroyed by the Spanish invaders," wrote the Mexican writer Roberto Cabral del Hoyo (42-43).

The Aztec sense of fatalism, the inadequate leadership of Moctezuma, and the use of modern weapons and tactics by the enemy enabled to Spaniards to destroy them. The nature of the conflict that Cortes unleashed, which pitted thousands of Indians against other Indians in a fratricidal war, also contributed to their defeat. But the infectious diseases brought unwittingly by the Europeans probably did more damage to them than these causes combined.

The fatalistic attitude of the Aztecs also contributed to their end. As historian William McNeill has described it, "a disease that killed only Indians and left Spaniards unharmed could only be explained supernaturally, and there could be no doubt about which side of the struggle enjoyed divine favor" (Dor-Ner 233).

The Spaniards captured Cuauhtemoc and brought him before Cortes for punishment. They had never forgotten that he had been the leader of the revolt that caused their early defeat and the death of their fellow Christian soldiers. The lost of their treasure during the retreat also had angered them. Thinking that gold was plentiful in the Aztec empire they tortured the Aztec leader, to force him reveal the source of their wealth.

The Spaniards never realized that the golden

artifacts they had received, or had seen in the Indian palaces, were the accumulation of centuries. There was no large quantity of gold in central Mexico, and most of the treasures that decorated the Aztec temples came from far away regions of the empire.

The Spanish burned Cuauhtemoc's feet and hands with boiling oil, and applied the same torture to his faithful vassal the Lord of Tacuba. Cabral del Hoyo writes that "unable to stand the pain the Tacuba chieftain looked at his emperor as though asking permission to speak. Cuauhtemoc understood his intention and asked ironically: `Do you think I am lying on a bed of roses?' The Tacuba ruler remained silent without a word of complaint" (44).

The Aztec Chief suffered stoically the Spanish punishment and treatment, and even earned the admiration and respect of his enemies. Since he did not care for the pain received and was nothing to reveal about hidden treasure, they stopped the torture. He remained a prisoner until 1525, when Cortés ordered his execution and those of other Mexican chieftains while visiting Itzamkanac, in the Mayan territory.

With the destruction of Tenochtitlán, the conquest of the rest of the empire was easy. Subsequent Spanish expeditions dominated without difficulty other Indian territories such Michoacan, Coatzacoatl, Oaxaca, Tehuantepec, Panuco, Tuxtepec and the Pacific coast. Cortés established himself in Coyoacan while Mexico City was being rebuilt under the new Spanish administration.

The Mexican writer Antonio Caso portrait the Aztecs as "administrators, legatees, dominators, and disseminators" of the Mesoamerican culture that existed before the arrival of the Europeans. He also writes that the Aztecs were in the midst of a flourishing era, and while they had not yet reached the same cultural level of other civilizations, they were progressing at a faster pace.

George C. Vaillant, on the other hand, views the clash that occurred in the Valley of Mexico in the summer of 1520 as a confrontation between two highly developed but divergent civilizations.   The Aztecs had assimilated the cultures of the Maya, Zapotec, Culhuas, Toltecs, Texcocans and of many other ancient societies that preceded them. Cortés, therefore, defeated a nation whose technical and artistic achievements rivaled those of Europe.

These are fair assessments and the remaining chapters

Figure 15 Warrior's shield (Codex Nutall)

will explain them and the extent of the Aztec culture and civilization that was destroyed by Cortés. They also will analyze realistically the impact of the European conquest of Mesoamérica from both the Indian and the European points of view.

Figure 16   Colossal head from San Lorenzo, Olmec
sculpture.

3

The Legacy from the Past

The Pre-Columbian Civilizations

Long before the discovery of America, many highly civilized Indian communities lived in central and southern Mexico, in the lowlands of Guatemala and in the northern part of Belize. These societies left behind a glorious imprint of ceremonial centers, pyramids and ruins that still fascinate foreign visitors and excite the intellectual curiosity of those who try to decipher their mysteries.

When the Spaniards explored the Western Hemisphere, they discovered many regional differences among the Indian tribes that occupied the American continent. While some native groups had just barely advanced beyond the Stone Age, others had attained a sophisticated level of civilization that could be compared with fifteenth century's European societies. The Indian cities and religious centers of Copan, Palenque, Chichen Itza, Uxmal, Monte Alban and Teotihuacan are, perhaps, the best examples of the cultural advancement of the Mesoamerican Indians.

John Lloyd Stephens wrote in 1841, after seeing the city of Copan, that historians said "America was peopled by savages; but savages never reared these structures, savages never carved these stones."

Recent investigations have solved many of those mysteries. They also have shown that war, human sacrifice and religious dogmatism were also part of the common inheritance of these people. As Curt Muser has noted, the study of this region is very recent and full of historical contradictions. "New stylistic studies continue to challenge established beliefs. It is this

Figure 17   Classic example of Olmec sculpture with child features. (INAH)

modern detective work that makes the study of New World Civilizations so interesting" (Muser xiii).

One hundred and fifty years ago hardly anyone dreamed of the existence of these Indian communities. Years of hard work, however, have restored some of their ancient religious centers, buildings and monuments. Many of these archaeological sites exhibit the past glory of the American Indians. Others exemplify their struggle for survival on a rugged and alien land. Only among the Inca of Peru and their Northwestern neighbors can one find a similar legacy of success and failure in the Western Hemisphere.

Northern and Southern Cultures

One cannot compare these cultural areas and arrive at the same conclusions. In Middle America, a concern of the theocratic rulers of the region was the construction of elaborated religious ceremonial centers. Mysticism and ritual were used extensively by to Indian priests to control the people and make them obey their rulers. In contrast, one of the principal concerns of the Inca authorities was the efficient control of a vast empire through the centralization of political and economic power. The Inca ruled a secular society that consisted of an aggregation of welfare states and thousands of obedient people.

Farming was another example of the differences between the two regions. In the Inca empire the farmers worked the land collectively. At harvest time, they divided the product of their crops between themselves, the government and the clergy. The local authorities redistributed the grain among the workers and provided them with shelter, clothing and provisions when it was necessary. On the other hand, in Middle America the farmers planted and harvested their crops in communal groups. They paid tribute to the government on a regular basis.

When Cortés landed on the eastern shores of Mexico, the Indian communities of Middle America had endured the hardships of survival and were in various stages of social and political development. Among those that lived in Central and Southern Mexico were Mayan, Totonac, Tlaxcalan, Huastec, Mixtec, Zapotec, Tarascan, Chichimec and Nahua groups. Many other tribes also lived in the northwestern region of the country.

Figure 18   Jade figurines found in La Venta. (INAH)

Mesoamerica

In 1943 the archaeologist Paul Kirchoof studied the area where these societies lived and named it Mesoamerica. The geographical region that he classified includes central and southern Mexico, Guatemala and Belize; the western part of Honduras, El Salvador and Nicaragua; and the northern part of Costa Rica. Anthropologists consider the Indians who lived there as the most advanced societies of the Western Hemisphere (Coe, et al. 84-85).

Kirchoof's definition also identified some common characteristics of the people who lived in the region. Among these was the use of books made of maguey fiber or tanned deerskin, the employment of ritual and solar calendars, and the participation in religious games. They also wrote in hieroglyphic symbols and practiced human sacrifices. The Mesoamerican Indians used maize or Indian corn as a staple food and had complex and fatalistic religious beliefs.

These Indians also had a well-developed knowledge of astronomy and mathematics, a deep understanding of poetry and a sentimental attachment to natural artistic beauty. They based their cultural development on mutual exchanges and on the achievements of earlier generations (Muser 99).

The Aztecs

The Aztecs were building a military theocracy at the time of the Conquest. These Indians attracted the interest of the Spaniards more than any other group. Their wealth excited the Europeans dreams for treasures of gold and silver and fortunes of incalculable value. At its peak the Aztec empire dominated most of central and southern Mexico.

Aztec merchants maintained a trade network that extended to the lowlands of the Pacific coast of Guatemala. The Aztec capital city of Tenochtitlán had a population of more than 200,000 inhabitants, which in the fifteenth century may have been larger than any European urban center.

The residents of Tenochtitlán handled very successfully the problem of urban growth, although the

Figure 19   Colossal Head No. 6 from San Lorenzo.
These monumental sculptures are the most famous works
of the Olmecs. (INAH)

city only covered about ten square kilometers and was located on reclaimed swamp land. That city is today the home of more than 20,000,000 people and is the largest urban center in the world. The Aztec empire may have included a population of 25,000,000 people, according to recent investigations.

These Indians inherited most of their social, political and commercial skills from the classic pre-Columbian cultures that preceded them. The earlier groups also influenced their military mentality and their religious beliefs and practices. They gained from the Maya most of their architectural and scientific knowledge, the use of the calendar, and the techniques of farming and harvesting crops.

Intellectually, the Aztecs lived upon the achievements of previous generations. They made limited contributions to the use of the calendar, the study of astronomy or the science and mathematics. Their writing never went beyond a simple pictographic style. But, in organizational ability, commercial insight and bravery in war they surpassed all their neighbors. That could explain why they succeeded in creating and efficient tributary state in less than two hundred years.

The Aztecs did not learn, however, the basis of good political statesmanship. They never realized the importance of "winning the hearts and minds" of those whom they conquered. As a result, "the Aztec empire contained the seeds of its own destruction" and had already begun to collapse years before the Spanish landed in the Western Hemisphere.

A Fantasy in the Wilderness

In Middle America the Indians built their cities and ceremonial centers with care and exquisite taste. The quality of engineering and workmanship, especially in Tenochtitlan, was so high that it even surprised the Spanish conquerors.

According to the historians and chroniclers of the Conquest, the beauty of the Aztec city amazed the first Europeans who saw it. "We did not know what to say when we see those marvelous things, nor did we believe what our eyes were seeing," wrote the Spanish soldier Bernal Diaz del Castillo. "There were great cities near the lake and many canoes crowded the water. The causeways that connected the city had many bridges. . ." wrote the Spanish soldier (Diaz del Castillo 160).

The beauty of the Indian work also impressed the German painter Albrech Durer, who saw in 1520 the native objects that Cortés had sent to the Emperor Charles V. Surprised by its refinement, the famous artist wrote: "I, too, have seen the things brought to the Emperor from the new Land of Gold. . . and in all my life I have never seen anything which so stirred my heart as those objects. For I saw among them wonderful works of art, and I marveled at the subtle ingenuity of those men in a faraway land" (Anton 6; Hightower 66).

In like manner, another German artist, the writer Ferdinand Anton, recently wrote: "This is what one of the most significant artists of the sixteenth century thought of early American art. And yet, three and one half centuries later, the director of the Louvre refused to exhibit such objects in his museum" (Anton 6).

Still, most of the European settlers who came to North America on the wake of the Spanish conquest could not believe the extent and character of the American Indian civilization. The Frenchman Alexis de Tocqueville wrote three centuries later that only nomadic tribes inhabited the empty land without receiving profit from it. Nineteenth century writer William Pidgeon wrote that the Indians were lazy and their "natural indolence" and averseness to any manual labor was well known.

The Nature of Government

The Aztecs of Mexico lived in a military theocracy organized as a loose confederation of tributary states. This society was very similar to earlier Mesoamerican cultures where the ruler was both Emperor and High Priest. The Aztecs were as warlike as the earlier Toltec and Maya and practiced as many bloody rites as their common ancestors. They conducted continuous warfare and ritualistic sacrifices as other Indian tribes did before them. Their society, therefore, must be studied with the rest of the pre-Columbian civilizations since they were a part of them.

The Aztecs had a limited scientific knowledge off the effects of the environment. Their inability to rationalize the actions of natural forces on their lives probably molded their behavior and conditioned

Figure 20   Sculpture of the head of a young male, Palenque, Chiapas. (INAH)

their daily activities. It is also possible that their immediate surroundings affected many of their religious practices.

Since the Aztecs glorified war and trained their youth for perpetual military service, a "garrison state" mentality prevailed among the people. They respected the military class and warriors received the highest honors and most of the benefits of society. Since one of their responsibilities was to capture prisoners of war for the sacrificial stone, soldiers and priests had a very good relationship. Military chiefs, who distinguished themselves in battle, served for an indefinite period as political leaders.

Feudal lords ruled the provinces of the empire as representatives of the Emperor, who in turn ruled in Tenochtitlán as a High Priest. A Council of Elders helped and advised him in government matters. Other priests exercised great power as teachers and judges of moral and social responsibilities. Their decisions were always final.

The Search for the Past

During the first stages of the conquest of Mexico the Europeans concentrated their attention mostly on the Aztecs. That could explain why the Spaniards gave so little attention to the other Indian cultures that lay hidden in the boundless forests and valleys of Mesoamerica.

The Spaniards did not acquaint themselves with the ruins, monuments and people from other societies until they expanded their imperial controls to other regions of Central America. Since these other Indian groups offered limited treasures and their lands contained nothing that the greed of the conquerors could use, the Spaniards lost their interest in them.

After the Conquest, religious friars and inquisitive chroniclers began slowly to record the past that laid hidden under the dilapidated structures and ruins of Mesoamérica. Other scholars continued the earlier work during the nineteenth century. As they searched the archaeological records, their investigations increased the knowledge of the ancient Mesoamerican past and changed many views concerning the American Indian.

At the beginning of the twentieth century American and

Figure 21   Mask representing the solar deity Kinich Aahau.   (INAH).

European investigators revived the interest in these Indian cultures. New ethnological and historical studies about the Aztecs and other Mesoamerican societies began to surface in the United States, Mexico, and Europe. After the Second World War, this work increased very rapidly. During this time, Mexican and foreign researchers succeeded in piercing together the mysteries and secrets of many of the vanished societies.

The scientific effort was very productive. In recent years, it has furnished new clues and evidence of the origins, development and achievements of the earlier Indian cultures. It also has revealed that for more than 12,000 years complex human interrelationships and events shaped the history and destiny of Mexico and of most of Mesoamerica.

The investigators discovered very early that the Aztecs were not the architects of the high levels of Indian culture found in the Mexican highlands. These Indians had inherited their cultural characteristics and agricultural skills from those who had lived earlier in the Valley of Mexico. The Aztecs themselves acknowledged that fact in the chronicles of their native historians.

Recent Investigations

Modern investigators have found many important archaeological treasures hidden under the ruins of the cities ravaged by the Spanish invaders. These artifacts are being carefully studied and evaluated to understand the importance of the Aztec influence in Mesoamerica.

Using modern technological equipment and better research techniques, often borrowed from other sciences, scientists are reconstructing the ancient history of Mexico. They search for trends that can explain ancient cultural developments instead of just studying past occurrences and the effects of particular events.

Anthropologist Don S. Rice described this form of scientific investigation several years ago when he wrote: "Modern researchers want to contribute to the general body of social science theory regarding the nature of human behavior and the processes of cultural evolution" (Rice 127-135).

Figure 22   **Fray Bernandino de Sahagun.**

The Aztec Homeland

The region where the Aztecs lived in pre-Columbian America is today the Federal Republic of Mexico. Located south of the United States and extending toward Guatemala and Belize in Central America, Mexico has a total area of 761,604 square miles. It also has a population of more than 88,000,000 people, making it the third largest nation in Latin America after Brazil and Argentina.

Indians have lived in Mexico for thousands of years. Many of these native groups interacted with the early Spanish settlers who conquered the country to form the present racial characteristics of the country. The Indian longtime occupation of the land and the later relationship with the Europeans also influenced the nation's social, cultural, and historical development.

The racial element that emerged from the mixture of the Spanish and the native races shaped Mexico's political, cultural and economic development. Descendants of the first Indian and European settlers have lived together in an environment that has influenced their life and forged their will to survive.

Most of the history of the Mexican Indians has been characterized by a struggle against corruption, scandalous privileges and political control, exercised mostly by landlords and members of the conservative classes. They also have fought against poverty, violence, and the influence of foreign capitalism. Their struggle for recognition of their identity has always been part of the Mexican reality.

Racial Distribution

The Mexican government has not recorded officially the racial composition of the Mexican society since 1921. Authorities have tried to resolve this problem, but the scope and size of the project have made the task extremely difficult. Since precise ethnic information is not available, the linguistic characteristics of the Indian groups that live in the country has been the main source used to identify the nation's racial distribution.

On the basis of this standard, the population of Mexico has been estimated to be about sixty percent mestizo, twenty-nine percent Indian and nine percent Caucasian. This racial distribution indicates a high

Figure 23 Urn with a representation of a deity with a buccal mask. Temple of the Deer 7, Monte Alban. (INAH)

level of native ancestry among its inhabitants.

About seven percent of the Indian population speak an indigenous language. More than 950,000 Mexicans speak Nahuatl, the language of the Aztecs. In the southern part of the country over 500,000 people speak Maya, while in the State of Oaxaca there are 300,000 who speak Zapotec.

Otomi is the basic language of one-quarter of a million people. Another one-quarter of a million speaks Mixtec in the southwestern region. The rest of the Indian population speaks a variety of native languages, such as Totonac, Mazahua and Huichol. At least four percent of these groups also speak the Spanish language.

The Impact of Geography

Geography influenced, perhaps, more than any other factor the social, cultural, and trading development of the Aztecs. It also affected the relationship that existed between the Aztecs, their gods, and the Indian groups. The geographical setting is still very complex and diverse. It controls the climatic conditions and the weather patterns of the country.

Mexico is geographically divided into highlands and lowlands. Mountains, dry deserts and uninhabitable jungles are the dominant features of the territory. Underneath the mountain peaks and extinct volcanoes, lay agricultural fields where farmers grow sugar cane, cotton, maize and other important products during the rainy season.

The important geographical divisions of Mexico are a central plateau, the low lands of the coast, the southern Chiapas highlands, the Lower California Peninsula and the tropical region of Yucatán. About fifty percent of the land is arid. There are dry deserts in the North, mountains and valleys in the highlands, and rain forests in the South. Much of central Mexico is exposed to regular earthquakes and volcanic activity.

The weather in Mexico is unpredictable and the geographic diversity of the country contributes to a harsh existence. Less than fifteen percent of the land is suitable for agriculture and erosion limits the crops that can be harvested.

As Francois Chevalier notes, "it is a country of contrasts between the low-lying zones, where it is too hot, sometimes damp, and difficult access, and the

Figure 24   Zapotec figure from Monte Alban. (INAH)

temperate, healthful climate of the high plateaus which, because of their extent and the demographic importance of Anahuac, still constitutes the essential part of the land mass; but even so, their climate is often dry, their soil poor, and their mountain ranges numerous and forbidding" (Chevalier 12).

The Mexican Highlands

The Sierra Madre mountains are the most important topographic feature of Mexico. This mountain range begins in the Isthmus of Tehuantepec and splits into the Sierra Madre Occidental and the Sierra Madre Oriental. Along the Pacific coast these mountains extend for more than seven hundred miles from Southeast to Northwest. On the eastern side they extend all the way to the United States.

The most important peaks are Pico de Orizaba, Popocatepetl, Ixtacihuatl and Nevado de Toluca. Popocatepetl is an inactive volcano from which smoke sometimes climbs lazily from its crater. Since 1519, it has erupted ten different times. These peaks are between 12,992 and 18,701 feet in height.

Popocatepetl and Iztaccihuatl, to the Aztecs "smoking mountain" and "the lady in white," have been for hundreds of years important religious symbols to the Mexican Indians. According to Stuart Chase, the Aztecs believed that Popocatepetl was "the abode of departed spirits of wicked rulers, whose fiery agonies in their prison house caused the fearful bellowing and convulsions" (21).

In 1519, members of the Cortés' expedition climbed the slopes of the mountain to impress the natives, but were driven back by the sparks, burning ashes and the black smoke from the volcano. Two years later, however, the gunsmith Francisco de Montero succeeded in reaching the crest of the mountain while searching for sulfur to manufacture gunpowder.

The Western Landscape

In the west harsh, dry ranges, high plains, steep slopes and long cliffs make travel difficult. The early Spanish settlers who traveled across these lands met with many perils. Since most of the region was uninhabited and dangerous, they had to take with them ample supplies when they traveled. The excess baggage that they carried and the height of the mountains made their journeys extremely dangerous.

The Franciscan chronicler Fray Toribio de Motolinia, who traveled throughout this region, wrote that the area had so many mountains that a person could stand in the middle of a plain and see nothing but tall peaks and ranges as far as twenty miles away.

There is also an interesting anecdote about the immense and rugged landscape of Mexico. According to the story, Hernan Cortes visited Charles V in Toledo sometime after the discovery of the Aztec empire. The Spanish monarch asked him: "What is Mexico like?" Cortés, taking a paper from a report he was carrying, crumpled it, and showing the wrinkled piece to the monarch replied: "Like this Your Highness, this is what Mexico looks like!" Cortés referred, of course, to the rugged appearance of the country that was to become the Viceroyalty of New Spain.

Between the Sierra Madre Occidental and the Gulf of California is a region of low mountains and plains with a narrow corridor that extends to the Rio Grande de Santiago in central Mexico. Toward the Northeast the country is mostly desert and very dry. Creosote bush, prickly pear and thorny huisaches cover the bare hills and plains. In the desert of Sonora grow a large variety of native vegetation such as cacti, mesquite and opuntias. Landscapes are dusty, hot and weathered by the intense gusty winds that blow in the region.

The Rugged Mexican Highlands

The volcanic central plateau of Mexico is mostly composed of lava rock, basalt and limestone. Periodically, seismic tremors shock the area. In September 1985, two almost consecutive earthquakes devastated large sections of the Mexican capital and several nearby towns, causing more than 10,000 deaths and millions of dollars in losses. The region has many inactive volcanoes and high mountains with rugged crests that stand sometimes more than 18,000 feet.

One of the most impressive mountain peaks of southeastern Mexico is the Pico de Orizaba, or Citlaltepetl. The famous "Mountain of the Star" of the Aztecs dominates the southern edge of the central

Figure 25   Center view of the Pyramid of the Sun, Teotihuacan.

highlands. The area has deep canyons and ravines that turn barren and colorless during the dry season. In summer the rain changes the region into a productive agricultural land.

The zone between 3,000 and 7,000 feet above sea level is the *Tierra Templada,* an area of relative cool weather where a variety of grains and fruits are cultivated. Limited rainfall prevents full utilization of the land, except in those areas where artificial irrigation has been built. Most of the ancient Indian civilizations lived in the few areas where water was abundant.

Toward the coastline the elevation of the mountain ranges is higher in the West than in the East. The altitude decreases slowly toward the Chiapas highlands. Lowlands are mostly flat with wide beaches, sandbars, and some rivers. The coastal plains are hot and moist and the temperatures are very high. The *Tierra Caliente* , as the area is known, is poor for agriculture, especially in the low lands of Tabasco. The region, however, is developing very rapidly into one of Mexico's most important industrial areas because of new oil and mineral discoveries.

Some of these areas periodically suffer violent rainstorms that cause heavy floods and destruction. Hurricanes which blow from the Caribbean have ravaged the coastal plains often. In September 1944, a hurricane struck the Yucatan Peninsula, the Isthmus of Tehuantepec and Vera Cruz with heavy rains and winds of more than 120 miles per hour. The devastation was considerable. Deaths from drowning and disease ran into the hundreds.

On September 1988, hurricane Gilbert, the most powerful Atlantic storm ever recorded, battered the Yucatan Peninsula with winds gusting at 218 miles an hour that raised the sea level by twenty feet. As many as sixty people drowned during the flash floods that followed and the damage to the coastal plains was extensive.

The Southern Perspective

The southern part of Mexico has tropical forests that are very hot and humid, and a mountainous region of high plains and volcanic peaks on the Pacific coast. The outstanding characteristic of the tropical lowlands and

**Figure 26   Stone disk with skull from the Plaza of the
Pyramid of the Sun, Teotihuacan. (INAH)**

coastal plains is the thick rain-forest vegetation that hides the surface with low tangled tropical growth. Much rain falls on the southern region during the summer, creating mangrove swamps, underbrush and a diversity of plant life.

In the tropical forests, a variety of trees stand above the brush and the tropical plants. Shrubs of many kinds and beautiful wild flowers grow under the twisted branches and vines. Ferns and evergreens can be seen throughout the wilderness. Animal life is very common among the roots that grow above ground and strangle the trunks of the trees.

In this landscape of hot and humid surroundings, temperatures can reach more than 100 degrees during the day; but at night, especially during the rainy season, they drop considerably.

Throughout the year, there is an abundance of moisture, especially during the early morning hours. The coastlines are covered with dense fog that quickly disappears as the sun heats the land. Wide beaches and mangrove swamps are characteristic of the region. Showers alternate with sunshine during the rainy season. Without the cooling effects of the winds from the exposed coast, these tropical forests would be unable to sustain human life.

The Yucatán Peninsula

The Yucatan Peninsula is a region of thick vegetation and gentle rolling relief that lies before the mountain plateau of Guatemala in the southeastern part of Mexico. It has very few rivers, but its position between the Bay of Campeche and that of Honduras gives its climate a favorable tropical character. The weather is hot and dry with limited rainfall.

Tropical grasslands, desert shrubs and low branching trees dominate much of Yucatan. The land has a flat, porous, limestone plateau that is covered with a brown scrub brush during the dry season. Most of the vegetation is highly resistance to drought and the alkaline soil. Toward Quintana Roo it changes from thick bush to a light, humid jungle. Surface drainage is difficult, except during the summer months when tropical thundershowers flood the area. The rain water seeps down through the limestone into subterranean pools forming

Figure 27   Small temple-like structures, Teotihuacan.

cenotes, or sinkholes.

These artificial wells are interconnected by underground channels that form caves and soil depressions as they run into the sea. Many years ago, there was a romantic Indian legend connected with these *cenotes*. The people from Yucatan believed that before the arrival of the Spaniards the Maya sacrificed young virgins in times of drought by drowning them in these wells.

According to Mayanist Sylvanus G. Morley, young girls were thrown into the pits of sacred wells at daybreak. If they survived the plunge, they were rescued at noon and questioned as to what the gods had in store for the tribe. If the maidens did not reappear, it was considered an evil omen, and artifacts and rocks were thrown into the well (Morley, 17).

Years later, Edward H. Thompson and Dr. Earnest Hooton of Harvard University, studied the remains and artifacts found in the *cenotes*. The results of their investigations showed that people died in these wells but "not necessarily as offerings." Those who may have been thrown into the *cenotes* were rescued if they survived until noon. Since these victims had experienced a special relationship with their gods, it was expected that they forecast correctly the weather changes for the incoming year (La Fay and Harvey, 750).

One of this *cenotes*, the "Well of Sacrifice" has been popularized throughout the years as a Mayan ceremonial center and today is a popular tourist attraction. Located near the ruins of Chichen Itza, this cenote is part of an underground water system that consists of fourteen other wells. Thompson, who explored it in several occasions, found on its bottom a variety of artifacts and objects together with 43 incomplete human skeletons, of which 14 has been identified as male, 21 as children and 8 as females (Zapata Alonzo 47).

This land was once occupied by the Maya and by the Toltec invaders who came from central Mexico at the end of the tenth century. Today, the accomplishments of those civilizations are being recognized by five Central American nations. They created *La Ruta Maya*, an ambitious regional project that will preserve the cultural, historical, and environmental heritage of the area.

Southwest of the tropical lowlands, the Chiapas Highlands, with their abrupt slopes, short streams, and deep depressions, stands parallel to the sea. This area is part of an almost continuous mountain range that threads south through the humid tropical regions of Central America to join the Andes mountains in the southern hemisphere. These highlands are very different from those of the central region. They are tropical and have little volcanic characteristics.

The closeness of the mountains to the sea results in a faster weathering process that exposes large sections of bedrock to the wind. Most of the time, the ground is covered with mesquite thorn scrub. While some areas are abrupt and rocky, others are low leveled gentle plains. The country that borders the mountains is warm and dry and can be used only for cattle raising.

Climatic Conditions

The climatic conditions of Mexico are either tropical or subtropical. The altitude is more important than the latitude in determining weather patterns, which resemble more temperate zones than those of a subtropical region. While dry and arid conditions prevail in about one-half of the territory, in areas of heavy rainfall the vegetation is tropical.

The mountains form barriers that diminish humidity. In the summer and fall weather patterns are determined by the flow of humid air from the Gulf. During winter, relative humidity is low, temperatures are cool, and frost covers many parts of the highlands.

There are no specific patterns of rainfall in Mexico; most of the country lacks adequate rain at least part of the year. Rain is usually light some years and extremely heavy on others. As historian Lesley Byrd Simpson has accurately described: "Average precipitation means very little. Years may go by with heartily enough rain to water the maize crop followed by a succession of disastrous floods and such high humidity that the grain sprouts in the ear" (6)

There are very few rivers and lakes in Mexico. As Simpson writes, "those that flow through the *barrancas* are feeble streams during the dry season and raging brown torrents from June to November, useless for transport and too far below the surface of land to be used for irrigation" (4).

These erratic weather changes must have influenced the Aztec mind. Since they could not understand the causes of

Figure 28   Courtyard of the Palace of Quetzalpapalotl, Teotihuacan.

the extreme variations, they sacrificed human victims to their gods to insure an adequate amount of rain during drought, or no rain at all during periods of heavy floods. Perhaps that may have been the reason they sacrificed so many children to the rain-god Tlaloc and made him one of their principal religious deities.

The Geographical Influence

At the beginning of this century North American and German geographers subscribed to the belief that man is a tool of natural forces, especially the climate. Their "determinist" theory emphasized conditions that were favorable or unfavorable to civilization. A temperate climate, for example, was considered essential for human progress, while the humidity, high heat, and monotony of the tropics had a detrimental effect on life.

This idea was not a new one. Two thousand years before, Aristotle, Hippocrates, and Herodutus thought that the rise of the Hellenic civilization and the fall of the mighty empires of Asia Minor were related to the weather and confirmed the excellence of the climate of Greece.

Geographers Ellsworth Huntington, S. F. Markham, Stephen S. Visher and others expanded these views by adding that mysticism and religious activity thrived in the semi-arid regions at the edge of the tropics. Since the Valley of Mexico is periodically shaken by violent earth convulsions and is located in a semi-arid region at the edge of a tropical environment, did climate and geography influence their inhabitants?

While today some of the earlier climatic theories are no longer valid and the effect of the environment on the American Indian may be the subject of academic discussion, a detailed study of the Mesoamerican Indians may disclose a relationship between their way of life and the threat of natural forces.

Some authorities believe that the abandonment of the Mayan ceremonial centers and the end of many of their settlements can be attributed to climatic changes. The height of the Mayan civilization occurred during a period of relative dry weather. The decay of their cities, according to H. G. Barnett, began when rainfall increased and the tropical forests advanced so fast that they,

Figure 29 Chac-mool, or reclining figure, with receptacle to receive human hearts. Chichen Itza, Yucatan.

literally, engulfed the great cities. Increasing rain patterns affected not only forests, but lakes and rivers, producing alternating eras of drought and flood.

Climatic conditions may have also affected the cultural advancement, social organization, religion practices and the trading activities of the Mesoamerican Indians. Victor W. Von Hagen, observes that geography and climatic changes play an important role in the building of imperialistic cultures, such as the Aztecs. According to Von Hagen those who live in the harsh lands, scoured by wind and hail are restless people and have imperialistic ambitions. On the other hand, people who live in the luxuriant warmth and sensualism of the tropics have a limited expansionist mood. The need to survive influences considerably the outcome of a particular society (56).

To the Aztecs, who came from colder zones, their struggle for survival may have shaped their social, political and religious development. When they arrived at the Central Valley of Mexico, the best lands were already occupied and they had to force their way in by war and conquest. To quote Von Hagen, "so into the lakes of Anahuac in the year Ome-Acatl, 2 Cane (A.D. 1168), moved this god-tormented tribe, this `Aztec' people who were to systematize rapine and war into a tribute-state and forever leave their impression in the Mexican land" (Von Hagen 23).

Figure 30   Atlante with raised arms from Chichen Itza.

4

The Search for the Ancient Americans

Early Migrations to the New World

It is generally accepted that the original inhabitants of the Western Hemisphere immigrated from Asia. For thousands of years nomadic hunters crossed the Bering Strait and the Alaskan highlands and settled in the New World. These earlier migrations probably occurred about 30,000 years ago, according to available scientific evidence.

An American-Soviet research team working in the Aleutian Islands discovered in 1974 many stone artifacts that were at least 9,000 years old. These objects were very similar to the prehistoric stone implements commonly found in the Gobi Desert of Inner Mongolia. Their location in southern Alaska was the first direct evidence that the earliest Americans came from Siberia across the Bering Strait.

Scientists agree that during the Pleistocene Era ice deposits covered most of North America. The sea level in the Bering Strait decreased significantly exposing large sections of land. Masses of ice traveled South as far as the valleys of the Ohio and the Missouri rivers.

An ice-free corridor that extended for hundreds of miles and known as Beringia apparently served as the continental bridge that allowed man to enter the New World. Nomadic hunters probably arrived in the Western Hemisphere during that time.

There is considerable disagreement about when man crossed the Bering Strait. In 1974 archaeologists discovered in Hueyatlaco, near Puebla, Mexico, stone tools believed to be 250,000 years old. Their discovery conflicted with existing archaeological theories and the scientific community never accepted the scientific claim.

That year, Dr. Jeffrey Bada of the University of California, using a technique called amino acid racemization estimated a skull found in Del Mar near San Diego to be 48,000 years old. Scientists also doubted this claim and sent the skull to the Scripps Institute in La Jolla for further study. Later tests determined that the Del Mar Man was about 5,400 years old.

Other Discoveries

Canadian geologist Archie MacS. Stalker discovered several years later the remains of a young child presumed to be at least 50,000 years old. Skepticism also followed Dr. Stalker's claims. The archaeologist never produced further proof to justify the "Taber Child" antiquity (Canby, 351).

Recently, archaeologist Richard MacNeish claimed to have found in Southern New Mexico the remains of extinct animals, butchering tools, and other evidence that man was in the New World at least 36,000 years ago. Researchers also have found evidence in Pedra Furada, Brazil, that suggests man's occupation of some regions of the Southern Hemisphere as early as 25,000 years ago.

The most acceptable evidence found so far about man's arrival in the New World is from the Yukon's Old Crow Basin in northern Alaska. Implements of caribou antlers made 27,000 years ago show unmistakable evidence of human alteration. They were used to hammer bone and stone into manmade tools. Researchers also have found in the same area the remains of domestic dogs, at least 30,000 years old (Canby 344)

The First Americans

The first Paleo-Indians that came through the continental land bridge had the standard mongoloid features found in most native Americans. They had black eyes, straight black hair, a bronzed skin, wide cheek bones, and "distinctively curved incisors characterized by anthropologists as shovel-shaped." They lived by hunting the herds of mammoths, bison, and other wild beasts that inhabit the northern territories.

Initially, these Paleo-Indians did not advance much

from a traditional nomadic existence. The cold weather and other climatic conditions forced them to move rapidly to the South. The location of stone artifacts and remains of butchered animals in Valsequillo, Mexico, confirms this view (Canby 352).

Over a period of many centuries, the nomadic tribesmen moved southward through Canada, the United States, and Central America until they reached the southern tip of Chile. During their long march across the American continents, they established few permanent settlements. Although they may have used some form of agriculture, they depended on hunting and food gathering for survival.

Organized Settlements

Where the food and water were adequate, these Paleo-Indians formed villages and organized a rudimentary community life. Scholars disagree about when these early communities appeared initially. The most acceptable date of human settlement in the Americas is 15,000 years ago. Other claims seem exaggerated and based on personal convictions rather than scientific data, or cannot be verified (Fagan, 14-17).

Contrary to expectations, there are very few archaeological sites in North America that researchers can use to confirm the period of earlier Asian migrations. The only archaeological artifacts that scientists have found north of Mexico that can be authenticated beyond any doubt are about 17,000 years old.

These are the famous Meadowcroft Rockshelter artifacts and projectile points discovered on a charcoal concentration southwest of Pittsburgh several years ago. Researchers have documented that humans occupied that site 12,000 years ago. In southern Chile prehistoric communities of hunters and food gatherers appeared 13,000 years ago. Two thousand years earlier their ancestors had traveled almost to the tip of South America.

Primitive Societies

Scholars believe that the earlier inhabitants of the Western Hemisphere developed their primitive societies without any interference from the Old World civilizations. There is no definite proof that the

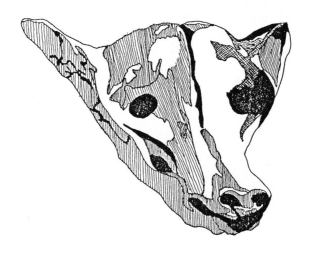

Figure 31 Carved animal fossil found in Tequixquiac, Valley of Mexico

original inhabitants of the Western Hemisphere had contacts with the peoples of Asia or Europe before the arrival of the Spaniards in 1492. Most of the evidence presented to prove the claim of foreign influence in the Western Hemisphere is very controversial.

There has been no discovery in ancient America about the use of the potter's wheel, the raising of cattle, or the domestication of farm animals. Most significantly, the American Indian lacked natural immunity to European diseases before the fifteenth century. He did not know until then how to use the Old World alphabetic writings.

Pre-Columbian societies also learned very late the use of metals such as bronze. As a result most of them lived in a Neolithic environment when the Europeans arrived for the first time in the New World.

The European View of the American Indian

For more than four hundred years American and European scholars debated the origin of early man in America. After the discovery of the New World, Church officials tried to explain the origins of the primitive people of the Western Hemisphere. Many Spaniards saw the Indians as "dirty dogs" with no religious or political rights. Others called them "noble savages" who deserved a fair treatment and a prompt conversion to Christianity.

According to historian Lewis Hanke "no other controversy so universally embroiled Spaniards during the sixteenth century or so well illustrates the climate of public opinion." As a result very few people agreed then on the nature of the American Indians.

Hanke writes: "Practically every important figure in the New World and many in Spain delivered a judgment on the capacity of the Indians. Humble friars and renowned theologians. . . arose to defend the Indians from the charge of irrationality. One of the greatest battles. . . took place in Valladolid in 1550 and 1551 when Juan Gines de Sepúlveda and Bartolomé de Las Casas fought bitterly over the question whether the Aristotelian theory that some men are by nature slaves applied to the Indians" (Hamke 11).

Other Speculations

Professor Barry Fell, writing about the speculations

Figure 32 Mixtec Funeral Ceremony.
Cocoa offering for the deceased (Codex
Nutall)

of the Church about the Indians, says: "The failure of the Bible to account for them and their continent was made good by the inference that Amerindians are the descendants of Babylonians, expelled from the Old World on account of the sins of their ancestors" Church authorities, and later the British antiquarian Lord Kingsborough, concluded that the inhabitants of Middle America were the descendants of the Lost Ten Tribes of Israel (Fell 16).

In 1811 the German naturalist Alexander von Humboldt recognized many Asian characteristics in the physical appearance of the American Indians and declared that they descended from Mongolian stock. The noted anthropologist Ales Hrdlicka also was an early exponent of the theory that the North American Indian is of Asiatic origin.

Many other investigators have written that the American Indian is of Chinese, Malay or Polynesian origin. They believe that man appeared in America thousands of years ago as a result of transoceanic travel across the Pacific Ocean.

In recent years, anthropologist Zelia Nuttall maintained that Phoenician traders probably set up colonies in Central and South America. Harold Sterling Gladwin also believed that the American Indian had contacts with Mediterranean cultures for hundreds of years. The Mesoamerican tradition of the "bearded white men who came from the East in ships" was frequently used to proof that ancient mariners from the Middle East traveled to America.

In 1931 Doctor Max Uhle of the Academy of History of Ecuador held that the Indian culture probably started in Central America. Several other scholars also debated the issue during the same year.

Anthropologist Lewis Spence accepted the "Lost Atlantis" theory by saying that survivors from that mythical region settled in Central America after the collapse of their civilization. Doctor Leo Wiener suggested, on the other hand, that shipwrecked mariners from Africa landed in Mesoamerica after drifting over the Atlantic Ocean currents.

Wiener used as arguments the apparent representation of Africans in Olmec art. He also used the prehistoric Hueyapan head with its Black race characteristics, and the references of Columbus to seagoing traders from Guinea, to justify his theories. He also held that the word canoe, smoking tobacco and the sweet potato came to America from Africa.

Present Scientific Views

 Most of the earlier views of the Paleo-Indian origin are no longer acceptable. Anthropologists now believe that the first Americans came from the northeastern part of Asia. Scholars also accept that the ancestors of the native American Indians were very efficient hunters. They knew how to track, kill, and butcher a prey; to make grooved or fluted stone points for weapons; and to use fire.
 These primitive people used special hunting techniques, spear throwers and stone-tipped lances. Writer Thomas Y. Canby has even suggested their depredations "may have caused the   extinction of the creatures they stalked" (330).
 Initially, the earlier nomadic tribes, did not advance much beyond the Neolithic age. It was not until 5000 B.C. that they discovered the techniques of agriculture. With this advancement permanent settlements began to take place in Mesoamerica and   Peru. The Indians cultivated maize, beans, squashes, chili peppers and other agricultural products in enough quantities to   allow the settlement and establishment of organized societies in Mexico and Central America.
 By 2000 B.C. maize had become a major source of food in Middle America. In South America, the cultivation of cassava, peanuts, maize and potatoes also permitted the development of highly organized agricultural societies.

Recent Investigations

 In recent years, Mexican scholars have investigated many sites searching for further traces of early occupation. Their research confirms that the principal migrations into the Western Hemisphere occurred during the last Ice Age.
 For thousands of years, primitive hunters stalked large grazing animals in central Mexico armed with very efficient spears. More than forty years ago Mexican paleontologist Juan Armenta Camacho found several stone artifacts and mastodon bones near the Valsequillo dam in Puebla.

One of the bones had a curious engraving that is at least 22,000 years old. In 1962 archaeologist Cynthia Irwin-Williams found on the same place evidence of human occupation that also shows a similar age.

In 1967 Dr. José Luis Lorenzo found in Tlapacoya, southeast of Mexico City, obsidian blades and other cultural remains that rivaled those at Valsequillo in age and authenticity. Archaeologists have found in Santa Isabel Iztapan stone tools and weapons dating to 10,000 B. C. Many of these artifacts were buried next to the bones of prehistoric mammoths, proving the existence of man in central Mexico during the Late Pleistocene Age (Canby 352).

Investigators also have found human remains, stone tools and weapons as old as 8,000 B.C. in Tepexpan. Excavations still in progress may even extend further the dates of the presence of man in the central highlands of Mexico. So far, the record does not go back much further than 12,000 years B.C.

Archaeological investigations also have shown that evolution from hunting and food gathering to settling farming villages was slow. Progress did not occur as fast as in the Old World because the Indians did not have cattle, pigs, goats, or sheep to use as a source of food. Also, there were no horses, mules or donkeys for use as pack animals. Agricultural yields were probably low since rain was inadequate, the soil was poor and natural fertilization was limited.

While the Indians knew about the principle of the wheel, no wheeled vehicles other than toys were constructed. The Mesoamerican Indians had no use for them because they did not have domestic animals to pull their loads.

Preclassic Period

By the year 2000 B.C., nomadic tribal groups began to appear in the Mesoamerican region to set up the beginning of the Preclassic Period. Agricultural settlements that produced corn, beans, squash, chili peppers, and amaranth seeds emerged to form the basis of the first villages. The primitive farmers who lived on them also hunted and fished, but left no permanent imprint of their society, except clay figurines that may have begun the rise of religion in Middle America.

Figure 33   Temple of the Warriors, Chichen Itza, Yucatan.

With agriculture firmly established by 2000 B. C., various cultures rose, flourished, and declined in the Mexican Plateau. The cool, beautiful and immense Valley of Mexico, located 7244 feet above sea level, was a refuge for many tribal groups. Lake Texcoco, the lagoon of Xochimilco, and many natural springs and rivers provided abundant water to the settlers.

As the Indians expanded their agricultural knowledge, they discovered the region's potential for development. Better organized settlements emerged along the margins of the lakes and rivers. Nomadic tribes settled in small communities near the Gulf Coast as early as 1500 B.C. These Indians used primitive forms of agriculture that was characterized by the digging stick. They also burned the forest lands to plant corn, beans, chili peppers and squashes.

Throughout the years, the poor quality of the soil and poor farming methods caused erosion, deforestation, and other related agricultural problems. Shortages of food forced many tribes to develop better organized societies under the direction of priest-rulers.

Between 1200 and 600 B.C., some of these tribal groups built large temples, pyramids and expressive sculptures in the Gulf Coast and central Mexico. They produced the first hieroglyphic writing in the Americas and painted large wall murals in a variety of colors.

Anthropologist Ignacio Bernal considers some of them "among the most extraordinary sculptors that Mesoamerica ever produced." Their cultural contributions had a considerable impact on succeeding tribal groups.

Olmecs' Earlier Contributions

One of the pre-Columbian societies that settled the hot and humid plains of the Gulf Coast was the Olmecs, perhaps the most mysterious and oldest of the civilizations of ancient Mexico. These Indians extended their influence through out Mesoamerica. Between 1500 and 1000 B.C. the Olmecs built San Lorenzo and La Venta as mayor ceremonial centers. The ruins of their ancient buildings, beautifully decorated with elaborate stone carvings, can still be found today in the area.

Throughout Mesoamerica, the Indians valued the pottery made by the Olmecs. Clay and jade carvings of religious motifs and half-human, half-jaguar figurines have been

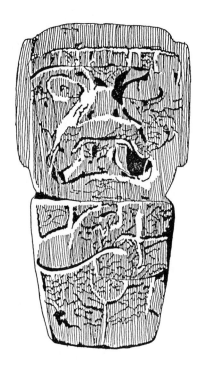

Figure 34 Prehistoric stone axe found in
Veracruz

found throughout the central and southern regions of Mexico. Olmec religion influenced extensively the Toltec, Mayan and Nahua civilizations.

Many of the early Indian societies used the Olmecs' building techniques. While the Olmecs pictographic writing has not yet been deciphered, enough information is known about them to say that they were the first Mesoamerican Indians who could calculate dates over extended periods.

Recent investigations, however, are changing many of the views held about the Olmecs. There has been a radical change in the interpretation of evidence and even the term Olmec has been questioned by many scholars.

Anthropologist Wendy Ashmore observes that few now regard the Olmecs as the "mother culture" of Mesoamerica, and many question the existence of an Olmec civilization at all. The Gulf Coast cultures "are now more widely viewed as part of a network of multiple, co-evolving complex societies." Their influence to the cultural development of central of Mexico was probably less significant that previously accepted.

While the Olmecs extended their civilization to the central highlands of Mexico and to other parts of Mesoamerica, very few of their archaeological sites have been found outside the coastal region. Their presence in the central highlands apparently was due to commercial interest and not to military control.

Archaeological evaluations of known Olmec sites in the Valley of Mexico confirm that these Indians lived peacefully for many years among the primitive people of the highlands. Anthropologist Jacques Soustelle wrote that they were met with little resistance when they first appeared in that area because their prestige was high and they showed no interest in war or military conquest.

Preclassical Cultures

The Olmec civilization ended about four hundred years before the birth of Christ. Other important settlements developed later in Mesoamerica and the Mexican highlands, and agricultural villages changed into larger organized communities. These earlier groups remained peaceful and had few expansionist ambitions. They did not practice war as an instrument of aggression.

Several preclassical cultures limited themselves to the cultivation of maize and to the manufacturing of pottery of utilitarian quality. Other became highly complex societies as shown by the construction of magnificent ceremonial centers. One important achievement from this period was the further development of hieroglyphic writing and the performance of complex mathematical calculations. The true city also emerged during this time at Teotihuacan. Later, in the Classic period, this urban center will dominate most of the Central Valley.

Between 600 B.C. and A.D. 100 highly superior cultures appeared in the central highlands. Their members built pyramids, ceremonial centers and pottery of high quality. They established permanent villages and introduced platforms and altars to serve as stages for ceremonial dances and religious rituals.

One structure that remains from this period is the ninety feet high, four-stepped circular stone platform at Cuicuilco, the first major ceremonial monument in the Valley of Mexico. Lava from the nearby Xitle Volcano buried the site some 2000 years ago.

At Ticoman the first recognizable gods appeared as clay figurines. Near the lakes, the building of chinampas increased the agricultural yield. This traditional Mexican farming method uses artificial islands of mud, dirt and tree branches for farming.

The Classic Period

The Classic Period in Mesoamerican history began about 100 B.C. and ended about A.D. 900. During this period Teotihuacan emerged in the Central Highlands as an urban center of great importance. Several other Indian cultures developed near present-day Veracruz.

Priests ruled the ceremonial centers of Papantla, El Faisan, and Remojadas. At El Tajin the Huastec Indians built a metropolis with temples and pyramids, and game courts where the people played the sacred game of *tlachtli*.

Monte Alban became an important Zapotec urban and ceremonial center in the southern part of Mexico. Its inhabitants did a variety of advanced medical and dental practices and metallurgical techniques unknown in other

Figure 35   Maya Puuc architectural design in mosaic form, Uxmal, Yucatan.

areas of Mesoamerica. The Zapotecs are still the dominant cultural group in the state of Oaxaca.

The Mixtecs also settled in the same region of Mexico. They were famous Indian artists and investigators can document their history to A.D. 692. During this time religion, art, trade, mathematics and science rose to new heights.

Elaborate funeral rituals and the traditional ball game, later adopted by the Aztecs, also date from this period. In the Yucatan and Guatemalan lowlands, Mayan societies unfold rapidly, culminating in the development of the most important Indian civilization in Mesoamerica.

The Maya

The Maya dominated Guatemala, eastern Chiapas Tabasco, the Yucatan Peninsula, the western parts of Honduras, El Salvador, and Belize. They were the largest homogeneous group in Central America and their language is still spoken by hundreds of thousands of natives.

Their astronomical and mathematical calculations established the pattern for later Mesoamerican scientific and religious inquiries. These societies also produced highly accurate calendrical systems and could record time to infinity. Natural themes and realism dominated their art. Their writing was complex and highly developed. Until recently, they remained almost unknown.

Maya architecture included the corbel vault and the roof combs. This type of engineering was used in the construction of ceremonial centers and sanctuaries. Pyramids were four-sided, stepped structures built to honor rulers and gods. The mortuary pyramids, such as those of Tikal and Palenque, had nine stages representing the nine levels of the underworld. The Maya used pyramids to entomb honored rulers or as centers for religious ceremonies. Many of the tombs contained grave offerings of ceramics, weapons, and tools.

Tikal was one of the largest and most impressive of the Mayan cities. Built in the dense forest of the Peten, Guatemala, it contained more than 3000 buildings in an area of no more than sixteen square kilometers. It had a population of perhaps 39,000 people at the peak of its power, with another 10,000 living in the outskirts of the city.

Figure 36   Warrior with tatooed face and headdress.

The residents of this urban center used intensified agricultural methods to support themselves instead of the standard slash and burn system of the other pre-Columbian societies. Researchers also have found the presence of large quantities of obsidian throughout the city. This suggests that the inhabitants were mostly stone workers. They specialized in hand-made crafts and in the manufacture of ceramics.

Importance of the Maya

The Maya occupied Tikal continuously for more than one thousand years. They built palaces, residences, ball courts, terraces, five temple pyramids and several market places. Archaeologists have found near the city more than two hundred carved stelae and hundreds of altars and burial places.

There were also religious centers for every 50 to 100 dwellings. Agriculture and trade were very important to the Maya. Bartering became the principal means of commercial exchange and value was established by demand and rarity instead of need.

Throughout the southern region of Mexico and the low lands of Central America there were many Mayan cities and ceremonial centers similar to Tikal. The most important were Palenque, Bonampak, Piedras Negras, Seibal, Copan, Chichen Itza, Uxmal, and Tulum. These sites served as administrative, commercial and religious centers. Public administrators and priests lived and worked in them while the rest of the people lived in the immediate vicinity.

The priests directed and controlled commercial transactions and business. The commoners did the principal tasks of society, such as farming, fishing, trading and doing public works. The Maya used criminals, debtors and prisoners of war as slaves.

The principal administrator or ruler was the Ahau or "truth man." He had the power to appoint the town chiefs and their deputies, to direct military operations, and to serve as a High Priest or senior religious official. The importance of these Mayan rulers continued even after death. The people considered them god-like during their lifetime, and death only intensified religious worship.

Many pyramids have been found in Yucatán, Belize and Guatemala that contain the remains of Mayan rulers or members of the aristocracy. In Yucatan one can see the remains of paved highways and canal systems that were used for trade and communication. Every city had circular underground cisterns lined with stone to preserve water.

Mayan Influence in Mesoamerica

Of all the pre-Columbian civilizations that emerged in Mesoamerica before the arrival of the Europeans, the Maya reached the highest degree of cultural development and scientific knowledge. Their civilization went into decline around A. D. 800. By A.D. 900 most sites had been abandoned and their population scattered throughout the lowlands of Mesoamerica. With the decline of Mayapan in 1450, Maya power collapsed and disappeared.

There are many theories about the reasons for the Maya decline during this period, none of which have been accepted as a final explanation. Cultural decadence, inferior architecture, and preoccupation with military and religious matters marked the end of that noble race. The survivors, divided into smaller groups resettled in other areas of southern Mexico. When the Spaniards reached Yucatan in the sixteenth century, they found many Mayan cities and stone buildings already in ruins.

Since there was no single Mayan geographical unit, but a series of regional centers or city-states that struggled among themselves for political control, perhaps constant warfare played a major role on their disaster.

As Peter Winn has suggested "a generation ago, our image of the ancient Maya was that of a peaceful people ruled by anonymous priest-astronomers whose eyes were fixed on the stars and their minds focused on the passage of time. The discovery of mural paintings showing warfare, captives, and human sacrifice led scholars to conclude that the Maya were as warlike as their central Mexican contemporaries, and were similar in their blood rites" (23).

Winn further suggests that the Mayan history parallel that of the ancient Greek states, where war and the struggle for regional power resulted in the end of their political system.

Others believe that by the twelfth century the classic Mayan civilization had long been in a state of decline from which it never recovered. Cultural paralysis, foreign invasions, a population explosion, and ecological abuse probably have a part in the collapse of the Classic

Figure 37   House of the Turtles, Uxmal, Yucatan

Figure 38   House of the Magician, Uxmal, Yucatan.

Maya civilization. The full story, however, will not be known until more studies are made of their hieroglyphic writing system.

Teotihuacan

In the central highlands Teotihuacan, an agricultural community located 28 miles northeast of present-day Mexico City, also became an important urban center and the nucleus of a commercial empire that extended as far as Guatemala and Honduras. A complex ceremonial system of pyramids and beautiful palaces, it dominated central Mexico and much of Mesoamerica for more than 600 years.

Two of its most important trading posts of Teotihuacan were Kaminaljuyu in Guatemala and El Tajin on the Gulf Coast. These commercial outposts traded mostly with the Maya and the Indian groups that lived in the Yucatan Peninsula and southern Mexico.

The products of their artisans, such as small clay figurines and painted cylindrical pots, have been found throughout Mesoamerica. Wealth was based on commercial trade and on the ownership of obsidian mines that produced the raw material for weapons.

The Pyramids of the Sun and the Moon

Teotihuacan was a planned city of massive ceremonial structures. One of them, the Pyramid of the Sun, is 207 feet tall, 740 feet long and 730 feet wide and covers and area of 540,200 square feet. It consists of more than two million tons of crushed rock, dirt, stone and tile. Archaeologists believe that its construction kept 10,000 laborers busy for twenty years.

The original pyramid was very different from the one that is seen today. At the turn of the century, an untrained and anxious archaeologist tried to restore the monument to impress the foreign visitors expected for the celebration of the centenary of the Mexican independence.

When he could not complete the task on time, the archaeologist rushed the pyramid repair work by `peeling it like an onion,' as Frederick Peterson described the restoration process. His workers removed thousands of rocks and stones from the structure exposing its interior

Figure 39   Palace, Nunnery Quadrangle, Uxmal, Yucatan.

Figure 40   Palace of the Governors, Uxmal, Yucatan.

to rain, which damaged it considerably (61-62).

Later repairs of the pyramid only served to increase the initial damage and destroy the remaining cut-stone facing, called *talud and tablero*. It also changed the pyramid original symmetry. Peterson writes, "What we see today is not the pyramid, but the core" (62).

In 1960 archaeologists made several borings in the stone facing of the monument and discovered an early structure buried underneath. They believe this may be a burial place, although this has never been confirmed.

The Pyramid of the Moon, rising on the eastern side, is smaller. It measures 492 feet long, 140 feet wide and 140 feet high and occupies and area of more than 68,000 square feet. The Indians used both pyramids as ceremonial shrines.

As many other ancient monuments, their constructions follow the shape of the land. In the Indian religion, the giant steps of the Pyramid of the Moon symbolized a path to the after world. Polychromatic murals painted with brilliant red, turquoise and yellow hues adorned the Temple of Quetzalcoatl, another important structure in the city. Its great stairway was decorated with feathered serpent heads, small mussels, and snails. Masks of Tlaloc, the rain-god, completed the decorations. Porticoes with carved pillars ran along the sides of the court. This temple was one of the most impressive buildings of ancient Mexico.

The *Ciudadela*, a sunken ceremonial courtyard located near the Temple of Quetzalcoatl, was the center of the city. A wide causeway, known as Micaotli or the Street of the Dead, extended in a north-south axis for several kilometers. Another avenue was laid out at a right angle to the first causeway, dividing the area into quarters. Many buildings and temples bordered the roadways that make up the main arteries of the city.

Influence of Teotihuacan

In Teotihuacan, Indian art had a strong religious development. Most of the sculptures and paintings in the temples and palaces depicted divine themes. Religious symbols of jaguars, snakes and eagles, and of priests making offerings to their gods, were widespread throughout the city.

Figure 41 Model of Tenochtitlan at the time of the
Conquest. (INAH)

Figure 42 A closer view of the rattlesnake trapezoids in
Lakin-East Temple, Uxmal, Yucatan.

Paintings of religious deities, warriors and fertility rites decorated most of the buildings. These artistic and religious motifs were copied extensively throughout the rest of Mesoamerica and influenced the architectural and ceramic forms of most of the Indian groups of the region.

Besides the religious monuments, temples, palaces, and other buildings, the city had more than 2300 multi-roomed, windowless apartment-like dwellings that served as living quarters. These structures covered more than twenty square kilometers of territory in a grid-style plan of streets, streams and buildings. The Great Compound, or marketplace, was located where the principal streets intersected the center of the city.

While the expansion of Teotihuacan as a major commercial center occurred mostly during the first centuries of the Christian Era, there is much controversy among researchers concerning the true beginning of this city. Recent investigations made by the Mexican anthropologist Ignacio Bernal place the beginning of the foundation of Teotihuacan 250 years earlier than was formally accepted.

The period, which Bernal calls Teotihuacan I, probably represents the beginning of the construction of the Pyramids of the Sun and the Moon, the outlining of the Street of the Dead and the establishing of the organized government.

Bernal writes, "The population density of Teotihuacan -- apart from the temples or public buildings -- must have been substantial. At its zenith it had over 200,000 inhabitants and occupied more than 32 kilometers. The fantastic quantity of accumulated constructions, ruins, objects, in a word, all signs of human life, suggests a population cluster on a scale hitherto unknown in Mesoamérica" (40).

Farming was the principal occupation of the residents of Teotihuacan, but the peasantry played no role in its administration. The merchants, priests, military leaders and government officials made up the elite. At the height of its development the population included hundreds of skilled workers, craftsmen, warriors, and many other specialists.

The influence of Teotihuacan in Mesoamerica lasted for more than six hundred years. Its art, architecture, religion, and social structure influenced every later

Indian civilization. The Aztecs were so impressed by this city-state that they named it the "place where the gods are made" and still made religious pilgrimages to it, seven centuries after its destruction by foreign invaders.

The Post Classic Period

After A.D. 700, most of the classic societies began to loose their commercial and political influence throughout Mesoamerica. War, natural disasters, foreign invasions and internal political problems caused the end of Teotihuacan and the Mayan centers.

Barbarian invaders burned and looted Teotihuacan at the end of the seventh century. Since there are no written records or inscriptions of historical value the evidence of what occurred in that city is limited. Its destruction marks the disintegration of Middle America's Classic Period.

The next group of Indians that found their way to the central highlands and southern lowlands of Mexico were the Nahua, of which the Aztecs, Toltecs, Chichimecs, Alcohuas, Tepanecs, and several others were but a limited representation.

These warrior people brought considerable turmoil to the Central Valley of Mexico. They rehabilitated the centuries' old societies that they met with their vigor and violent ways. With the end of the classic period the old cultures also adapted themselves to the new militarist way of life. The priests lost some of their power to rising young warriors, but it continued to flourish under new ideologies and religious cults.

The Nahua adopted many old customs and traditions of the Classic cultures, such as the cult of Quetzalcoatl, who became the most widely accepted creator god of the Postclassical societies. They also adopted the rain-god Tlaloc, an ancient Mesoamerican divinity. He became the patron deity of rain, floods, drought, hail, ice, and lightning, and as such, a helpful and beneficial but dangerous god.

The use of metals expanded throughout the Post-Classic Period. Knowledge of metal working probably reached Mesoamérica from Panamá or South America. Some basic materials used in the construction of weapons and artifacts apparently came through trade with the Indians

Figure 43   Atlantean basalt figures, Temple B, Tula.

of northern South America.

The early peoples of Mesoamerica apparently benefited from the trade with other parts of ancient America. The knowledge of the cultivation of manioc or cassava in Mexico probably came from Peru, where the tropical plant has been used as a staple food for hundreds of years.

Afterward, the Toltec state rose in central Mexico around A.D. 900 to set the militarist ideal of the Postclassical period. Based in the sacred capital of Tula, the Toltec state rose and fell in central Mexico between the tenth and the twelfth century.

The political unity of central Mexico gave way to chaos after the twelfth century. Internal economic and religious problems, droughts, the pressure from displaced peoples and renewed barbarian invasions destroyed the Toltec Empire. About 1150, Tula was abandoned to foreign invaders.

Other Aztec Predecessors

Many of the Indians that moved to the central valley of Mexico were contemporary of the Aztecs, while others preceded them by hundreds of years. The Totonacs lived in central Veracruz and northern Puebla. Their capital Cempoala, a city-state of more than 30,000 people, was a thriving commercial center that paid tribute to the Aztecs. They were the first ones to ally themselves with Cortes during his march to Tenochtitlan. the Tlaxcalans, also enemies of the Aztecs, lived in central Mexico. They, too, battled Cortes and his allies, but later joined him against the Aztecs.

The Huaxtec split from the Maya of Yucatan earlier in their history and settled north of Veracruz. They became almost isolated from their southern relatives, but their artistic styles influenced the Late Postclassic period of Mesoamerican culture.

Out of the confusion of Toltec refugee groups and renewed warfare in the Valley of Mexico, five city-states: Atcapotzalco, Zaltocan, Texcoco, Colhuacan, and Xico, rose to share the fragmented power of the Toltec state. Not until the Aztecs appeared in the central highlands and used their skills and military might in the fifteenth century to conquer their neighbors would total domination of the Valley of Mexico be accomplished by a single tribal group.

Figure 44   Ruins of the Toltec capital of Tula. Temple B is on the background.

5

Journey from Aztlan

Origins of the Aztec Nation

In the sixteenth century the Spaniards found in Central Mexico a group of people who were strangers to the area. These Indians had migrated hundreds of years before and did not consider the region where they lived as their original home. Most of them spoke Nahuatl, a Uto-Aztecan language of northwestern Mexico.

For more than three hundred years that language had been the principal means of communication in Mesoamerica. Even now, millions of the residents of central Mexico speak Nahuatl. In North America, several Indian tribes, among them the Shoshoni, Paiute, Pima and Hopi also speak dialects of that language.

Several historical traditions of the Nahua suggest that they came originally from northern Mexico. For hundreds of years these people had lived as nomadic, uncivilized people dedicated to hunting and fishing as a way of life. The alien environment where they lived apparently hardened their spirit and made them a fierce and warlike people. Like other Mesoamerican Indians, the Nahua had no difficulty in abandoning their settlements to secure better ones when conditions required it.

These Indian groups, which included the Aztecs, began to migrate to central Mexico at the beginning of the ninth century. Most of them considered themselves as migrants from a mysterious place called Chicomoztoc, or the Seven Caves, which were located somewhere in the western part of the country. Legends of their struggle have evoke many stories and even whole chapters in the Mexican folkloric literature.

Figure 45   Ruins of a burnt palace, Tula.

While those legends are very consistent and interesting, the beginnings of their civilization are uncertain. For many years, investigators have attempted to find the origins of these ancient societies. But myth, legend, and the limited amount of historical evidence that is available have made the task very difficult.

The Aztecs and the Spanish chroniclers called the Nahua-speaking people Chichimec, or "Sons of Dogs," because they lived as uncivilized people in the northern deserts. The Spaniards later applied the term to all the groups that migrated South, including the Aztec themselves. The Chichimecs who invaded in the twelfth century the settled areas of central Mexico were a nation of nomadic warriors.

The Aztecs, who came from a region of western Mexico known as Aztlán, entangle the narratives of their initial journey with those of the Nahuatl immigrants. They added to the historical records many heroic and mystic accounts of their ancestry to fit their expanding political interests, and to convince the people of their noble heritage. As a result, their stories of the migration cannot be authenticated. The accounts that exist are mostly from the colonial period and must be used with care. Some tales are based on the native folklore or in the tales told to the Spanish by the Indian themselves.

The quest for scientific knowledge has also been difficult because most of the archaeological ruins of Tenochtitlan lay beneath the tall buildings, city streets and stores of Mexico City. In recent years, however, a wealth of new scientific information has surfaced as result of the work of many investigators. In spite of the renewed efforts, the task of investigation still is incomplete.

The National Institute of Anthropology and History of Mexico has been in the forefront of modern research. Workers have uncovered many of the remains of the Great Temple of Tenochtitlan. The ruins of that important religious center were discovered in 1978. The study of those archaeological ruins has changed our knowledge of the Aztec world.

The Place of the Herons

The Mexican anthropologist Wigberto Jimenez Moreno believes that the Aztecs came from the present state of

Nayarit. Many historians also have mentioned this region, located about 450 miles northwest of Mexico, as the probable location of Aztlan, their mythical birthplace.

There are many linguistic similarities between the language of the Cora and Huichol Indians who live in that region and the Nahuatl spoken by the Aztecs. The geographic features of the area also seem to match those used by the Aztecs to describe their homeland. Aztlan, or the "place of the herons," was also the source for the Nahuatl word Aztec or "people of heron place."

Investigators have been unable to agree on the exact location of Aztlan. The German naturalist Baron Alexander von Humboldt placed it in the northwestern section of the United States. The Frenchman Abbe Carlos Brasseur de Bourbourg and the historian Francisco Clavijero believed that it was located in northern California. Historians Lorenzo Boturini, Hubert H. Bancroft and J.M. Aubin also placed it in California.

The Spanish chronicler Jose de Acosta and the Codex Ramirez placed Aztlan in the northern part of Sonora, Mexico. The Franciscan Jeronimo de Mendieta and the Mexican historian Hernando de Tezozomoc wrote that Aztlan was located in the Jalisco province in western Mexico. Other historians have placed it in many other areas, from Southern California to central Mexico.

The Village of Mexcaltitan

Modern Mexican scholars suggest the possibility that an island village named Mexcaltitan, located in the west coast of Mexico, may have been the homeland of the Aztecs. This unique river settlement closely resembles the one that the early Mexicans described as their homeland.

The chronicles of the early Spanish missionaries who interviewed the Indians after the Conquest reveal many similarities between Mexcaltitan and Aztlan. Some characteristics of Tenochtitlan, the famous capital of the Aztec Empire, were very similar to those found in the island village.

The animal and plant life that surround Mexcaltitan also seem to fit the description of the Aztec homeland. Graceful herons and egrets, and scores of other water birds, as described by the Aztecs, live among the lily pads and marshes. In spite of the similarities, there has been no scientific evidence to prove the argument.

Other Possibilities

Toward the southern side of the San Pedro River, there are other possible areas for the location of Aztlan. The mangrove swamps along the Rio Grande de Santiago, or the swampy vegetation of the low lands near San Blas, could have been places for their homeland. The Aztec sense of beauty, their love of flowers, birds, and butterflies showed a preference for wetlands.

They probably selected Lake Texcoco for the end of their journey because it may have been similar to Aztlan. Geographers Terry G. Jordan and Lester Rowntree write that "migrating people often are attracted to new lands that seem environmentally similar to their homelands" (Jordan and Rowntree 205).

When the Aztecs migrated from Aztlan to the Valley of Mexico, they must have followed a southeastern route. The path of their migration is inaccurate and largely surrounded by legend and superstition. They probably traveled across the present states of Jalisco and Michoacan, well known for their many lakes, lagoons and marshes. The regional lakes of Chapala, Patzcuaro and Cuitzeo, and others that are now dried or have changed into deep valleys, may have also attracted them during the journey.

No one knows exactly why the Aztecs leave their homeland in a journey across the mountains that brought them suffering and anguish. The motive for their departure was probably in Emperor Moctezuma I's mind when he asked the Aztec historian Cuauhcoat for an explanation.

The old man replied: "Our fathers lived in a happy and beautiful place. They could feast on all types of duck, hens, and crows, and enjoy the singing of the red and yellow feathered birds. They could eat many kinds of fish and enjoy the coolness of the trees at their pleasure. After they left the region, everything turned against them; the underbrush cut their bodies, the stones scraped their feet, the fields were full of vines and thorns. Snakes, poisonous insects, and mountain lions were their constant companions" (Chavero 579).

Figure 46   Detail from the Wall of the Serpents at Tula.

Droughts and Weather Changes

If the story provided by Fray Diego Duran is true, Aztlan must have been an idyllic place. Why, then, did the Aztecs leave their paradise? What were the reasons for their neighbors to due the same? Placing aside the mythological wishes of their gods as a reason, changes in the weather may have forced them to migrate.

Man seldom moves from areas that are satisfactory to his life style. He prefers a sedentary existence and dreads to move to new and unfamiliar places. He may not change to a new location to start a new life if he is satisfied with his present surroundings. Unless threatened by weather variations, enemy threats, or other causes, he will stay in a known location.

Anthropologist Nigel Davies has studied the effects of droughts and aridity on the northern Indian settlers of Mexico. As he points out, the North American arid zone was expanding in all directions between the twelfth and the fifteenth centuries; this change must have disturbed the subsistence pattern of the nomads living in sensitive border zone between savanna and steppe climates.

Davis further suggests that the advancement of the arid zone, inadequate amounts of rain, and other related factors may have triggered the barbarian invasions that destroyed the Toltec empire. Their migrations occurred about the same time that the Aztecs traveled to central Mexico.

Many ancient writings of the Toltecs talk about intense droughts during the period of migration. "Tula, the Toltec capital, suffered severe crop failures after seasons of devastating frosts and droughts," writes Jonathan Kandell (25).

The Tira de la Peregrinacion

There are two well-known Aztec hieroglyphic writings that are considered genuine that partially describe the Aztec migration. Unfortunately, these early pictographic writings contain a substantial amount of mythological tales that make the historical narrative questionable. The chronology of dates and events is also confusing an unreliable.

The first one, in several colors, shows in cycles of fifty-two years the Aztec pilgrimage and the locations where they rested. This painting belonged to the Spanish Jesuit scholar Carlos de Siguenza y Gongora. It was published for the first time in Italy during the seventeenth century.

The second hieroglyphic was drawn in black ink with a red line connecting the different drawings. It also details part of the Aztec journey. The *Tira de la Peregrinación Azteca*, drawn at least one hundred and fifty years after they moved to central Mexico, contains a chronology of the most important events of that pilgrimage. Scholars have used this document extensively to study the Aztec migration. It has been published several times and now is in the National Museum of Anthropology in Mexico City.

There are other sources, such as the *Codex Vaticanus 3738*, that can be used to study the Aztec pilgrimage. Pedro de los Rios, a Dominican Friar, made this post-Columbian codex about 1562. It is preserved in the Library of the Vatican in Rome. It contains a limited description of the Aztecs'pilgrimage from an area known as Chicomoaztlan, located in the old Tlapaltec territory. Investigators believe that Aztlan may have been a part of that territory.

There are many other documents that describe the Aztec migration. Most of them are based on the same two documents previously described and, with few exceptions, the details are the same. There are no facts of the historical journey that can be authenticated. The documents that are available do not provide any additional information on the pilgrimage.

The Religious Pilgrimage

Fray Diego Duran, a Dominican priest, wrote that beginning in the year A.D. 820 six Indian nations left the seven caves where they lived in northern Mexico; and, after a journey of more than eighty years, they reached the highlands. These tribes did not leave together, but in subsequent waves. A seventh group, the Aztecs, went to the same area three hundred and two years later.

The Aztecs, according to Duran, left their home under divine guidance of their war god Huitzilopochtli. During the journey four selected priests carried a wooden idol of their god. His spirit spoke to the tribe through the priests (Duran 21-26).

Another source, the Codex Boturini, mentions that eight Indian tribes (the Codex Ramirez says seven), representing the Nahua nation, migrated to the South of Mexico. Traveling by canoe and by foot, these tribes marched for sometime without a definite destination until they arrived at Coluacan, where they rested for the first time.

In that place they built an altar to their hummingbird god of war Huitzilopochtli, who spoke to his followers through the tribal priests. He ordered them to carry his idol on their backs and take care of his needs.

The Spanish historian Fray Juan de Torquemada writes that the pilgrims continued their journey, and later rested near a large tree where they built another altar to their god. Several days later, the tree crushed to the ground, dividing itself into two parts. The Indians accepted the event as a manifestation of Huitzilopochtli's wishes to divide the pilgrims into two groups.

The priests selected two of the tribes, which they reformed into a different group called Mexica or Azteca. They also ordered the rest of the people to continue their journey on a separate direction. To please Huitzilopochtli, the head priest sacrificed several women. The religious ceremony was so successful that the war god rewarded them with an abundant hunt.

The Codex Boturini

The Codex Boturini continues the description of the journey. Apparently, the Indians moved afterward to Chocayan where they stayed for sometime. Then the Aztecs settled at Coatepec near Tula, and lived there in semi-permanent homes. Huitzilopochtli's sister Coyolxauhqui insisted in remaining there with the rest of the tribe. In the struggle that followed between the two deities, Huitzilopochtli killed and dismembered his sister. This myth had many variations and was very important to the Aztecs (Matos Moctezuma 39-41).

The Aztecs arrived to Tollan or Tula in A.D. 1165, the year in which northern barbarians destroyed the city. From there the Aztecs moved to Atlicalaquia. Fourteen years they lived as farmers in that area. After this period, they moved to Tlemaco.

The Aztecs continued their journey, and as they

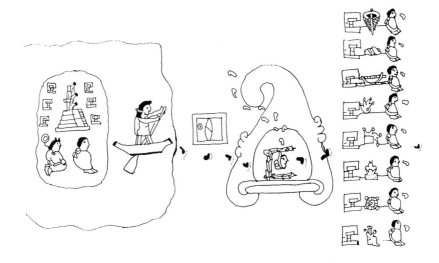

Figure 47 The beginning of the Aztec's journey (*Tira de la Peregrinacion)*

moved, they sacrificed human beings to insure their god's benevolence. They later moved to Tolpetlac, where they learned the use of maguey, and the manufacture of alcoholic beverages.

Their journey continued unabated for several more years, until they reached Acolman. They settled in Chapultepec, a region of central Mexico that had many strategic advantages, good hunting, excellent fishing, and the availability of salt.

A year later, the Aztecs decided to conduct a religious ceremony by sacrificing several human beings to the god Huitzilopochtli. To do so, it was necessary to secure prisoners of war. They raided the neighboring tribes for victims, but their enemies defeated them. Soon after that, they had to abandon the area, becoming a tribe of homeless wanderers.

The following year they were captured by another tribe, who reduced them to slavery. Their captors, however, went to war against the Indians of Xochimilco. During that conflict, they utilized the Aztec as warriors. The newcomers fought with great courage to regain their freedom. The even proved their warrior's skills by cutting the ears of their fallen victims. The narration of these events, which D. Lorenzo Boturini published for the first time in 1746 in the *Catalogo del Museo Indiano*, ends at this point.

The Codex Ramirez

According to the Codex Ramirez, a manuscript of the sixteenth century and a more reliable document as far as dates are concerned, the Nahuas left their homeland in different groups about A.D. 820, and traveled periodically for eight years to reach the central valley of Mexico, arriving in that area in the year A.D. 902.

The Aztecs, arrived at the central highlands 302 years after the first Nahua groups. The Code Ramirez notes the year as A.D. 1204. More modern sources place the arrival time during the year A.D. 1168. Since their journey was not continuous, they settled temporarily along the route until their guiding religious deity told them to go to another place.

The present historical records do not provide adequate information about the route that the Aztecs followed in their journey to central Mexico. The geography of the western area of that country, however, may confirm the belief that the Aztecs must have traveled to the southeast during the earlier part of their migration. They probably used a route close to the present Mexican section of the Pan American Highway.

Some Speculations

Following trails that had been used by many Indians for hundreds of years, the Aztecs must have limited their wanderings to a few places. The high mountain barriers and steep ravines that border the trails probably prevented it. Traveling in family groups, with children, the sick and the elderly, in an unfamiliar alien environment and without knowing what would be their final destination, their journey must have been a challenge to them.

Even if they followed at the beginning the narrow coastal strip of land wedged between the ocean and the Sierra Madre Occidental the mountain and river barriers probably made their pilgrimage extremely difficult.

Near the Rio Grande de Santiago, rivers and streams cross the plains that, in flood season, create serious hazards to the traveler. Near the coast, marshes and lagoons also make travel difficult. In some of these areas today, the brush and the thicket of small trees, tangled growth of cactus, and other shrubs, make any journey difficult.

The Michoacan Sojourn

From the Rio Grande de Santiago to Michoacan the Aztecs probably followed a corridor that is bordered by high mountain peaks and valleys, some of them of nearly 9,000 feet. So forbidding are the mountain barriers of this area that even today travel is very difficult except along the Pan American highway.

This area has many dormant volcanos. On February 20, 1943, near the village of Angahuan, 105 miles southeast of Guadalajara, a volcano sprung out of a cornfield and within six days its cone measured 525 feet in height. The lava of the Paracutin buried over nine square miles of farmland and two nearby villages.

The Tarascan Indians who lived in Michoacan did not accept the Aztecs when they arrived in their territory.

Since in the arts of war they could withstand their enemies successfully, the Tarascans effectively prevented Aztec settlements in Lake Patzcuaro, one of the most important lakes in the central highlands. The Aztecs left the area soon after the first encounters and continued their journey toward the Valley of Mexico.

The Aztecs departed Michoacan carrying an effigy of Huitzilopochtli in a portable shrine. The route that they now took has been the subject of controversy for years. The small lakes and short rivers that the Aztecs found east of Michoacan was the proper territory for their life style.

Judged by the standards of the other Nahuatl-speaking people who had arrived in the central highlands much earlier, the Aztecs were uncivilized. Unwelcome and shunned, they continued their journey until they reached Tollan, the Tula of the Toltec empire.

The Toltec Empire

The Aztecs entered the domain of the Toltec rulers when that empire was on the verge of collapse. The Toltec state had risen in central Mexico around A.D. 900 to set the militaristic ideal of the Post-Classical period. They represented a mixture of Chichimecs, Nahua, and Nonoalcas who had migrated from the northwest to establish themselves in the central valley of Mexico.

Based in the sacred capital of Tula, the powerful Toltec state influenced the political, commercial, and cultural characteristics of Mesoamerica as no other civilization had done before them. Their direct political control centered mostly north of the Valley of Mexico.

The Toltecs practiced a religion based on human sacrifice, such as the Aztecs did many years later, and introduced the first historical period of the Valley of Mexico. Their first ruler, Mixcoatl, was an extraordinary leader whose influence and qualities affected considerably the Toltec state. He developed a society based on militarism and warfare, efficient land cultivation, and a strong government control.

His son, Ce Acatl Topiltzin, who took the name Quetzalcoatl to honor that ancient god, expanded the borders of the Toltec state beyond the frontiers of the central valley and built the great city of Tula. His political control, however, centered mostly north of the

Figure 48   Monolithic Atlantean supports, Temple B, Tula.

Valley of Mexico.

The Glory of Tula

In Tula, Topiltzin changed the emphasis of the people from religious to military and civil matters. Toltec power and prosperity reached the highest point in their history. During his nineteenth year's rule, the Toltec king made his capital a center of learning and splendor.

According to a legend quoted by Alfonso Caso in his book *El Pueblo del Sol*, "Tula was an eternal paradise, where cotton grew in different colors, where agricultural grain was so large that the imperfect seeds were used as combustible in the steam baths." Topiltzin built elaborated temples, revived the idea of monumental architecture, and established a tributary state. His atlantean columns in the great temple of Tula can still be seen today.

To the South, Toltec traders maintained commercial ties with Guatemala, Honduras, Nicaragua. To the North, their influence stretched from northern Mexico to the southwestern part of the United States. It is speculated that the Toltec influence may have reached even the Mound Builders of the Mississippi Valley. After A. D. 1000 these Indians transformed their simple burial sites into lavish mounds with temples structured after the truncated Toltec pyramids. Archaeologist Ewil W. Haury believes that "Hohokam symbols, found nowhere else in the Southwest, derive from the calendrical symbols common in Mexico."

Toltec art glorified the military with colossal warrior pillars, serpent columns, and reliefs of fierce jaguars and eagles. This city-state set the standards of militarism, trade, political organization, religious dogmatism, and social organization that the Aztecs used to develop their empire.

The Toltecs apparently believed that a race of giants called Quinametzins once ruled the earth and build great cities such as Teotihuacan. Probably the legend originated when they uncovered the bones of extinct mammoths in the region and could not explain their origins. The Spaniards even accepted the belief and sent to their king the bones of an elephant as proof of the existence of giants in the Western Hemisphere.

The End of the Toltec Empire

The political unity of central Mexico gave way to chaos after three centuries of Toltec rule. Internal economic problems, the pressure of displaced peoples, and renewed Chichimec invasions undermined the empire in the twelfth century. Droughts also played an important part in its end. The Toltec chronicles tell of many years of crop failures as a result of poor weather conditions.

The problem of religion became acute in the Toltec empire by the end of the millennium. Many Toltecs were followers of Tezcatlipoca, while others owed allegiance to Quetzalcoatl. For the Toltecs, this god was far more kindly than the other members of the Toltec pantheon.

Quetzalcoatl was the cultural hero who once instructed the Nahuas in agriculture and the arts. He was also the lord of wind and rain and the patron of merchants. He ruled with mercy and justice, opposed human sacrifices, and encouraged the development of arts and learning. The deity first appeared on the temples and pyramids of Teotihuacan, and later in the Toltec religion. According to an Indian legend, Quetzalcoatl was going to return some day to impart further knowledge in the arts and the cultivation of the soil.

On the other hand, Tezcatlipoca, the other Toltec deity, was the god of night. He was also the god of death, demons, and destruction. He intervened directly in human affairs and was the protector of sorcerers and witches. This god was the brother and adversary of Quetzalcoatl and demanded human sacrifices for his satisfaction. He had many followers in the Toltec state.

Internal Strife

The cult of these two deities created a great internal religious strife. Those devoted to Quetzalcoatl and those who preferred the fierce god Tezcatlipoca fought a bitter conflict. The struggle reflected the divisions that existed between traditional theocratic leaders and the military groups that attempted to change the system (Caso 41).

Those that honored the war god were victorious, and Topiltzin was sent into exile. The cult of Tezcatlipoca replaced that of Quetzalcoatl. Both gods became later very prominent member of the Aztec religion.

Following Topiltzin departure, other kings continued to rule the demoralized Toltec state. The ancient splendor and importance of the empire disappeared with further internecine conflicts. Huemac, the last king, also abandoned the city, ending the long dynastic rule of the Toltec kings.

The Barbarian Invasions

About 1160, Tula was abandoned by its residents and later destroyed by northern barbarians. One factor that helped in its destruction was the absence of fortifications. Tula was a ritual and commercial center easily accessible to everyone. There can be no doubt that this setting contributed to its end.

The foreign invaders that destroyed Tula were members of agricultural groups that had been raiding the Valley of Mexico for hundreds of years. The Chichimecs were not simple barbarian nomads, as it was long speculated. They had productive farming settlements in the mountains and practiced a strong material culture. They raided the Toltec settlements in search of fertile land and better fishing and hunting areas. These raids were probably the result of the prolonged droughts that dried their fields and destroyed their crops.

The Chichimec invasions brought intense tribal warfare into the seemingly well- organized urban societies of the Valley of Mexico. Their raids have been compared with the invasions of the "barbarians" that destroyed the Roman Empire. The Chichimec invasions changed the political stability of central Mexico and created the basis for the emergence of the Aztec empire. The region was still politically unstable when the Spanish invaders arrived at the beginning of the sixteenth century.

Political Instability

After the Chichimec debacle, the Toltecs that survived the destruction of Tula founded the city of Chicken Itza in Yucatan, as the capital of a new Toltec state. In the Valley of Mexico the collapse of Tula resulted in a period of political instability that lasted for more than two hundred years.

Figure 49   Ball Court at Tula.

The glory of the Toltec empire did not disappear completely after the fall of Tula. The Toltec heritage continued to influence the groups that wandered or settle in central Mexico. Among them were the Aztecs, who had arrived in Tula before its political and religious crisis.

The Toltecs accepted the Aztecs as serfs and mercenaries. When the Chichimecs attacked Tula, the Aztecs reveled against their masters and joined in the scramble for the spoils. During the Tula sojourn they added many gods to their religion. They continued the practice of human sacrifices and copied the cult of Tezcatlipoca and Quetzalcoatl from the Toltecs. The Aztec inherited the folk history, the painted codices of the Toltecs, their militarism, and their techniques of empire building.

Out of the confusion of the disintegration of universal rule and renewed warfare in the Valley of Mexico, different states rose to share the fragmentary power of the fallen Toltec state. Not until the Aztecs appeared in the central highlands and used their skills and military might in the fifteenth century to conquer their neighbors would total domination of the Valley of Mexico be accomplished by a single tribal group.

The Refuges from Tula

The Aztecs entered the Valley of Mexico as refugees from the disaster of the Toltec empire on or about A.D. 1218. Their pilgrimage, however, did not end there. For the next one hundred years they continued to search for a place to live. Then they still were a small, poor and unimportant tribe with scant resources and no definite plans.

According to anthropologist Ignacio Bernal, they lived in primitive simplicity. Quoting older sources he writes, "Their garments and loincloths were of palm fiber, their sandals of woven straw as were their bows and their sacks." In spite of these hardships, the Aztecs learned the ways of their neighbors and improved their fighting abilities. They also learned new skills and experiences, continued to add foreign gods to their religion, and studied time and the ancient calendar (Bernal 93).

The native tribes that occupied the region rejected the new arrivals and opposed their settlements. They believed that the Aztecs were a dangerous group, cruel, deceptive and practitioners of bloody rites. These tribes also objected to their presence near them and disliked the refugees' violent behavior.

As Bernal says, the Aztecs had "acquired a well-deserved reputation of being a quarrelsome, cruel, unfaithful to their word, and women-stealers." The Spanish chronicler Fray Bernardino de Sahagun adds that for some of these reasons "nobody wanted or welcomed them, the people turned them away in every village, or refused their requests for help because they did not know them."

The outcome of that open hostility was the creation of a very suspicious society that distrusted its neighbors and was always ready for war. The experience also played an important part in the Aztecs' tribal, social and economic development. They disdained death and used armed forays and war to support themselves, according to the *Annals of Tlatelolco*.

The ordeal also conditioned them to resist when required, or to compromise when there was no other choice. It also prepared them for the practice of a violent and bloody religion, since they attributed their survival to the guidance and protection of Huitzilopochtli, their war god. As Miguel Leon-Portilla has written, "besides the Nahuatl language, the most important heritage they brought was their indomitable will."

Figure 50   Model of Aztec temple in Tenayuca, similar
to the Great Temple of Tenochtitlan.

6

The Aztec Empire

Struggle for Supremacy

Around 1280 the wandering tribe settled temporarily near the cities of Azcapotzalco and Tlacopan. There they shared with others a well-watered surrounding and a fertile land. To protect themselves from the harassment of their enemies they fortified the hills of Chapultepec, or the Hill of the Grasshopper, and began a new life.

The Aztecs arrived to Lake Texcoco during a period of relative peace. Before their arrival, the Valley of Mexico had experienced constant warfare. For over two hundred years, the residents had fought continuously for better lands. They had struggled to protect themselves from the northern invaders and the ambitions of their neighbors. The weaker groups retreated into less productive lands, paid tribute or integrated themselves with the larger ones.

Gradually stability overtook the great central valley. The Chichimecs settled down in the area of Lake Texcoco. The Toltecs who had survived the destruction of Tula joined forces with them and conquered the remaining tribes. This coalition succeeded in gaining the upper hand in central Mexico for many years. The Chichimecs founded the cities of Tenayuca and Texcoco and the Toltecs extended their influence to Culhuacan.

The Culhua became the dominating force in the southern area of Lake Texcoco. As descendent of the Toltecs, they retained the influence and pride of their ancestors. During this time, the Tepanecs also began to build a

Figure 51   Atlante with raised arms from Tula. (INAH)

state in the same region, but they did not launch their bid for power until much later. The Valley of Mexico was gaining political stability when the Aztecs made their appearance on the shores of Lake Texcoco.

The Hill of the Grasshoppers

For more than a generation the Aztecs lived in peace with their neighbors. As their power increased, they became involved in local conflicts with disastrous results. Nigel Davis observes that their bid for conquest was premature. At that time they were not yet powerful enough to challenge their neighbors and were obvious candidates for the privilege of paying rather than demanding tribute from others.

According to the *Annals of Cuauhtitlan*, when the Aztecs began to raid the local communities in search of women, booty, and captives for their ceremonies, a coalition of the people of Culhuacan, Azcapotzalco, Tlacopan and Coyohuacan raided their settlement.

The members of the coalition succeeded in getting the Aztec warriors out of their fortifications. Then, they attacked the women and children first to demoralize the defenders. In spite of their efforts, the Aztecs lost the battle to the superior forces, which promptly destroyed the settlement.

There are many versions of this event and the accounts differ about who was responsible for the final expulsion of the Aztecs from Chapultepec. Most colonial documents agree that an alliance of local groups evicted them from that location.

The *Annals of Tlatelolco* also show that the Culhua seized many survivors and carried them off as slaves to their city-state. The Culhua also sacrificed the Aztec chief Huitzilihuitl. The rest of the outcasts, including the women and children, went to Culhuacan, Xochimilco and other areas. Those that went to Culhuacan settled in the wasteland of Tizapan and lived there a very harsh existence as servants.

Slavery at Tizapan

The Aztecs' new home was a desolate, rocky, barren land of thorny vegetation, snakes and poisonous insects. Aztec traditions say that Huitzilopochtli taught them

Figure 52   Monolithic statue of the Rain-God Tlaloc.

how to hunt, roast and eat the snakes, and cultivate the volcanic soil.

Several years later, the Culhua went to war against the city-state of Xochimilco. Impressed by the Aztecs ability to survive, they sent many of their soldiers to the war. The mercenaries fought "without shields or lances" according to a historical account. Apparently, the Culhua did not trust their vassals too much, or expected that they may not return from battle.

The Aztecs, however, defeated the Xochimilca and returned victorious with prisoners of war and the ears of their slain enemies. Released from bondage, and with their prestige recovered, they began a new life as mercenaries of the Culhua.

There are two interesting legends about this period of Aztec history. After the battle, according to one of the stories, an Aztec chief asked the ruler of Culhuacan for the hand of his daughter. The girl's father accepted the marriage proposition and delivered the maiden to her future husband.

In a religious ceremony, the Aztecs sacrificed her as a bride of their war god Huitzilopochtli They removed her skin very skillfully, covered a priest with it, and invited the Culhua for the celebration. When the father of the bride discovered the death of his daughter, and the flaying incident, he became very angry and swore revenge. The Culhua, allied with the Tepanecs, attacked the Aztecs and forced them to flee the area.

A second story says that the Aztecs returned from battle with several prisoners and invited the ruler to a ceremony in honor of Huitzilopochtli. The bloody, ritualistic sacrifice that followed horrified the Culhua king so much that he considered the Aztecs as dangerous savages and ordered their expulsion from the kingdom. His soldiers persecuted them constantly until they were finally out of Culhuacan.

The End of the Journey

The Aztecs fled to the lakes where they made rafts to cross to the other side. Another romantic legend, not well authenticated, describes in part the Aztec subsequent odyssey. According to the Spanish chronicler Fray Diego Duran, after leaving Culhuacan, the Aztecs went to Lake Texcoco searching for a new place to live.

One night a priest dreamed that Huitzilopochtli wanted the tribe to continue the pilgrimage until they could find an eagle devouring a snake on top of a cactus.

In the year *2-house*, according to the Aztec calendar, an Indian chief named Ocelapan saw the prophetic event taking place on a small island in Lake Texcoco. Since the eagle represented light and goodness and the snake all that was evil, they took the sign as a message from heaven to stop there and build their nation (Duran, II,44).

A symbol of that event appears today on the center of the Mexican national flag, and is Mexico's national emblem. The writer Jonathan Kandell writes that, "this legendary version of the Aztec arrival in the Valley of Mexico is still taught as factual history to Mexican schoolchildren" (Kandell 27).

The Beginning of the Empire

The Aztecs selected a very poor place to start their new life. It was surrounded by swamps and had poor agricultural land. The area had remained uninhabited because it lay on the borders of the three most powerful Indian states of the region. A hostile occupation by any one of them would have resulted in open hostilities.

Soon after their arrival, the Aztecs build a temple for their tribal god. They also built the first simple dwellings of what was to become later the city of Mexico-Tenochtitlan. The Aztecs named it after Mextli and Tenoch, the two priests who guided them during the long pilgrimage. The future capital of the Viceroyalty of New Spain and of the Mexican republic became in less than 500 years the most important historical and commercial city of Central America and the largest city in the world.

Thirteen years later after their arrival, a Nahua group left Tenochtitlan due to lack of space and built on an adjacent island the city of Tlatelolco. They constructed there a huge marketplace with temples and palaces that rivaled those of Tenochtitlan. Tlatelolco became an important trading center and a landmark for the Nahua merchant class. Tenochtitlan incorporated it in 1473 as part of the growing Aztec empire.

Figure 53 Foundation of Tenochtitlan
(Codex Ramirez)

Compromise for Survival

To protect their small settlement the Aztecs established a precarious truce with Tlatelolco, which had become their rival. They also accepted the domination of the Tepanecs of Azcapotzalco. Their city-state was then the most important political center in the valley of Mexico. The Aztecs paid regular tribute to their masters and served them as hired mercenaries. With the Tepanec as allies, they took part in the destruction of their old enemy Culhuacan in 1367.

By 1376 they were sufficiently strong to proclaim a separate kinship while continuing to pay tribute to the Tepanecs. They obtained a member of the defeated ruling family of Culhuacan to rule as their king. Acamapitchtli, who claimed to be a direct descendent of the Toltecs, became the ruler of the Aztecs.

Under their first three rulers, Acamapitchtli (1376-91), Huitzilhuitl (1391-1415), and Chimalpopoca(1415-26), the Aztecs participated in many military engagements. Their activities strengthened the supremacy of Tezozomoc, the Tepanec king.

As mercenary allies of Azcapotzalco, they conducted a ruthless and continuous warfare against other city-states, sharing with their overlords the booty of their conquests. The Codex Mendoza shows many drawings about the Aztecs' activities during this period. The painted manuscript depicts among them warriors provoking war and receiving trophies for capturing prisoners.

Further military actions took the Aztecs as far as the Gulf of Mexico. With the destruction of Texcoco in 1418, they stopped serving Azcapotzalco. The Indians had learned well the technique of empire building and were ready to begin their aggressive pursuits.

Tenochtitlan also had prospered very well with the trade and spoils of the recent wars. The city grew very fast with the arrival of artisans, weavers, laborers, sculptors, and merchants from other provinces. Historian Hubert Herring, comments: "The canny little god of the Aztecs perhaps foresaw, and rightly, that the unification of the valley would vastly facilitate further conquests by Tenochtitlan when the proper moment came. It was a diabolical tactic: Azcapotzalco laid the foundation for the Aztec Empire and, in doing so, burned itself out" (Herring 47).

The Triple Alliance

During the rule of Chimalpopoca, the Tepanecs attempted to strengthen the control of their empire. In a sinister plot they conspired to assassinate the Aztec king and t o force the exile of Nezahualcoyotl, the ruler of Texcoco.

The failure of the Tepanec plans threw the empire into a political upheaval. Nezahualcoyotl returned to claim his right to rule, but other contenders opposed him. The internal divisions that followed split the state. When several cities revolted against Azcapotzalco, the skillful Aztecs switched loyalties.

Under Itzcoatl (1428-40), the fourth Aztec ruler, they joined the enemies of Azcapotzalco. In 1428 the tribal chief Tlacaelel, who later became a counselor, lead an army of Aztec warriors and coalition forces against Azcapotzalco, crushing the forces of the proud empire. By 1429 he had established the supremacy of the Aztec nation in the Valley of Mexico.

Soon afterward the Aztec ruler allied himself with Texcoco and Tlacopan. The triple alliance agreed to settle their differences and to divide the spoils of war two shares for Tenochtitlan, two shares for Texcoco and one share for Tlacopan. The arrangement brought Tenochtitlan more power and riches.

The Aztecs, who had won the reputation as the best fighters of the region assumed the military leadership of the alliance and became its dominant partner. Tlacopan, the third member of the alliance, was relegated to an inferior position.

A Center of Culture

Texcoco served as the intellectual, artistic and literary heart of ancient Mexico. Under Nezahualcoyotl, the poet-king, it flourished as the most remarkable center of culture and learning. It had an Academy of Music that directed the arts and sciences. Poems, dances, musical compositions, literary works and paintings must have its approval before they could be performed or exhibited.

This academy expanded Indian education and controlled the purity of the Nahuatl language. It approved the

Figure 54 Chimalpopoca, Third Aztec
Emperor (Codex Ramirez)

qualifications of teachers and supervised their work. It held literary and musical contests and selected judges from the Alliance to evaluate the competitions.

Nezahualcoyotl built a palace of 300 rooms, patios, art galleries, museums and conference rooms. His pleasure gardens located in Texcotzingo had a zoo and a collection of unusual plants. The king also designed and built many waterways for irrigation and bathing. He directed the affairs of state sitting on a beautiful golden throne. The monarch had forty wives, sixty sons and fifty-seven children.

The Spaniards and their Indian allies destroyed most of the art treasures of Texcoco when they entered the city. They burned the royal archives, the chronicles of the ancient kings, the financial records, the descriptions of military campaigns, and every piece of literature found in the libraries. For centuries, the first bishop of Mexico, Fray Juan de Zumarraga, was accused for this destruction. But in the nineteenth century, the Mexican historian Joaquin Garcia Icazbalceta demonstrated that Tlaxcaltecan Indians and not the Catholic priest actually were responsible for the devastation of the Mexican historical heritage.

The Chosen People

The Aztecs believed that they were the chosen people of Huitzilopochtli, the sun-god. They always based their prosperity and achievements on that god's guidance and protection. They also believed that their destiny was to rule as conquerors, and to serve the only god who could save mankind from its impending disaster.

To justify these claims, the Aztec emperor Itzcoatl ordered, years before the destruction of Texcoco, the rearrangement of the existing historical accounts. He believed that the ancient records underrated the Aztec achievements and neglected their religious traditions. To correct the error, he ordered the rewriting of history.

The Aztecs recorded and validated their accession to power, revised their ancient cosmogony, and justified human sacrifices as a necessity for the salvation of the universe. Subsequent rulers rationalized their power by claiming to descend from the Toltecs.

The destruction of the ancient historical records make difficult the study of earlier Aztec's history. On the other hand, the records that survived are mostly free of mythological tales. They can be used to study the political changes that occurred during the last centuries of the empire. These records provide valuable information on their military, economic and social developments. They also authenticate dynastic changes with some level of certainty.

After 1436 the Aztecs embarked in an expansion of the empire. First, they consolidated their control in the Valley of Mexico; then, they moved South and East. Under Moctezuma I (1440-69), the grandfather of Moctezuma II and fifth Aztec ruler, the Aztecs extended their conquests to Puebla, Morelos, and Guerrero in the Southwest and to Veracruz in the East.

Eventually, the Aztec incorporated into their expanding empire the Valley of Oaxaca and its nearby territories. Further territorial gains extended the empire from the Atlantic coast to the Pacific ocean.

During Moctezuma's rule 489 cities and towns paid tribute to the Triple Alliance. Towns gave thirty to thirty-three per cent of their total production. Farmers and craftsmen paid the same rate in grains or manufactured goods. The government also collected luxury goods, raw materials, exotic articles, cocoa, gold, and gemstones.

Most of the tribute and taxes collected were used to support the government, the army, and the nobility. The conquered provinces also furnished victims for religious sacrifices.

The Expansion of the Empire

Axayacatl who ruled between 1469-81 continued to expand the Alliance. In spite of constant revolts from conquered tribes and a military defeat by the Tarascans, the Aztecs consolidated their power. Netzahualcoyotl, the ruler of Texcoco and an ally of the Aztecs died in 1472 after an illustrious reign.

Tizoc (1481-86), the seventh Aztec ruler, lasted only for five years. During his brief reign he continued to expand the empire, but was poisoned when his forces lost a military campaign. An enormous basalt stone located in the National Museum of Anthropology in Mexico City commemorates his victories.

Ahuitzol (1486-1502), the eighth Aztec ruler, extended

Figure 55   Xiuhtecuhtli, the Old God of Fire. (INAH)

the empire to the Maya domains and the highlands of Guatemala. He integrated most of the Mixtec territory into the Aztec nation between 1486 and 1500. He also conquered the territory of Tabasco and all the lands along the Gulf of Mexico.

Only few states remained outside the Aztec empire. Tlaxcala, the Tarascan region of present-day Michoacan, and the Zapotecs of Tehuantepec maintained their independence. The states of Metztitlan, the Yopis and the small nomadic groups of the Northwest also escaped the Aztec influence. Ahuitzol's reign was the apogee of Aztec culture and history.

In 1502, Moctezuma II, also known as Moctezuma Xocoyotzin, began the reorganization of the empire. His reign produced many changes in the Aztec state. He organized the empire into provinces and selected governors to rule them in his name. He created a complicated administrative machinery of tax collectors, courts of justice, military garrisons, messenger services, and religious leaders. Moctezuma II increased the payment of tribute creating serious dissatisfaction among the people. He also reduced Texcoco and Tlacopan to inferior partners in the alliance.

Moctezuma's armies won many new victories, extending their control to Central America. The Aztec ruler assumed more power that his predecessors. He maintained a ruthless control, forcing nobles to work as public administrators. He began military academies, selected schools for the nobility and enforced strict ceremonial rules. His subjects could not even touch him or look directly at his face without his consent.

A weak and insecure ruler, Moctezuma II had more interest in sorcery and mystical experiences than in making war. His inability to lead the people during their worst political crisis resulted in the downfall and destruction of the Aztec empire.

The last Aztec ruler was Cuauhtemoc, the "fallen eagle." He became the leader of his nation in 1521, when the Spaniards were destroying Tenochtitlan. Cuauhtemoc led the Indian groups that resisted the Spaniards; but, after weeks of heroic street fighting surrendered his forces to Cortes.

Initially, he received an adequate treatment from his enemies, but four years later they accused him of treachery and hanged him. He is probably buried near the church of Ixcateopan in Guerrero.

Tenochtitlan

The city of Tenochtitlan became the capital of the Aztec nation. This city was the hub of an economic empire that extended from northern Mexico to the highlands of Guatemala. Built on the southwest corner of Lake Texcoco, the seat of the empire can only be approached by three broad stone causeways. Massive wooden bridges, that were drawn up during emergencies, protected the island from enemy attacks.

The city covered approximately ten square kilometers and by 1519, had a population of more than 200,000 people. Tenochtitlan was founded on reclaimed swamp land without any particular plan. Five different administrative jurisdictions, or campan, divided the city. Each division consisted of four barrios or wards, called calpulli, for a total of twenty. The calpulli divided the city of more than 60,000 houses and buildings with their own independent administrative systems.

Dwellings were seldom more than two stories in height and their walls were covered with a fine coat of cement. The merchants, government officials, and priests made their houses of stone and cement, but without windows. Most of them had courts of marble or polished stone.

The homes of the rich were large and had bath and gardens. They were constructed of red tezontle, a soft lava rock that was whitewashed and polished to a brilliant luster. The square structures had central courts and terraced tops, and were separated from each other by small bridges, narrow roads and interconnecting canals.

The best houses were built on an elevated platform with stone facing to protect the occupants from rising waters. The poor people lived in small houses of unpolished rock and adobe. These homes had only straw roofs, dirt floors, mud walls and no decorations.

There were few streets, but the residents communicated with each other by using canoes that traveled along narrow canals that reached all parts of the city. Alfonso Caso writes that the Aztec resolved their sanitation problem by stationing large boats in specific areas to collect and carry the waste. The residents used it as fertilizer. The residents conserved the urine in closed containers and used it as a mordant in the dyeing of clothing.

Engineering Wonders

The city suffered periodic inundations during heavy rains because the Valley of Mexico had no natural outlets. One of the valley's larger lakes, Zumpango, was twenty-five feet higher than the city. Even the Spaniards had problems with the rising waters during the rainy season.

The floods of 1553, 1580 and 1604 were so devastating that The Spaniards considered removing the city to a higher level. Only the potential loss of millions of dollars of property prevented this action.

To correct the problem of flooding, the Aztecs built a dike more than nine miles in length and six meters wide. The massive stone dam, designed by Nezahualcoyotl, stretched across Lake Texcoco from Atzacualco, in the northern shore to Iztapalapan on the South. This engineer marvel was constructed of stone and clay and had a strong stockade on the sides to brake the force of the waves. It created an artificial lagoon where the city stood like an ancient Venice (Piho 65).

The east side of Lake Texcoco lacked a natural outlet and was very salty. The west size received the drainage from several springs and rivers and the water remained fresh. The dike divided the lake along the two sections, regulated the water level that entered the western area and controlled the floodwaters during heavy rains (Martinez 67).

A stone aqueduct supplied Tenochtitlan with fresh water from Chapultepec. Another aqueduct several miles in length connected the sister city of Texcoco to several reservoirs. These systems of dikes and aqueducts not only supplied Tenochtitlan with potable water, but also regulated the level of salt in the lakes.

The Temple of Sacrifices

A walled area of seventy-eight major buildings intersected the three causeways at the heart of the city. The center of government and religious activity, it had huge painted temples, palaces, schools, monasteries,

Figure 56 Tzontemoc, the Sun-God, descending from
the sky at sunset. (INAH).

courtyard and pools. In the middle was a massive pyramid-temple made of limestone and rock, painted red and blue.

It was some 130 feet high and over 300 square feet at the base, with dual shrines dedicated to Huitzilopochtli and Tlaloc. Before the statues of these tribal gods, the priests placed a special stone for the sacrifice of human beings.

The selection of these two gods to command the seat of Aztec power shows the importance that the Aztecs gave to war and agriculture. Other structures in this inner city were a temple dedicated to Ehecatl, the God of the Air, and a wooden rack used to hold the skulls of sacrificial victims. Outside the walls was an enormous building that the Spaniards called "the palace of Moctezuma." The Aztecs considered the ceremonial center sacred ground. Only selected priests, nobles and servants could live and work there.

The beauty of Tenochtitlan, the orderliness and cleanliness of its people, its buildings and markets, and "the wide and straight causeways" so impressed Hernan Cortes that he compared it with Sevilla and Granada. In one of his letters to the King of Spain he wrote: "Its impressive size and magnificence no tongue could describe."

The European's Views

The organization of the Aztec capital also amazed the historians and chroniclers of the Conquest. As has been previously discussed, the Spanish soldier Bernal Diaz del Castillo wrote with great care about the splendor of the temples and palaces of the city.

Diaz del Castillo described Tenochtitlan from the top of the Great Temple. After observing that "it was a wicked and cursed place," he wrote: "We could see the three causeways that entered the city, and the aqueduct from Chapultepec that provided the city with sweet water. We also could see a multitude of canoes moving to and from the mainland, loaded with provisions and merchandise, and the houses, separated one from the other by small wooden drawbridges. We also could see the towers of the temples of the nearby cities that looked like fortresses" (Diaz del Castillo 173).

These tales fascinated the Europeans. The first

Figure 57   Copy of Moctezuma II headdress, made of
Quetzal feathers. Original is conserved in Europe.
(INAH)

Figure 58   Mixtec ceramics. (INAH)

printed description of Tenochtitlan appeared in Europe in 1522. It was the famous *Carta de Relacion* that Cortes wrote to the King of Spain after the conquest of Mexico. Two years later, a map of the city attributed to Cortes appeared in a book entitled *Praeclara Ferdinandi Cortesii de Nova Maris Oceani Hispanica Narratio*. The map showed the city in the center of a lake, with drawings of temples, palaces and small houses, which looked as those of the small villages of southern Spain.

The legends on the map described the attitude of the Spaniards toward the city and the Aztec world: *"Templum ubi sacrificant,"* or "temple of sacrifices," and *"capita sacrificant,"* or "capital of sacrifice." That European attitude toward the native Americans was to remain unchanged for the rest of the sixteenth century.

The Organization of the Empire

The Aztec empire consisted of many separate urban communities. At its peak it extended from one ocean to the other, from northern Mexico to the independent Maya states of Yucatan and Guatemala. It was approximately 80,000 square miles in size. Conservative estimates place its population at about twenty-five million people. The anthropologist Adolph F. Bandelier called it "a loose confederacy."

That definition may not be entirely correct because the Aztecs held the empire by force, not by loyalty. Most of its subjects never were free members of the Aztec state and Tenochtitlan terrorized them into submission. On the contrary, the Aztec's subjects hated and detested their conquerors and only waited for the right opportunity to revolt against them.

The Aztec state controlled and directed every aspect of Indian life. The position of Tenochtitlan in the Valley of Mexico centralized communication and commercial access to the main cities and towns of Mesoamerica. That location also protected the city from foreign invaders (Wolf and Hansen 13-14).

The geographical advantage and trading facilities of Tenochtitlan also served as a catalyst for the further expansion of the empire. Religion played an important role in influencing the people and justifying the power of the nobility. Selected members of that class directed

Figure 59   Model of the marketplace at Tlatelolco.
(INAH)

the bureaucracy that was responsible for the collection of taxes, the distribution of food, the management of trading, and the supervision of justice.

The Aztecs administered the empire very efficiently and had a complex bureaucratic system. The government permitted both private and community property, but large sections of the land were set aside for the support of the priests and the army. The largest portions were held by the ruler and nobles. The Aztecs allowed local groups composed of several families or clans to work and inherit land, but they had to contribute part of the agricultural yield to the state. Rarely the government permitted the individual ownership of land.

Religion also justified expansionism and the necessity for wars and sacrifices. It provided a rigorous and inflexible system of social and moral order to rule and control the Aztec state. Since religion was also in the hands of the ruling class, there was no conflict of interest between church and state. Probably the pervasive force of religion created the imperial mood of the Aztec state and the surplus energy necessary for the construction of so many temples and ceremonial centers.

The Aztecs accepted many of the ideological views of others and made few changes in the customs and traditions of those who they conquered. They seldom attempted to assimilate them. Some of the conquered people retained their autonomy. Cholula, Tehuacan, Chiapas, the Zapotecs, and part of the Mixtec preserved their power by recognizing Teotihuacan as the principal authority and paying tribute to it.

While the local rulers had to subordinate their rule to the state, they continued to enforce the local laws. Aztec subjects could retain their traditional ways, their gods and their leaders as long as they remained at peace and paid the required tribute. Failure to do so would bring rapid retribution from the powerful imperial army.

The Flowery Wars

The Aztecs also waged war without provocation to intimidate their subjects into submission and ensure an adequate supply of captives for their religious ceremonies. It was customary to start a war when a new ruler rose to power. The purpose of the conflict was to capture prisoners for sacrificial ceremonies. If there were no insurrections or revolts, the tradition required the beginning of "a flowery war" against the Tlaxcalans, or other selected enemies.

This tribe had never been conquered. They had entrenched themselves in the mountains of eastern Mexico and had built a massive wall to protect their settlements. Aided by the Otomies and other peoples, they had defied and foiled every attempt to destroy them.

Since the Tlaxcalans honored the same god as the Aztecs, they also fought to defend their territory and to capture sacrificial victims. The participants called these campaigns *Xochiyaoyotl*, or "flowery wars," since they were fought to honor Huitzilopochtli and the Aztec metaphor for blood was "flower."

The Aztecs conducted these conflicts under special rules and against selected adversaries. They chose the battlefield and the day of the engagement in advance after consultation with astrologers. The soldiers, dressed in exquisite garments, using multicolor shields, feather headdress and ear and nose plugs, fought half drunk with stone-edged clubs and axes until both sides had their quota of captives. The battle was then stopped and the opponents returned home. There was no further animosity between the contestants, nor an exchange of prisoners was carried out.

Captives welcomed their fate since their sacrifices permitted them to ascend into heaven and be in the company of the sun-god. At times they even called the victor "father" and the captor addressed him as "son." Aztec warriors received rewards for the number of prisoners that they took in battle, but no account was ever kept of those slain in the battlefield. Flowery war victims entered the paradise of the sun, according to an Aztec legend.

Internal Crisis

There are no reliable estimates about the number of captives that the Aztecs sacrificed, but it has been calculated that at least 10,000 of them were taken prisoners for that purpose every year. According to anthropologist Frank B. Livingstone, there were about 15,000 deaths a year as a result of war and the practice of human sacrifices.

This constant drain of human resources, the

dissatisfaction with the tribute system, and political and economic problems were causing an internal crisis on the eve of the Spanish Conquest. There was insecurity and distrust among the Aztec leaders, according to Caso, and "in the tributary states discontentments increased and revolts occurred regularly."

By the beginning of the sixteenth century, farming also had become a significant problem. Caso writes that resupplying Tenochtitlan with food, and the rich objects demanded by the ruling class, had become a heavy burden to the rest of the empire. The need for firewood destroyed many wooded areas and caused severe land erosion. Primitive methods of agriculture aggravated the problem and many farmers abandoned the farms to become artisans and improve their quality of life.

Sherburne F. Cook has even suggested that the increase in war and human sacrifices during this period may have been an attempt by the government to reduce the population. This is doubtful, however. Years of constant warfare, human sacrifices, and increased infant mortality, were reducing the empire's population to unacceptable levels.

The Aztecs never attempted to unify the empire politically until the beginnings of the sixteenth century. At that time the Aztecs tried to unite the territories by brutal militarism, as the Inca has done in the Andean world, but it was then too late. The historian Arnold J. Toynbee observes that the establishment of an indigenous universal state by the Aztec empire-builders at that time was forestalled more by their lack of unity and purpose, and their internal problems, than by the effects of the Spanish conquest.

Figure 60 The Sun Stone, also known as the Calendar Stone. (INAH)

7

The Aztec Society

The Emergence of the Aztec State

The structure of the Aztec society went back to the early years of tribal wandering. The Central Valley of Mexico was then under considerable political turmoil and survival depended on strict discipline and adequate organization. Surrounded by enemies everywhere, the Aztecs lived during that time a precarious existence.

To protect the tribe from danger and maintain social order, the elders established a mystic-militaristic system of rigorous laws that demanded absolute obedience, conformity and full participation in the society.

The Aztecs' religious beliefs also played a major role in their struggle with other groups. Since they waged war to gather prisoners for the sacrificial stone, their activities created hostility and fear. Armed conflict, however, served very well their objectives. It produced territorial gains, wealth, power and victims for their gods.

Anthropologist Richard E. Leakey has observed that materialism undoubtedly provides a favorable environment for warfare. Since the Aztecs were not idealists, they accepted war as a "highly successful way of a gaining material advantage."

The Aztec society was not a tribal-kinship structure, but a marked hierarchical system that was progressing very fast at the time of the Conquest. They differ from other Mesoamerican civilizations in the way they

Figure 61   Coyolxauhqui. Stone sculpture found in the Great Temple. (INAH)

structured their system.

The upper class, merchants, warriors and members of the clergy shared most of the political and economic power. "If the foreign invasion had not occurred," writes Jacques Soustelle, "the trading class, in particular, might have become the chiefs of a bourgeoisie that would have either become part of the ruling class or would have displaced it and taken its power" (Soustelle 75).

Divisions of Society

The Aztecs divided their society in three classes. At the very top stood the tlatoani, the head of the state. He claimed to descend from the rulers of Tula. These Indians traditionally glorified their ties to the imperialistic Toltecs to enhance their past and assert their authority. That historical lineage accorded the emperor special prestige in the society. He was the most important political, religious and military leader of the empire.

The Aztecs did not consider the tlatoani as a god, nor did he inherit the throne automatically. A council of elders selected the emperor from the closer relatives of the previous ruler. To be chosen, the candidate had to be a military leader, or an important member of the priesthood. The council consulted many people before the election to insure that they select the best candidate.

Once chosen, the emperor became a high priest, the commander of the military forces, the senior justice of the court of appeals and the director of the town market. He ruled the nation with the assistance of the Tlatocan, or Great Council. This advisory board was the most important political body in the Aztec system. It met every eighty days to decide all the important state matters (Davis 102).

The tlatoani was not immune to political problems. He could be deposed for a variety of reasons. As has been noted, during the final days of Tenochtitlan the people stoned emperor Moctezuma II to death after accusing him of treason and cowardice.

The Last Elected Emperor

Moctezuma II, the last elected emperor, succeeded his uncle Ahuizotl. The people celebrated his coronation for many weeks with festivities that included mass executions. The emperor established a despotic rule from the beginning of his reign. He imposed higher taxes and tributes to the conquered states and expanded the administrative management of the empire. He also eliminated the commoners from the court, forced many nobles to work and established a strict ceremonial procedure. The emperor's army enlarged the territories of the empire as far as Honduras and Guatemala.

Those who wished to see him must seek permission from the council. If the advisory group approved the petition, the person went to the palace, removed his shoes, bow three times in front of the emperor, and said: *"Tlatoani no, tlatoani, hueitlatoani,"* that is, "lord, my lord and great lord" (Vega 17).

If a commoner ever looked directly at Moctezuma, he faced death. According to Fray Diego Duran, the emperor believed that commoners must never look at the face of a god. Once an Indian worker told Duran: "Father, I would not lie to you, I have never seen the face of the emperor. I would have die as the others did if I have done so" (Duran, II, 407).

The Aztec prince lived with great ostentation and splendor in a magnificent palace. The building provided rooms for the administrative work of the councils, advisers and judges who aided the monarch in the management of his daily affairs. Hundreds of attendants, bodyguards, artisans and clerics always accompanied the emperor. His servants carried him in a sedan chair during public appearances.

The tlatoani appointed most of the administrative staff of the government. He also promoted the high-ranking military officers, planned war activities and distributed the wealth of the empire. His officers collected the tribute and taxes of the people and managed the affairs of the state.

Initially, the Aztecs did not have a chief of state of their race. Their elected Acampichtli as their first emperor because he was a member of the royal lineage of the Toltecs. Chimalpopoca, and Itzcoatl, the subsequent rulers, were both of uncertain ancestries. It was not until 1440, or 121 years after their first appearance in the Valley of Mexico, that the Aztecs had a truly Mexican ruler.

Figure 62   Sculpture of Coatlicue, Goddess of Earth and of Death. (INAH)

Functions of the Tlatoani

The emperor and the council members controlled the legislative processes of the empire. A highly trained group of professional officers did most of the administrative work. This bureaucratic system included many tax collectors, military officers, accountants and judges.

The well-defined administrative structure maintained hundreds of official records and functioned as well as any modern system. Land assignments and litigations were especially important. The government maintained record on every legal case, with "maps, plans, genealogical studies, statements, reports and whatever else was required to justify claims for particular sections of land" (Soustelle 13).

The government maintained a staff of scribes and record keepers to insure the accuracy of these documents. The Europeans destroyed most of them because they suspected they contend evil matters. The burning of these documents and archives has been attributed to the religious zealots who arrived in Mexico in the wake of the Spanish conquest.

Historian Burr C. Brundage writes that the Aztecs view their government as a "lordship" instead of a viable political institution. According to the writer, there were no words for "nation" or "state" in the native Nahuatl language.

Apparently, the vested interests of the privileged class and the priesthood were the main concerns of the government. The Indians engaged in frequent wars to appease their gods and expand their commercial interests. They seldom did so to improve the living conditions of the people or the prosperity of the state.

Functions of the Cihuacoatl

The second highest official among the Aztecs was the Cihuacoatl. He was the emperor's adviser in all political, economic and criminal matters. The Cihuacoatl was not a member of the Tlatocan or the Great Council. He attended its deliberations as a representative of the emperor. He played the role of a modern prime minister and was responsible for the administration of the Treasury.

As a "senior criminal justice officer," he decided the outcome of the most important legal cases. As a financial officer, he was responsible for the collection and distribution of taxes and tributes. The Cihuacoatl was also the second officer in command of the army. Though he was a man, he had the extraordinary name of the Snake Woman.

Structure of the Calpulli

The larger unit of political and social administration was the Calpulli. There were twenty units in Tenochtitlan, and the division was very useful as a military organization and land tenure system. The Calpulli's territory was held in communal ownership, but divided among the households for tillage and harvesting.

The farmers who used the land could maintain it as long as they cultivated it. When a family separated herself from the Calpulli, the abandoned lands were redistributed to other members of the community. This territorial unit, as French writer Jacques Soustelle has called it, varied considerably in its individual characteristics. It may have consisted of a dozen farmers living in an isolated region, or a larger section of urban territory. Those in the heartland of the country lived in agricultural areas.

In towns and cities the Calpulli were mostly units of expert craftsmen, local farmers and urban workers. In Tenochtitlan, they were aggregated in phratries or "barrios" for administrative purposes. Each division was primarily a military organization with an official appointed by the Great Council.

The Calpulli as a Family Organization

The Calpulli also constituted the basic form of family social organization. Its members had no private property and the security and welfare of the group took precedence over those of the individual. These Calpulli were feudalistic in nature. They paid tribute to the government in food and manufactured goods and provided laborers and soldiers to the state.

A council of household leaders under the direction of an elected official governed the Calpulli. This adviser also represented the unit during the meetings of the

**Figure 63   Temple of Ehecatl-Quetzalcoatl found in
1967, Mexico City.**

Minor Council. The Calpulli officials appointed military leaders to train and lead the unit as a fighting force. An executive civil officer called the teachcauh directed the distribution of land, the storage of grain, and the legal matters of the community. He also presided over most festivals and religious ceremonies.

The Minor Council had considerable powers. It could declare war or establish peace. It resolved disputes among Calpulli members and served as administrators of the land units. They met in Tenochtitlan every twenty days to make recommendations to the Great Council.

The teopixque directed the religious affairs of the Calpulli and supervised the local rituals. This priest also managed the educational activities of the Telpochcalli, the official school for children and warriors. The members of the Calpulli elected all the other officers of the unit.

There was some degree of local democracy in the electoral process, but the basic consideration for a position was fitness for responsibility. The elected officials had no local political autonomy and had to follow the instructions of the central government.

The Social Organization of the State

The pilli or pipiltin were the nobles of the empire who had royal ancestry. Among them were the emperor and his family. The emperor permitted these nobles to own their private lands. The tecuhtli, or honorary lords, were the most powerful members of the society. They included among themselves the leading merchants of the empire and those individuals who held high positions in the hierarchy of religion and government.

The members of this privileged class "lived in large houses, wore fine clothing, ate the best foods, and provided the best education and training for their children." Their homes were luxuriously furnished, surrounded by beautiful gardens, fountains and private baths. They used most of the local economic resources and received a larger share of state tribute (Beals and Hoijer 341).

The tecuhtli held important positions in the government. Almost all of them had titles and offices conferred for life. While their sons could not inherit these titles or their privately owned lands, the tlatoani normally appointed these youngsters to special positions in the government. By the end of the fifteenth century, "it had become increasingly common to appoint sons of tecuhtli to the offices and status of their fathers."

Thus in fact, if not in legal theory, the tecuhtli were on the way "to becoming hereditary lords and a small but powerful class of wealthy landowners" (Beals and Hoijer 341). Tradition allowed members of the council and high-ranking military officers to tie their hair with red leather during official occasions (Beals and Hoijer 341).

The Middle and the Lower Classes

There was a middle class that consisted of wealthy farmers, craftsmen, merchants, military leaders and political officers. Its members, known as macehual, represented most of the people and formed the main framework of the Aztec society. These individuals served in the military forces during emergencies. When they excel in their services to the state, the emperor raised their social status to tecuhtli.

As honorary lords in the privileged class, the new tecuhtli did not pay taxes. They shared part of the rich tribute that flowed into Tenochtitlan and received additional land grants from the emperor. As tecuhtli, they could attend the meetings of the Tlatocan and participate in the government of the country.

The Spanish chronicler Alonso de Zorita, a member of the colonial judiciary system, described Indian life before the Conquest in idyllic, romantic terms. According to him, the Aztec rulers were fair and gave great attention to the welfare of the people. He believed that the tribute system was reasonable because it was based on total production and not in the number of Calpulli members. According to Zorita, the government never forced the Indians, to work very far from their families. Lords understood very well the personal misfortunes of the people and the Indians were happy (Zorita 27-39).

This view contrasted strongly with the real life of the Aztec peasant. In fact, the lower class, or mayeques, owned no property or farm lands. They were for the most part unskilled laborers, ex-slaves, or serfs, attached to private or state-owned rural estates. They did most the menial tasks of society, lived in groups and worked as tillers of the soil. During their spare time they build roads, temples and palaces. When they become disabled, or had a serious misfortune, they had no other recourse but to sell themselves or their children into slavery.

The common people lived in sun-dried brick houses covered with palm or maguey leaves. Their homes had dirt floors and no windows, and were very cold during the winter months. The Indians built their houses around a patio and raised them on a platform for protection against floods.

The lower class also included people who had been banished from the Calpulli, foreigners and war captives. Debtors, and "those who sold themselves into slavery or were sold by their parents by reasons of poverty," also belonged to this class. This group of people did not participate in public affairs, received a share of the tribute, or hoped to raise their standard of living. Those expelled from the calpulli could never return to the unit.

The common man possessed more personal freedom that the upper classes. In the Aztec society, the higher the rank, the less time a person had for taking care of his personal life (Beals and Hoijer 341).

The Plight of the Agricultural Worker

More than two-thirds of the members of the empire were farmers, but those who lived near Tenochtitlan and in the city itself were considered urban dwellers. While the peasants lived an unpropitious life, the residents of the city dedicated their time to craftsmanship and industry. Neither one nor the other went hungry. The farmers normally harvested sufficient food to feed their families and the rest of the population.

The peasants worked for the government in their spare time building pyramids, temples and palaces. Many of the unskilled laborers involved in the construction of religious monuments came to Tenochtitlan from distant parts of the empire. To the women, the major concern was the health and safety of the family. They dedicated a considerable amount of time in domestic affairs, planting crops and working in community projects.

The Aztecs gained personal wealth and professional status through promotions and appointments. They received special awards for significant military accomplishments.

Figure 64   Excavations at the site of the Templo Mayor.

The upper and middle class received political appointments private estates, and ample recognition. "Birth played its part," concludes Jacques Soustelle, "but it was still personal merit that raised a man, and lack of it that lowered him" (Stuart 139).

The children of those who were successful could enter selected schools, such as the Calmecac, and participate in special activities. A large majority of the children of affluent people joined the army or the priesthood after completion of their specialized training.

There was a major difference between farmers and urban residents. Craftsmen had a higher status than those who worked in the fields. Among the middle class, the most important occupations were military and business careers. State officials, especially those who worked directly for the emperor, had considerable prestige in the society.

The Spaniards overcome Tenochtitlan more by psychological warfare than by the force of arms. But the rapid destruction of the rest of the empire may be attributed to the role that the aristocracy played as the dominant force in the political and economic affairs of the state. When the Spaniards destroyed Tenochtitlan they also ended the influence and control of the privileged class. Throughout the years, a selected leadership had directed the military forces and the government. Without their advice the rest of the people did not know what to do.

The provinces made no efforts to continue the war against the Spaniards, nor to struggle somewhere else to maintain the state's political integrity. Many of the distant regions saw the collapse of Tenochtitlan as an end to their economic woes. Many welcomed the event as a relief from bondage. Those who paid the larger taxes had the greatest enjoyment. Only in the area of Yucatan did the Maya continue to fight the Spaniards for another half a century.

The Importance of the Nuclear Family

Among the Aztecs the family was an important part of society. Young people had to marry at an early age. Women joined in matrimony between the ages of fifteen and eighteen. Men normally waited until they reached their twentieth-first year to make a decision.

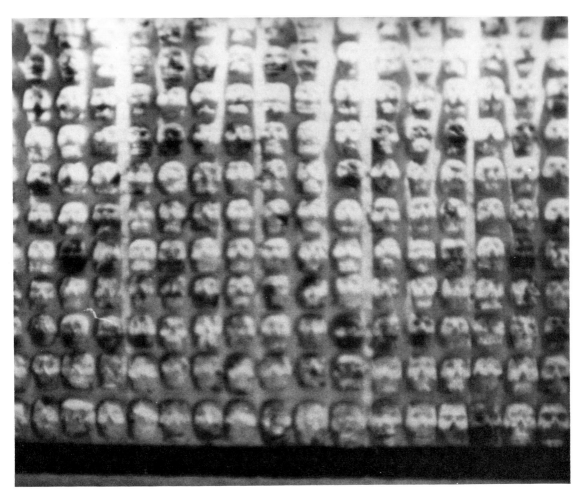

Figure 65   Skull-rack, altar, or "tzompantli," Great Temple.

The family was an important part of the Aztec society. Those who refused to get married received a severe punishment. If found guilty of the offense, they had to abstain from further sexual relationship and could not even court a member of the opposite sex.

The community permitted divorce, but the system was not officially sanctioned. Counselors attempted always to reconcile those who sought separation. They told them that the action was an affront to their families, an offense to the gods and a disgrace to the community.

Fray Diego Duran, who chronicled the life of the Aztecs, very skillfully, explained that the Indians allowed polygamy as long as the husband planted a field of corn for each of the wives that he desired. Military officers who distinguished themselves in battle could have as many wives as they desired. In Tenochtitlan, the people considered multiple marriages as a prize for heroism.

Polygamy was based on the ability of the husband to support his family. The poor people, however, did not practice it regularly. The aristocrats, merchants, and government officials were the principal practitioners of the practice. The children of polygamists did not carry a particular stigma. They could inherit the fortune and titles of their fathers despite the low legal standing of their mothers. The exception was the emperor himself. He could have as many wives as he desired, but he must always designate one as the principal spouse. Only her children could inherit the throne.

The Rearing of Children

The birth of a child was a very special occasion. The Aztecs welcomed children to the world with joy, poetry and flowers. "The rigid structure and ultimate purpose of each Mexica life were proclaimed at birth," writes historian Gene S. Stuart.

A midwife helped the mother and the infant during childbirth, while the father buried the new born placenta in the earth. Four days later, according to the Codex Mendocino, the woman carried the child around the room mat and placed him in a basket. She then set next to him a small bow with arrows and a shield to symbolize manhood. If the child was a girl, the nurse set a spindle, a work-basket and some yarn or a broom close to

Figure 66   Mayan burial site with religious offerings.
(INAH)

the child. The midwife named the new-born baby according to a very strict religious discipline.

The child education began at a very early age. The mother trained him until he was three years old. After that, the father assumed the responsibility until the age of six. Parents taught their children to respect the elderly, to be truthful to others, and to maintain self-control.

They punished the children very harshly when they disobeyed instructions. Punishment normally consisted of tying the child over wet sand for several hours, or pinching him repeatedly with maguey spikes. Discipline at public schools was also severe. At the age of seven, the child began to help his parents, both in the home and at the work place. When he was fifteen, the parents allowed him to go to the Telpochcalli, or house of youth, where he learned the basic responsibilities of citizenship. Those inclined toward the priesthood entered the Calmecac.

Young girls also received a very disciplined education. They learned to do domestic chores, serve the gods and behave correctly. Women were told to be tender, modest, preserve simplicity and always be clean. After the age of six, they also learned spinning and weaving and to do simple sewing. This training symbolized life, death and rebirth in a continuing cycle, and represented the nature of Mother Earth.

Young women learned to cook at an early age. Most of the women wore simple white dresses without adornments. Their parents advised them that: "Only courtesans and harlots shaved their faces and used colors." Adolescents selected for the priesthood had to be chaste and virtuous, but could leave the discipline when they desire to get married. During special celebrations and festivities, the Aztec women used home-made jewelry and brightly colored clothing (Vega 24).

Social Behavior

Pandering was a serious crime that was punished with great severity. Procurers of sexual favors had his hair burned in public. If the violator was an influential citizen, he received the death penalty. The Texcocan king Nezahualpilli ordered once the death of a woman who brought to the palace a lover for one of his daughters.

Figure 67 Disobedient child is beaten with a stick (Codex Mendocino)

The Aztecs regarded prostitution as improper behavior but tolerated it. Only single people could keep concubines. The penalty for adultery was death. While desertion and divorce were punishable, "a man could obtain the right to cast out his wife if she were sterile, were subject to prolonged ill temper, or neglected her household duties (Vaillant 125).

According to the Spanish chronicler Alonzo de Zorita, a man could get a mistress just by asking her parents to allow the girl to live with him and have his child. If the parents agree, the young maiden moved to his household and lived there until she had the first child. After the baby was born, the parents asked the father to marry their daughter. If he refused, they ended the arrangement and he could not see her nor the child again.

Other Social Characteristics

The Aztec society considered drunkenness a serious vice. It was view as a dangerous social problem and as the principal cause for crime. When authorized by the local officials, the people could drink octli, or pulque, a potent alcoholic beverage made from the sap of the maguey plant.

The Aztecs considered the fermented brew to be divine, but a person could face death for gross abuse of it. Today, in Mexico City only licensed *pulquerias* sell this liquor, which spoils very fast and must be drunk the day it is made.

The Codex Mendocino mentions that an elder person could drink up to four cups of pulque if he was seventy years old, sick, or under a physician's care. Fray Jeronimo de Mendieta wrote that women drink when they were sixty years old, or during the first days of childbirth. Physicians normally gave medicines to their patients in a cup of pulque.

During the celebration of special religious festivals, weddings, or parties, the authorities permitted the participants to drink two cups of pulque if they were thirty years of age or older. Those who worked in the forests carrying heavy loads also drink pulque after work. Except the yaoyizquez, or combat officers, military leaders could not drink alcohol.

In spite of these restrictions, almost everyone drank in the privacy of their homes. Duran writes that the

Figure 68 Father sitting on a palm-leaf mat. Aztec's gliphs always showed men sitting on mats. Mats never appeared under female figures.

authorities prohibited drinking pulque in public places because people who drank excessively caused many problems. The punishment to those who disobeyed the law was humiliation, chastisement, and social disapproval. Their heads were shaved and their homes destroyed. Those who continued to drink after the initial punishment were stoned or beaten to death.

Slavery

Slavery was another important institution in the Aztec society. There were several categories of slaves, among them, prisoners of war, public debtors, criminals, servants and children enslaved by private owners. Many had accepted voluntarily their condition as result of extreme poverty, starvation, or debts that could not be paid. Their willingness to do so could be attributed to the mildness of Aztec slavery.

Historian William H. Prescott wrote that it was common for parents, with the master's concern, to use other sons to replace the one in bondage. (50). Parents sold their children into servitude when famine or starvation threatened the welfare of the rest of the family Merchants bought or sold slaves in open markets (Bandelier 628-29).

The Aztec priests usually sacrificed prisoners of war, and the army even fought battles to capture victims for the sacrificial stone. Lawbreakers who had been spared from execution became privately-owned slaves. The law permitted the enslavement of people as restitution for injuries that they had caused to others.

Slaves could be freed if they paid to their owner the cost of their purchase. Those who ran away and turned themselves in voluntarily to any official justice would be set free. If a slave was captured by a person who was not a member of the owner's family, the guardian claimed the fugitive as his own and used him as a servant.

A pregnant slave received freedom if her owner was the father of the child, or if he married her. If a slave escaped and entered a royal palace he also was set free. Proprietors could also emancipate any slave whenever they wanted, and most of them did so when they were about to die.

The Aztec judicial system punished the mistreatment of slaves very harshly. Aztec law defended slave rights tenaciously. Those who entered slavery voluntarily as result of debts received a contract witnessed by at least four persons. The document contained the duties and responsibilities of each slave and the terms of his servitude. Slaves could not be mistreated, or resold to another person without their personal consent.

Owners could place wooden yokes around the necks of dangerous slaves to prevent their escape. They could sell any slave who attempted to escape. If the slave continued to be a problem, he could be sacrificed during a religious ceremony (Prescott 50).

Slaves were considered personal property. They lived in lands owned by their masters and could have a family, own property, or held other slaves. Their children were always born free: "An honorable distinction, not known. . .in any civilized community where slavery has been sanctioned," according to Prescott (Prescott 50).

Social Standing of Women

The social standing of women in the Aztec society was limited. Society considered them inferior to men. Women, except those selected for the priesthood, could not participate actively in religious ceremonies, nor enter the business profession. They could own property, gain redress in the courts of law and influence matters of government concern. Women worked mostly in industry, farming and in private homes (Vaillant 125).

In spite of these limitations they were not abused. Recent investigations conducted by Inga Clendinnen on the role of the Aztec woman indicate that "Mexica women enjoyed effective protection, and exercised a degree of individual autonomy in the small liberties and decisions of everyday life that possibly surpassed that of men" (Clendinnen 206).

While some of Clendinnen's work may be speculative, as reviewer Peter Winn observes, the new assessment of the Aztec women tends to show that they, too, played an important role in the Aztec society.

The Spanish historians and chroniclers of the sixteenth century who studied the Indian domestic life wrote that the Aztecs were emotional and sensible. They loved literature, music and poetry, and was not unusual to see a warrior carrying a bouquet of flowers for his wife. Artisans produced works of art in beaten gold and

Figure 69 Detail of stone relief from Teotihuacan.

pure silver that far surpassed anything done in Western Europe.

The Aztecs congratulated each other on special occasions such as the birth of a child, marriage, a promotion, or on any good fortune. They gave costly presents to their friends. According to Sahagun, the Aztecs regulated their personal visits to their neighbors and acquaintances with the precision of oriental courtesy.

Students of the ancient Mesoamerican civilizations are also impressed by the government efficiency. The emperor had a communication system that kept him informed of the important news of the empire. His carrier service provided him with fresh fish from the Gulf twenty-four hours after being taken. Moctezuma also could enjoy tropical fruits from the southern edge of the empire while they were still in season.

Writers expressed their literary views in pictographic form. Professional scribes did drawings on coarse paper made from the maguey leaf. Aztec literature was quite extensive and some of it has survived to this day in the form of historical codices. One of these works, the *"Songs of Huexotzingo,"* is a poetic lament to future generations. It concludes: " Will I leave only this, like the flowers that wither?/ Will nothing last of my name, nothing of my fame, on this earth? / At least the flowers! At least the songs!

These magnificent words of hope and inspiration are carved today on a stone wall in the National Museum of Anthropology in Mexico City for everyone to see and to remember!

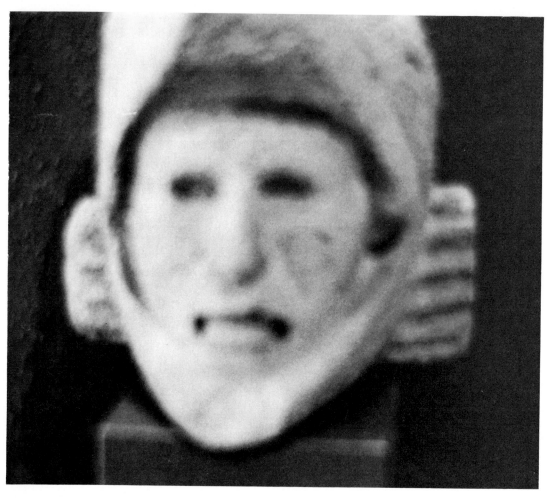

Figure 70 (Sculpture representing an Eagle Warrior.
(INAH)

8

THE ANCIENT JUDICIAL SYSTEM OF MEXICO

A Responsible Ruler

Nezahualcoyotl, the poet-philosopher who ruled Texcoco, a member of the Aztec empire, was an important lawmaker in ancient Mexico. He was very strict about the enforcement of laws, and "tempered justice with mercy," according to historian William H. Prescott. There are many stories about Nezahualcoyotl's judicial ethic and personal interest in the welfare of his subjects.

The ruler often disguised himself as a common man and walked among the people to inquire about their personal lives. On one such occasion, while walking in the woods dressed as a hunter, he met a young lad who was gathering firewood. The ruler asked the boy why he did not go to the other side of the forest where the kindling was plentiful, dryer, and better. The child responded that the other sections of the woods belonged to the emperor and it was prohibited to enter those lands. "If I do so, I will lose my life," said the boy.

Nezahualcoyotl asked the boy who was the ruler that forbid such a thing and he replied: "He is a miserable man who takes away the things that our gods have given us." The monarch then told him to go to the other side of the forest to get his firewood; no one was going to tell the Emperor about it.

The young man, disturbed by the suggestion, admonished the stranger because he was telling him to disobey the law. Returning to his palace, Nezahualcoyotl summoned the child and his family to reward them for the lad's honesty. Few days later, he ended the prohibition of gathering firewood in the royal preserves (Alva Ixtlilxochtl, 129).

Another story about this monarch says that he was so concerned with the welfare of his people that often he visited the market square to purchase goods that the farmers were unable to sell. He paid them more than their regular prices to improve their lives and lighten their misery.

These anecdotes have appeared in many forms since the historian Fernando de Alva Ixtlilxochtl told them for the first time in his book *Historia de la Nacion Chichimeca*. The stories not only describe the Aztecs' reluctance to disobey the law; they also reveal the concern of Nezahualcoyotl, and his desire to reward good deeds. They show the severity of the Aztec punishment, the people's familiarity with the laws and the structures of the Mexican legal system.

A Severe Legal System

The elders who had migrated with the tribe years before created the harsh system of laws that concerned the young wood gatherer. Since the Aztecs did not have written codes of law, the people memorized them.

Common law and legal experience was the basis for the Aztec legal system. Conserved in the minds of the people, the laws were a part of the customs and traditions of the tribe. Throughout the years, the Indian leaders made very few changes in those codes. The original legal doctrine continued in effect until the end of the empire.

In the Aztec society, the rule of law predominated over every aspect of life. It was expected that everyone knew the basic tenures of the legal system. Violators paid a prompt retribution for their deeds and judges enforced the laws faithfully. These magistrates settled disputes and litigations quickly with no partiality and little mercy. After every trial, they released the facts and decisions to the public (Soustelle 149; Prescott 49).

This procedure resulted in a high level of law awareness. The Spanish Jesuit historian Francisco Javier Clavigero wrote that everyone knew the laws so well that there was no need for judicial books. Parents never stopped teaching their children the contents of the laws to prevent involuntary transgressions (Clavigero 201-204).

Teachers taught their students respect for their

elders, to love truth and to obey the laws. The harshness of many codes and the pervasiveness of the system concerned everyone. Death was the penalty for many criminal offenses.

Changes in Common Law Practices

In later years, the Aztecs formed a political union with Tlacopan and Texcoco. To reform their laws, the Mexicans made several important changes in their legal system. They adopted many of the codes that Nezahualcoyotl had revised and supplemented them with their common experiences.

The ruler of Texcoco created eighty new legal codes and eliminated many older ones. He reorganized the government and the functions of the state into councils of war, finance and justice. The new laws allowed common citizens to participate for the first time in the administrative activities of the government (Martinez 248).

When the Aztecs accepted these changes, they copied them in folding books using pictographic writing. They did this work with such care and professionalism that Spanish tribunals later accepted the statutes as evidence in colonial trials.

In spite of the changes, the harsh legal ethic of the empire continued unabated. The system forced the people to live under constant anxiety and social pressure. Rules of conduct were clear. Those who committed theft in a marketplace, or a crime in a highway, received the death penalty. Capital crimes also included murder, the practice of black magic, and the impersonation of high ranking officials.

If the victim of a lesser crime had a family, the wife could pardon the criminal, but he became her slave for life. Death was the penalty for high treason. Those that were guilty of this crime died without mercy. Their bodies were quartered, their wealth confiscated, and the parents and family members sold into slavery. Anyone accused of using the military standards without authority lost their personal property (Clavijero 217).

Sexual offenses such as homosexuality and bestiality were capital offenses The law also punished with the death penalty incest and marriages between relatives. The only exceptions were relatives who took the widow of

Figure 71 Human sacrifices. Victim
dying on stake-platform (Codex Nutall)

a dead brother to their household to live with them. The Aztecs believed that public honesty would have been seriously compromised if members of the same family were allowed to marry or live together as sexual partners.

Civil and Criminal Laws

The Aztecs believed that men who dressed as women or women who used men's clothing were homosexuals, and punished them severely. Adultery was such an immoral crime that the offense always received the death penalty. The Aztecs seldom used torture to force a confession. A witness swore in the name of Huitzilopochtli to tell the truth, knowing that if he lied the court could punish him with death. If the criminal was an important person, or a member of the aristocratic class, the Aztecs tarred and feathered him and burned his hair. He was later executed in private (Bray 84).

The Codex Mendocino shows those guilty of adultery being stoned to death. Strangely enough, if a man killed his wife for being an adulteress, he also lost his life for taking the law into his hands. Entering a secluded area where young maidens lived or attended school resulted in the maximum punishment (Clavigero 218).

Once, the eldest daughter of a ruler invited a young man to enter a room where her sisters were playing. He stranger talked with them for a short time and left when the palace guards arrived. The guards never caught the intruder, but the ruler ordered the strangulation of his daughter because she had violated the law. Even children were not exempted from punishment. The penalty for striking a parent was slavery or death, depending on the severity of the transgression. (Peterson 124; Vaillant 98).

Other Penalties

Children who disobey their parents were sold as slaves. Abortion meant death to the woman who committed the crime and to the healer who gave her the medicine. Slavery was the accepted punishment for kidnappers and for those who had a personal fight in a public place.

Stealing was a major crime and, when committed with violence, it received the death penalty. The thief that could not return what he had stolen, was enslaved for

Figure 72   Brazier, Templo Mayor, Tenochtitlan.
(INAH)

life. Robbers who regularly stole merchandise in the marketplace were stoned to death.

If a group of men stole food from a warehouse, the one who entered the building first received the hardest punishment. Gamblers who refused to pay their debts were sold into slavery. Stealing maize was punishable with death or slavery because corn was the staple of life and a sacred gift from the gods. The Aztecs considered the pilfering of grain unnecessary. Farming was a communal affair and everyone could receive a section of land for their individual use.

To prevent crop stealing and to help the poor, Nezahualcoyotl decreed the planting of several rows of maize, squashes and beans along the roadside. The poor and the hungry used the products of these special areas. If someone took more than four ears of corn at once, or removed the kernels from the rows farther from the roadway, he was accused of stealing and put to death.

The law helped those in need, while those who wanted to take advantage of the lenient policy paid the full penalty. Maize was such an important crop for the Aztecs that even removing plants from the field before the harvest resulted in the death penalty (Bray 85).

Family Life and Legalized Society

The Codex Mendocino shows how habitual liars had their lower lip and ears cut. Slanderers received the same punishment. To steal objects used in official religious ceremonies such as gold, silver, or jades, was a mortal crime. This type of offense, however, was rare for it brought disaster, not only to the lawbreaker but to the community as well (Vaillant 98).

Aztec law also regulated extravagance in food and dress on religious and moral grounds. Contrary to the Maya and other Indian tribes of Mesoamerica, the Aztecs conserved the natural resources very well. To cut down a living tree or kill a forest animal without a reason was punished severely. Since communal ownership of the land was an accepted practice and only the harvest belonged to the farmer, the destruction of boundary markers was also punished with death (Gilmor 110; Bray 85).

Special laws directed the affairs of state and the foreign activities of the Aztecs. To kill a merchant while visiting a foreign region was a just cause for war.

Other statutes dealt with collections of tribute, appointment of governors in conquered areas, and the conduct of commercial transactions. Prisoners of war who returned to their military units had to contest charges of cowardice at the time of their capture. If found guilty, they received the death penalty. The Aztecs believed that there was no honor in being a captive of an enemy.

Business and Civil Laws

Civil codes recognized ownership of both movable and fixed property and divorces. Rights to a property were established by contract, royal concession, or inheritance. Pictographic details outlined the limitations of land areas and well known geographic landmarks established the owner's boundaries.

Contracts consisted of agreements, exchanges, land rents, loans, work commitments and donations. According to the Spanish historian Juan Torquemada, civil law permitted that women inherited personal property, but not political power. Such action would have resulted in internal divisions and unrest.

Inheritance laws distributed equally among the children the wealth of an individual. When the children were small, wrote the Franciscan Friar Toribio de Motolinea, the oldest one became the custodian of the wealth. He divided it with the rest when they became old enough. If none of the children married, the possession and subsequent distribution of the inheritance became the responsibility of the elder brothers of the deceased. Parental guardianship was authorized only to the father and was absolute while the child was under age. A parent could even go into voluntary slavery with his children.

The Nature of the Law

The Aztec laws applied equally to all members of the community. The justice system judged all citizens under the same standards and made no distinctions between rich or poor, merchant or common laborer. The upper class and the merchants had separate courts of law but their punishments were more severe because as privileged persons they had to set the example in all religious and public activities.

**Figure 73   Polychromed urn with face of corn goddess,
Templo Mayor. (INAH)**

Nezahualcoyotl, the ruler of our earlier story, decreed the death penalty for one of his sons who had committed adultery. Nezahualpilli, his successor, ordered the execution of four sons and the women involved. The Texcoco ruler believed that it was unjust to punish his people and not his children for committing the same crimes, and that all evil deeds had to suffer the same penalties (Martinez 55-59).

For the aristocracy, death by drowning was a common punishment. Nobles that were guilty of a serious crime died in this fashion. If the offender was a common man, however, he was enslaved for life. A nobleman accused of being intoxicated in a public place could expect the death penalty; a laborer who committed the same offense for the first time had his head shaved. Aztec justice was unmerciful and impartial. Deterrence was the principal element of the judicial system.

Criminal Justice System

Aztec criminal justice was so severe and swift that it required no penal institutions. They believed that lawbreakers should pay the society for their crimes in the hardest way. Convicts received no humanitarian treatment and had no opportunity for rehabilitation. Since the Aztec did not use money, it could not be used to pay fines or penalties. Punishment became the only form of retribution for crimes and it consisted mostly of corporeal discipline, slavery or death.

Prisoners sentenced to death for their crimes, or those scheduled to be sacrificed, were temporarily confined in wooden cages called Quahcalli, or houses of wood. These cells were located inside a building called the Petlacalli that had only one door and a dark, long galley.

With limited ventilation and no windows, it must have been a terrifying experience for the prisoners to stay in these confined quarters, completely alone and isolated from the rest of the society. Except this limited confinement, no other system of legal custody existed in ancient Mexico.

Lawbreakers could expect a brutal punishment from the Aztec judicial system. Fray Gerónimo de Mendieta, a Franciscan friar who studied the system, wrote that criminals were executed by striking them on the face after being tied hand and feet together. Others were strangled slowly and painfully while adulterers were burned alive.

Death by stoning was common for many crimes. Those sentenced were taken to the town square, where people were invited to throw stones at them until they died. Persons convicted of lesser crimes faced enslavement, amputation of limbs, mutilation, banishment from the community, destruction of their property, or shearing of the hair.

Judges also forced wrongdoers convicted of minor offenses to pay their victims with food, labor, or property. All stolen property had to be returned. If the article was of small value, its restitution settled the matter. If the article was of great value, had been damaged, or could not be restored, the thief became bonded to the victim until payment was completed. Most Mesoamerican civilizations practiced a similar method of economic restitution.

The Aztec judicial system was a highly structured and complex organization with both trial and appellate jurisdiction. Alonzo de Zorita, the Spanish judge who investigated the Mexican law, wrote that there were judges in each mayor town to represent the judicial system. The elders selected these judges for one year from the commoners who had shown leadership qualities and sound judgment practices.

The magistrates, with different names in each region, resolved the minor civil and penal cases in their towns and provinces. They had the authority to order the arrest of delinquents and to insured that lawbreakers were brought to trial. They also conducted criminal investigations for other courts, enforced the local laws, and tried to keep litigations from reaching the higher tribunals.

In some areas of the empire there were local appeal courts who revised the sentences, but most the important cases went to Tenochtitlan for final action. Besides the magistrates, the people also appointed special officers to watch over the conduct of certain families, and "report any disorder or breach of the laws to the higher authorities" (Prescott 46).

Aztec judges were individuals of a high moral character, strong religious convictions, and a righteous standing in the community. Often they were members of

Figure 74 Sacrificial knife with
turquoise decorations (British
Museum)

the military elite, tribal elders, or relatives of government officials. The provincial judges had limited jurisdiction. Cases that they could not resolve were sent to a higher court. Under these magistrates were other officials who served the warrants and citations, and carried out the judgments of the tribunals.

The judges of the lower courts held their trials in special buildings selected for that particular purpose. The residents of nearby towns came to have their cases heard and decided. Seated on straw mats, the law officers listened to the evidence presented and examined the witnesses. Their legal proceedings took sometimes many hours of investigation (Zorita 131-132).

Rules of Evidence

All procedures were verbal, but in certain cases evidence could be presented in pictographic writing. In the courts, there were scribes who were skillful painters. They did the task of recorders, and draw in native characters the development of the case, including the views of both the judge and the accused. They also outlined the various claims, declarations of witnesses and the final sentence. This detailed procedure was limited mostly to important cases, but litigants had an opportunity to have their lawsuits judged according to their merit.

Except in land disputes, legal documentation was seldom required. The judges accepted oral testimonies and depositions that were verified thoroughly by cross examination. Cases were handled quickly and the justices tried to reach conclusions and arrive at the truth directly.

The maximum time allowed to decide an action was eighty days; but, provincial and local judges normally ruled them in one day. The Aztecs, according to Zorita, did not use the court system extensively and they normally confessed to wrongdoing at the beginning of a trial.

The Legal System in Tenochtitlán

Tenochtitlan itself had a different system. A lower court composed of three judges ruled in all simple civil and criminal cases, except those of the aristocracy. This courtroom, called a Teccali, was located in the royal palace, where it did its official functions for the four calpullis, or townships of Tenochtitlan. The tribunal was in session continuously and was one of the most important courts of the judiciary system of ancient Mexico (Peterson 119).

Fray Bernardino de Sahagun writes: "In this place lived the senators and the elderly who listened to the petitions and arguments of the people. They tried to do their duty with prudence and sagacity as fast as possible. They saw the evidence and listened attentively to the witnesses before passing a sentence (Sahagun, VIII, 466).

Appeals from the Teccali could not be heard directly by the higher tribunal because some of its judges also were members of that court. This limitation, according to historian Manuel Orozco y Berra, allowed the Cihuacoatl, the second highest official in Tenochtitlan, to decide most criminal cases with the help of other judges. This Court of Appeals known as Tlacxitlan had four judges to handle the appeals from the lower courts. The decisions of this tribunal were final and no one could appeal his sentence.

The Cihuacoatl, however, could refer them to the emperor for a final determination since he had the last judicial authority. This prerogative was especially important in cases involving noblemen and privileged persons. The Cihuacoatl held office during life.

The judicial system of the Aztecs permitted appeals to a higher tribunal. Orozco y Berra also writes that the emperor had the final authority in all legal cases. He was the Supreme Justice and had the title of Tlacatecuhtli. Zorita speaks that he had a council of twelve judges who investigated the cases before presenting them to him.

Twelve additional senior officers were responsible for the arrest of important persons and the conduct of court business in other towns. These advisers also investigated matters of importance such as military conflicts and a questionable aristocratic behavior. This special counsel met every ten or twelve days to resolve any pending case before being presented to the Emperor. This court of appeals was located in Tenochtitlan.

The emperor, assisted by these judges, ruled on the cases that were brought to him. Those that involved crimes of the nobility or war activities had special importance. After some consideration, the emperor resolved them as the Spanish chronicler Bernal Diaz del Castillo says, "in a few words."

The emperor's legal advisers were known as the Tecutlatoque. Every one of these advisers, as Zorita wrote, had also twelve constables who were authorized to arrest the suspects of a crime as determined by the ruler or the judges. According to him, other individuals served as court messengers who, "carried out their errands with the greatest diligence, by night or day, in rain, snow, or hail, without the slightest delay" (Zorita 126).

The judicial authority of the emperor in these matters is expressed by a pictographic drawing in the Codex Mendocino. In a section of this work, a court of four judges sits before a man and a woman while the emperor is in a higher position denoting the status of his authority.

Towns that were too far from Tenochtitlan, or that did not form a part of the Aztec territory directly, had ordinary judges. These lower court magistrates also could arrest delinquents, resolve minor criminal cases and examine serious ones with independence. They withheld their sentences on important cases until they met with the emperor in Tenochtitlan.

After consulting with his advisers, the emperor made the final decision on these cases. Besides a magistrate, these smaller towns had a Tlayacanqui and a Tequilatla who acted as town mayors, and a Topilli or sheriff who helped in the enforcement of the judicial system. Most of these territories were located south of Tenochtitlan between Xochimilco and Atzapotzalco.

Tribunal of the Eighty Days' Speaking

Representatives from all the major cities met in Tenochtitlan every eighty day to act as a Great Council and to debate matters that concerned the judicial system and the Aztec empire. In sessions that lasted up to twelve days, they listened to the magistrates give an account of the cases decided in their courtrooms.

This court was known as the *Nauhpohaulltlatolli*, or Tribunal of the Eighty Days' Speaking, and not only

Figure 75 Human sacrifices. Offering hearts to the sun.

advised the ruler on the conditions of the empire but decided any legal case still pending. After the eighty days, the maximum time allowed for a case to be decided, a Tecpoyotl or official caller, informed the people of the nature and scope of the sentences.

The Tecpilcalli was a board of nobles that tried important military officers and decided court-martial cases. Another specialized court of law was the *Tlacxitlan*, which held final jurisdiction in cases involving the nobility. These special tribunals investigated and conducted their trials in private chambers to prevent the people from knowing the weaknesses of its leaders and the shame of the higher class. While the high ranking members of the aristocracy had a special legal treatment, the punishment for those who abused the privilege of their positions was harsher than that of the common men.

Judges and Court Officials

In Texcoco, there was a court with two judges who ruled on lower civil and criminal cases. A second court also composed of two magistrates, who did not sentence unless approved by the emperor, resolved appeals from the lower court. This second tribunal selected the cases for the emperor and made recommendations to him.

Judges received for their services a house, merchandises, revenue, and the products of certain lands set aside specifically for that purpose. Special workers planted their farms, collected firewood and provided water to them. While the judges received these benefits free, they could not dispose of the lands allocated to them. When they died or changed their responsibilities, the property and the assigned workers went to their replacements.

Judges and court officials could not accept any other form of payment, or receive personal favors or gifts from the litigants. They had to be impartial in all their decisions and incorruptible. Judges that did not obey their code of ethics received a strong reprimand from their fellow justices. If a judge committed a serious violation, he lost his job, his head was shaved, and his home and all his possessions were confiscated.

Partiality in any legal case was a serious offense. Nezahualpilli, dictated the hanging of a judge who showed special favors to a nobleman at the expense of a peasant. Another judge who had decided several cases of family members was executed (Bray 84).

The Aztecs developed an effective judicial system to deal with their problems and their responsibilities as an imperial society. Surrounded by enemies who paid tribute to them, they could not divert their attention to internal problems of law and order. For the Aztecs, a code of laws that served as a deterrence to crime was necessary. This system maintained the people subordinated to the rulers and to the state.

Since execution loomed fearfully in the minds of everyone, for it was the most common penalty, the Aztecs restrained themselves to live as they were told. Those who challenged the system or endangered the community received the death penalty.

The Use of Capital Punishment

Some scholars have argued that punishment in Aztec Mexico, with a primary reliance on the death penalty, was more than an attempt to prevent crime by deterrence. They have concluded that it was a system designed to curtail individual freedom and dissatisfaction with the actions of the ruling elite.

It has not been easy to understand what caused the destruction of earlier Mesoamerican civilizations. Perhaps, internal discontent with their ancient rulers contributed significantly to the end of these organized societies. Could the Aztecs have known that problem and tried to resolve it by strong judicial measures? Scholars of the ancient Mexican legal system probably will never be completely certain about the Aztecs' motives for punishment.

The danger and isolation in which the Aztecs lived, surrounded by enemies who constantly tried to destroy them, and the tributary economic system that they maintained demanded constant obedience from their subjects. Their religious fanaticism, which forced a fatalist view of life, also contributed a system of judicial law based on deterrence and fast retribution for crimes.

The Aztec systematic method of criminal control may have been necessary to them to assure the preservation of their violent society. Their system prompted greater

Figure 76   Brazier for religious ceremonies, Templo Mayor. (INAH)

public awareness of their social responsibilities. Fathers instructed their children, elders maintained constant vigilance, and priests warned potential violators.

The Aztec system of jurisprudence with several different tribunals to enforce legal obedience must have created many interpretations of the law throughout the Empire. There were no lawyers to interpret the legal codes and superior judges were wholly independent in their decisions. In fact, interfering with the legal process was severely punished by burning the hair of the intruder.

The Aztec society punished the important crimes with the death penalty. Even the murder of a slave was punished with death. As a result, the entrances to the Aztec dwellings were not secured by bolts, or fastenings of any kind, nor the occupants had to worried about a criminal assault (Prescott, 49).

The law encompassed all activities and affected everyone in the Aztec society, from rulers and nobles to farmers and housewives. It touched the lives of men, women, and children, from those who lived in splendid palaces to the poor ones who gathered firewood. It reflected, as the Aztec scholar Miguel Leon-Portilla tells us, "a striving toward the fundamental ideal taught at the Calmecac" of respect to others and "giving oneself up to what is appropriate and righteous."

**Figure 77   Modern "voladores," the spectacular Aztec
high pole entertainment.**

9

Feathered Serpents and Smoking Mirrors: The Dichotomy of Religion

Importance of Religion

One of the principal concerns of the Mexican Indians was religion. The Aztecs believed that good and evil struggled to control human existence. That life centered on a mutual relationship between gods and people, and faith had divine and human characteristics. They maintained that their lives were directed by higher powers who alone knew everything and could help or harm humans at will.

The Aztecs conditioned their lives to accept the power of their deities as very few societies have ever done. The gods alone could protect mankind from the perils of an uncertain fate. These deities had to be obeyed and worshiped as masters and custodians of the universe (Leon-Portilla, 118-122).

The Mexican Indians expressed their religious beliefs with such intensity and zeal that ritual, organized worship and sacred services took precedence over all other matters. Their society, as historian Burr Cartwright Brundage labeled it, was etched on the sacrificial stone.

Religious faith was prominent in every aspect of life. The gods directed morality, ethical conduct, and individual undertakings. They determined the success of business, military ventures and collective endeavors. Liturgy regulated the planting season, the proper time for marriages, and personal relationships. Native art, music and literature reflected the dedication and reverence that the Aztecs had for their gods.

Religion also influenced education, the dances and

ball games of the people, and the business practices of the merchants. The Aztecs even attributed illnesses, diseases and personal misfortunes to supernatural forces (Duran 156).

The Aztecs worshiped their deities with distrust and fear since they could not tell when the gods accepted pleas with kindness or rejected them with hostility. Ritualistic invocations sought to gain a favorable acceptance of daily existence and protection from the forces of evil. Ethical control, spiritual perfection, communal strength, and all the principal functions of society were directly or indirectly related to religion. The ritual, a combination of superstition, witchcraft, and magic, dominated their lives. Ceremonies were extraordinarily harsh and cruel.

Since the gods had the power of life and death over everyone, the well-being and the protection of the community depended entirely on their appeasement. As George C. Vaillant has described it, "the Aztec universe was conceived on a religious rather than a geographic sense" (Vaillant 178).

Organization and Functions of the Priesthood

The structures of the Aztec priesthood went back to the early years of tribal wandering when the clan elders established stringent laws to compel blind obedience. These priests became very powerful and wielded great influence over the people.

Throughout the years the priesthood developed into the most important class of the Aztec society. The gods spoke through the holy men. They alone knew how to please and persuade the divine rulers and to safeguard the people from peril, ward off floods, cure sicknesses and prevent crop failures. The priests determined the need for sacrifices or offerings for the divinities, and directed the people to do them.

A complex hierarchical organization of priests and sages was responsible for supervising the religious lives of the people. At the top of the structure was the Tlatoani who, besides being the major political and military leader of Tenochtitlan, also was the highest priest (Krickeberg 81).

As a chosen leader, he presided over all the important religious ceremonies. He had the attributes of

Figure 78 The Toltec God Quetzalcoatl

possessing magical powers, the ability to foretell the future, and the power to cure many illnesses. The Cihuacoatl, the second highest official in the government, took over the Tlatoani responsibilities during his absence.

The priests that directed the cults of the gods Tlaloc and Huitzilopochtli had the highest rank and were called Totec Tlamacazqui and Quetzalcoatl Totec Tlamacazqui respectively. They were chosen to these positions after serving for a long time in the Calmecac, the principal nobility and religious school of Tenochtitlan. The Aztec priests had considerable power and responsibilities. They organized rituals, supervised the training of specialists, and taught in the religious schools (Davis 114).

In Tenochtitlan and adjacent towns and villages, there were priests that collected tributes and served as custodians of the temples and sacred places. Many of them, according to the Spanish chroniclers, "wore cotton cloaks that reached to their feet, with their hair so long and dirty with blood that it could not be parted or disentangled." The soldier Bernal Diaz del Castillo wrote that "the priests cut holes in their tongues, pierced the earlobes, and drew blood from their arms and legs during ceremonies" (578).

Priests did not teach the idea of goodness with the same emphasis as it is taught today. This characteristic of western religious culture was unimportant to the Aztecs. Goodness was simply the act of faithfully observing the daily religious rituals without seeking personal gratification.

The wise men, or tlamatinime, predicted the future and "the inexorable end of human destiny" with the aid of the tonalamatl, or the book of horoscopes. These sacred books contained paintings of religious symbols and objects of worship, such as artifacts, altars and idols. Large colored drawings, bordered by thirteen squared spaces, contained names, dates, numbers, and representations of the gods and birds associated with them.

These manuscripts depicted the divinities who, according to Aztec religion, influenced the events and the weeks of the year. Unfortunately, very few pages of these "horoscope books" survived the destruction by the Spaniards. The most impressive of those that remain are

Figure 79 Priest with censer (Codex
Mendocino)

part of the Codex Borbonicus now in Paris.

The gods had the power to decide everyone's fate. Success or failure depended on the exact time of birth. As a result, parents consulted the wise men soon after a child was born to find out his future. "Four days later," as G. C. Vaillant has written, "the child's family held a feast both to celebrate his birth and to name the child. If the day of birth proved to be unlucky, custom sanctioned a religious fiction by which the naming ceremony was postponed to a more favorable period"(Vaillant 96).

Gods and Goddesses of the Aztec Pantheon

Aztec religious beliefs centered on the worship of natural objects and phenomena such as the sun, the moon, the Morning Star and the rain. The Indians regarded most celestial things as sacred and represented them with idols. Their principal deity was Huitzilopochtli, the Hummingbird on the Left, who was the god of war, the sun and the blue sky. This god struggled daily against the forces of evil to maintain the sun moving across the sky. He also led the Aztecs into military victories to preserve and maintain their empire.

The Aztecs also worshiped Tezcatlipoca, or Smoking Mirror. He was the ruler of the night, the benefactor of sorcerers and witches, and the messenger of death. This god was an evil being who always got involved in human affairs. He also was the patron of warriors and the divinity who bestowed wealth and honor to the Aztec nobility.

Quetzalcoatl, the Feathered Serpent, was one of the oldest and most respected of the Mesoamerican gods. This deity was revered by Maya and Toltecs alike, was the giver of life and the god of wind and heavens. He inspired men to study the stars, to use agriculture, and to develop the calendar, industry and the arts. He stood for law, order, and enlightenment. The Aztecs believed that one day he would return from exile to reclaim his domains.

The Indians also worshipped Coatlicue, the earth goddess and the mother of gods. She is represented by one of the most gruesome and horrible sculptures of Mesoamerican art. The statue that survived the colonial destruction has a monstrous head of rattlesnakes; a necklace of hearts, hands and skulls; and a skirt of snakes. The hands and feet have claws to "feed off the corpses of human beings." The statue symbolizes the deity's as mother goddess maintaining the balance between life and death. This monument is in the National Museum of Anthropology in Mexico City.

The god Tlaloc, He Who Makes the Plants Spring Up, was the ancient deity of rain and a divinity of all the Nahuatl tribes. Since rain was so important the cult of Tlaloc occupied a high position among the Aztecs. The people honored him far more frequently than any other god.

Tlazolteotl, the Filth Eater, was the goddess who cleaned men's souls by eating all that was bad and evil. She received confessions of transgressions and sins. Centeotl, or Divine Ear of Corn, was the deity of maize that presided over agriculture. Soothsayers and fortune tellers venerated her.

Xipe Totec, or Our Flayed Lord, was the god of the spring and the patron of goldsmiths. Xochipilli, the Flower Prince, was the god of love, music and dance. Xochiquetzal, the Precious Flower, was the goddess of beauty, flowers, grains and plants, and the patroness of weavers and women of easy virtue. These gods and goddesses played a very important role in the Aztec religion (Sahagun 31-52).

There were also many other deities in the extremely complex Indian pantheon. There were gods of the maguey plant, pulque, song and flowers. The Aztecs also worship gods of the moon, stars, earth and heaven; and gods that lived in caves, mountains and rivers. Even the Pochteca, the Aztec merchants, had their god of trade. The Aztecs probably venerated more than sixteen hundred deities at the time of the arrival of the Spaniards to the New World.

A "Doomsday Ideology"

Many times the Aztecs also adopted the deities of their enemies and neighbors. For them, there were no other deities; other gods being only representations of those whom they already honored. The priesthood restricted the introduction of foreign deities into the Aztec pantheon by bringing to Tenochtitlan the idols of the conquered people.

Figure 80 Tezcatlipoca

Religious rites and practices of former enemies received considerable attention. Those elements that could be absorbed were added to the standard practices. Foreign idols were placed under special religious patronage. The Mexican anthropologist Alfonso Caso believes that this practice could have developed into some form of religious monotheism if allowed to continue without interruption.

The distinctions among Aztec gods became obscured at times, especially when they were represented during certain times as reincarnations of other gods. The Spanish priests who came to Mexico in the wake of the Conquest used this characteristic of the Aztec religion to convert the Indians to their faith. Even today many of the local ceremonies are a mixture of Christianity and Indian lore (Caso 37).

The cult of the Virgin of Guadalupe, the patroness saint of Mexico, is a good example. The Indians accepted the religiosity of the miracle because the spirit of the Virgin appeared on the same hill where the Aztec goddess Tonantzin, Our Mother, once had a temple. Today, on this spot, thousands of Indians participate in annual festivities to honor the Virgin of Guadalupe with dances and ceremonies designed hundreds of years ago.

The Aztec religion has been called a "doomsday ideology," since it thrived on idolatry, terror and a violent philosophy. The priests and rulers used religion to strike fear, force obedience, manipulate the people and protect the empire. As in ancient Israel, religion was the sole system of law.

The priests were the principal magistrates of the judicial system. These judges had considerable influence and those who refused to accept their decisions were executed. The central theme of Aztec system was simple, direct, and explicit. The world was going to end in a cataclysm and the divine mission of the priests was to postpone that catastrophe. To this end the sun god had to be kept alive by feeding him human blood. He required a daily nourishment of human hearts to survive in the struggle with the forces of evil (Soustelle (103–107).

The Myth of Creation

According to one of the traditions about the original creation, the gods Ometecuhtli and Omecihuatl, "the

Figure 81 Xipe-Totec, Lord of the Flayed Ones (Codex Fejervary Mayer)

Duality Rulers," gave to the gods Red Tezcatlipoca, Tezcatlipoca, Huitzilopochtli, and Quetzalcoatl, their four sons, the task of creating mankind, the sun and other ruling gods. The divine couple also directed their sons to protect the four directions or cardinal points of the universe, and to defend everything within them, while they continued to rule the earth and the sky (Caso 19-20).

The distributions of power apparently created jealousy and distrust among the divine beings, especially between Tezcatlipoca and Quetzalcoatl, since both had the responsibility of creating mankind. According to Caso, the conflict between these two gods is the history of the universe. The destruction and subsequent recreation of the world were attributed to their successes and failures. (Caso 25).

The Aztecs inherited from their predecessors the belief that the history of mankind consisted of five ages, which they called "suns." These were Ocelotonatiuh, or Sun of the Tiger; Ehecatonatiuh, Sun of Wind; Tletonatiuh, Sun of Fire; Atonatiuh, Son of Water; and Ollintoatiuh, the Sun of Movement.

The first four of these eras were destroyed by cataclysmic forces. During the first one, Tezcatlipoca, who used as a disguise a tiger's mask, became the sun as other gods populated the world with acorn-eating giants. While ruling it, his enemy Quetzalcoatl stroked him with a walking stick and the sun god fell into the water, where he changed into a jaguar that ate the giants and left the earth deserted and without life (Caso 24).

The second time, Quetzalcoatl became the sun and ruled the world until Tezcatlipoca destroyed it with hurricanes and high winds. Most of the human beings died during this time, except for those who changed themselves into monkeys. The third time, the Divine Creators made the rain god Tlaloc the ruling sun, but Quetzalcoatl destroyed the world with a rain of celestial fire, which devastated everything and turned people into birds. The divine god then made the water goddess Chalchiuhtlicue, Tlaloc's sister, the sun in a newly created world.

The fourth time, Tezcatlipoca destroyed the world with torrential rains. People changed into fishes to survive the cataclysm. After this catastrophe, and with no sun to illuminate the sky, the gods met at Teotihuacan, the ancient religious center of central Mexico, to decide who

Figure 82   **Mixtec temple. Codex Nuttall.**

would be transformed into a reigning sun (Caso 29-32).

The task required that those accepting the challenge plunge themselves into a celestial fire, where one of them would be purified to shine as the new sun. After four days of fasting, two of the deities fulfilled the undertaking by throwing themselves into the raging blaze. One of them, Nanauatzin, finally succeeded and a new sun, and later the moon, reappeared on the sky.

But the sun stayed still and refused to move until the rest of the gods also cast themselves into the flames. The sacrifice of the gods to insure the motion of the sun became later a fundamental part of the Aztec mythology.

Quetzalcoatl created mankind again by descending into the cold world of the dead to assemble the bones of previous generations and give them life. He had to overcome many obstacles to accomplish his purpose. Mictlantecuhtli, Lord of the Land of the Dead, surprised Quetzalcoatl and forced him to run away. While leaving the underworld, the god abruptly fell, breaking the bones that he was carrying into many pieces. He sprinkled them, however, with his blood to recreate mankind again, but some men came out short and others tall because the bones were of different sizes (Caso 22).

The End of Mankind

During Ollintoatiuh, or the present age, the Aztecs expected the destruction of mankind by earthquakes, starvation and drought. The wise men believed that the predicted destruction of the world would occur exactly at the completion of a 52-year cycle on their Indian calendar.

The Aztecs prepared themselves to die at that time by destroying their possessions and extinguishing their fires. On the evening of that fateful day, a group of elderly priests marched in procession to the Hill of the Star near Ixtapalapa, on the southern part of the valley of Mexico, to do a strange and dreadful ceremony.

First, they waited silently and with great expectation for the passage of Aldebaran and the Pleiades across the zenith at midnight. These stars in the Constellation Taurus, which passes at the zenith precisely every 52 years, marked the end of the Indian time chronology. As the stars approached the middle point of the darkened sky, the priests did the New Fire Ceremony to assure the beginning of a new cycle (Sahagun 440)

The ritual consisted in sacrificing a young member of the nobility by removing his heart and kindling a fire on his open chest. Other priests, dressed in appropriate ceremonial clothes, lit bundled torches in the flames and distributed the new fire among the participants. About the New Fires, historian Nigel Davies wrote that if the fires were not drawn, the sun would have ceased to shine and the fifth world would have been destroyed.

According to Caso, "if Aldebaran and the Pleiades had not crossed the zenith, the stars and the planets would have descended to the earth and transformed into wild beasts, eaten mankind at the same time that powerful earthquakes destroyed the sun." Because of this great expectation, "the New Fire was awaited with anguish and dread" (Caso 32).

The Rekindling of the Fires

When the people finally realized that the world was not going to end during that time, they celebrated their good fortune. They began to remake the things that had been destroyed, to rekindle their fires, and to carry their flames to the temples and homes. With great rejoice they participated in thirteen days of festivities to hail the beginning of another life cycle. The last of these lurid celebrations occurred in 1507 during the reign of Moctezuma II.

Since the New Fire Ceremony occurred probably once in the life of an individual, no one questioned the failure of the predictions, nor the fact that the prophesy had failed before. On the contrary, the people were happy that they had survived the ordeal, and soon, the incident was forgotten. Skepticism changed to concern for the construction of new monuments.

The Aztecs sacrificed human beings to sustain the life of the sun, and to prevent the fifth destruction of the world. According to another legend, the earth god Coatlicue lived in obscurity after giving birth to the moon and the stars. One day, while sweeping a temple, she found a ball of soft downy feathers that she tucked under her blouse. Soon after that, the ball disappeared and she felt pregnant. When the moon god Coyolxauhqui and her 400 brothers, the stars, discovered what had happened

Figure 83 Mixcoatl, God of Fire

they became angry and decided to sacrifice their mother.

As they approached the temple to do their feat, Huitzilopochtli was born fully armed and saved his mother. He killed his brothers and dismembered Coyolxauhqui, and proclaimed himself the guardian leader of the Aztecs (Caso 23).

Because of that struggle, the sun had to continue fighting the moon and the stars every sunrise to force them out of the sky. After the daily celestial engagement, the souls of the warriors who had died in battle carried aloft the sun from the underworld to the middle of the sky.

In the afternoon, the spirit of women who had died during childbirth continued to guide the divine heavenly body across the sky, and at sundown the souls of dead mothers took him to his resting place under the horizon. The Aztecs believed that as chosen people of the gods they were responsible for providing human blood and hearts to the sun to fortify him in his struggle for survival (Duran 92).

Man had been created by the sacrifice of the gods, and so it was natural for him to do the same by offering his blood to them. The gods needed this nourishment because it was the only substance that could perpetuate their existence. As the selected "people of the sun," the Aztecs believed that it was their duty to nourish the celestial star.

Human Sacrifices

The religious beliefs of the Aztecs compelled them to live in a constant state of warfare with their neighbors. Though they also used war to protect their empire and to expand their commercial control, the main purpose of conflict was to gather sacrificial victims for their religious rituals.

During sacrifices, the Aztec priests brought their victims naked to the top of a pyramidal temple and stretched them on their backs over a sacrificial stone. One of the priests placed a yoke upon his throat. Unable to move, the prisoners waited without struggle for the end of their lives.

The priests opened their chests with obsidian knives and "with amazing swiftness tore out their hearts, ripping them with their hands." The priests lifted the

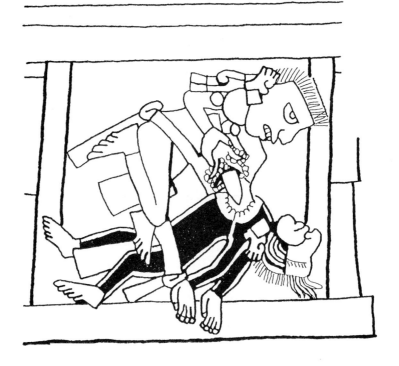

Figure 84 Priest removing heart from
sacrificial victim (Codex Nutall)

hearts toward the sun and offered it to him with prayers, omens, predictions and augurs. After the ceremony, the priests pushed away the body of the dead prisoner until it rolled down the steps. The distance between the sacrificial stone and the beginning of the steps was no more than two feet. At times the priests also practiced ritualistic cannibalism, with the victims' limbs serving as food and his head hung on a skull rack (Duran, Gods 92).

These ceremonies were not limited to Tenochtitlan. Duran writes that "the same sacrifices were practiced by the men of Tlaxcala, Huexotzinco, Calpan, Tepeaca, Tecali, Atotonilco, and Cuauhquecholan with the prisoners that they captured. All the provinces of the land practiced similar ceremonies" (Duran 32).

Every fall the priests sacrificed a young maiden to the god Chicomecohuatl, in symbolic fertility rites, to insure that the corn grew abundantly during the following year. The Aztecs also did a strange ritual to honor Xipe Totec, the god of spring.

To celebrate the beginning of the planting season, the priests sacrificed several prisoners who had been especially selected for the occasion by flaying their skins. Food beggars wore these skins as an outer garment for twenty days to symbolize the renewal of the earth with new vegetation and the ripening of the corn husks on the fields. Afterward, the priests buried the flayed skins in a cave.

Religious Rites and Festivals

During September, the Aztecs celebrated Teotleco, the "arrival of the gods." This festival honored the return of the deities who had gone away. At midnight, on the last day of the month, the priests went to the top of a temple to make a corn dough, which they put into a sacred bowl.

They could tell when the gods arrived by the appearance of a small footprint on the corn flour. All night the people waited in silence for the magic sign to appear on the flour. When the imprint finally appeared, the head priest proclaimed the arrival of the gods and the beginning of the festivities.

Immediately, hundreds of people in wards, districts and adjacent areas, began to sound their trumpets and

Figure 85   Ball Court Ring, Chichen Itza, Yucatan.

Figure 86   Tzompantli, or skull-rack, Chichen Itza, Yucatan.

play their drums and other musical instruments in celebration of the good news. They lighted fires on the roof tops, which gave an eerie look to the whole city, and danced with great joy.

On the following day, the priests honored the occasion by conducting human sacrifices, while men with painted faces and dressed in bat costumes danced and whistled wildly every time a victim was thrown into the fire (Sahagun 87-88).

The Aztecs periodically celebrated other religious festivals to honor their gods. During these celebrations, the priests sacrificed large numbers of slaves, prisoners of war, devout volunteers, women and even children. The leading gods needed appeasement, and the priests felt compelled to make daily offerings of human blood to them.

These sacrifices were not just isolated examples of the Aztec religious fanaticism. According to the noted Franciscan scholar and chronicler Fray Bernardino de Sahagun, who wrote extensively about the Aztec religious rites and rituals, the obsession with sacramental offerings even extended to lesser gods. Among them was Uixtocihuatl, the goddess of salt, who received once a year the sacrifice of a young maiden dressed and ornamented as the female deity (Sahagun 83).

Sahagun writes that the Aztec priests conducted these rituals in seven different places, and sometimes they also ate part of the victims' bodies after cooking them. In similar ceremonies, the ministers sacrificed more children during March, April and June.

Duran writes that during the festival of Huey Tozoztli, or Great Puncture, the priests also sacrificed children to Tlaloc. The priests slew six and seven year old infants to the sound of trumpets, conch shells, and flutes, and used their blood to sprinkle the face and body of their idols. On these occasions, all the nobility of the land attended the festivities (Duran 83).

Recent archaeological excavations of the ruins of the Great Temple of Tenochtitlán in Mexico City, confirm the ceremonial sacrifices of young children. Offering 48, found above Chamber III on Stage IVb has bones and skulls of forty-eight children, approximately three months to eight years old, sacrificed in honor of Tlaloc, the rain god.

The Dark World of the Spirits

The uncertainty of the death constantly occupied the minds of the Aztecs. They believed that the lifestyle and the nature of death, not moral conduct, determined one's final destiny. The souls of those who died in battle, by drowning, or during sacrifices drifted to one world; but those who died of natural causes went to another.

Warriors who died in combat or at the sacrificial stone went directly to Tonatiuhichan, the "dwelling place of the Sun." For four years they accompanied the god on his daily rounds, and after that period they returned to earth as birds of great beauty.

Mothers who died during childbirth went to a paradise called Cincalco, or the house of corn. Their spirits returned to earth several times in different forms. Those who died by drowning, during a lightning storm, or as a result of leprosy went to Tlalocan, the heavenly place of Tlaloc where people lived in happiness, abundance and contentment.

For the Indians "whose lives were at the mercy of drought, this must have been a wonderful prospect." The inhabitants of this paradise returned to earth as plants, flowers, rain or clouds.

People who died of natural causes went to Mictlan, the abode of Mictlantecuhtli and Mictecacihuatl, lord and lady of the emaciated. This place was the dark, mysterious land of the dead. But in contrast with Judeo-Christian teachings, which consider hell as a place where souls undergo eternal punishment, Mictlan was a final resting where souls did not suffer pain.

In a Dantean way, however, the souls of the dead had to pass first through nine different regions of terrible ordeals before they could reach Mictlan. The journey lasted four years and took the penitent across a wide river, between two clashing mountains, through an obsidian mountain ridge, and across a plain of very cold and icy winds.

During the remaining journey, the traveler faced many other perils, such as going through narrow trails and heated desert sands, fighting wild beasts, and escaping from arrow attacks. To help the soul during this journey, his relatives buried charms, amulets and a reddish dog with the dead body. They also bundled and cremated it and placed the ashes in an urn, which was buried close to the victim's last known home.

The Indians believed that the souls of those who died a natural death returned to earth as poisonous insects or beasts of pray. Only those who had a glorious death could expect an adequate retribution (Caso 78-90; Bierhorst 155;Sahagun 205-08).

Sahagun writes that those who died in combat or at the sacrificial stone were highly praised by their contemporaries, and many people desired to have a similar end. The souls of dead infants, on the other hand, went to a special paradise named Chichihuacanhuo, the wet-nurse tree, where they were nursed until their time became born again.

Since after-life was so uncertain, the Aztecs obeyed the rules of their religion and the instructions of the priests because they wanted to find happiness in this life and peace in the unknown world to follow.

The Aztecs' considered mountains, rivers and caves as sacred places. To them, mountain peaks and streams were the dwelling places of unpredictable gods who demanded supplication and offerings. Grottoes were the holiest of places and caves were underground passages to the womb of the earth.

Many Aztec mythological stories tell of ancestors emerging from caves and of brief encounters with deities and spirits of the death. Duran observed that the Aztecs had a compulsion "to go to the mountains to offer incense, food, wine and human sacrifices for protection against the wrath of the evil gods who inhabited them." Caves also were of immense importance to other people of ancient Mesoamerica. The Maya believed that they were entrances to an underworld inhabited by death and evil spirits (Duran 55).

The "People of the Sun"

The Aztec conception of destiny as, "the people of the sun," also motivated them to expand their territorial boundaries by conquering the neighboring weaker tribes. They justified their imperialistic designs with the need of providing victims for their sun-god.

As chosen people of Huitzilopochtli, they believed that they were the selected ones, those chosen to appease and nourish the gods to insure the survival of mankind.

Figure 87   Serpent head motif in the Temple of the Warriors, Chichen Itza, Yucatan.

War and the payment of tribute, therefore, became acceptable means of carrying out their sacred mission.

The Brazilian scholar Darcy Ribeiro writes, "these beliefs not only imbued the Aztecs with the ardor that made them capable of dominating other peoples, but also with a general world conception to which they sought to lead their subjects, and in which they were defined as supporters of the Sun and therefore of life and prosperity for all" (Ribeiro 109).

This sense of cult superiority, however, could not be understood by the other Indian tribes. Other members of the Aztec Confederation did not practice it. The residents of Texcoco worshipped mainly Quetzalcoatl and other benign divinities. To them, human sacrifices were repugnant. They preferred to pursue their religious activities through prayer, song, and poetry .

The Aztecs paid daily homages to their gods, not only with human sacrifices and related religious rites, but also with the wealth and offerings of many other people. The obligation to pay tribute to Tenochtitlan created many enemies in a very unstable political situation in the Valley of Mexico. It doomed to a final destruction the future of the empire.

In spite of their advanced astronomical knowledge, the Aztecs could not understand the disappearance of the sun under the horizon every evening, nor could they explain its timely return the following day. As is the case with most primitive societies, nightfall, violent storms, and unexpected changes in the weather terrified them.

The severe climatic conditions, immense natural barriers and unpredictable volcanic activity of Central Mexico, where tremors and earthquakes are common and smoke climbs lazily from craters, also contributed to their concerns. The hostility of the climate, the lack of sufficient rain during the dry season, and the rugged terrain affected decisively their religious beliefs.

As Caso has written, men resolve their needs in different ways and with different resources. For the Aztecs, myth, magic, and religious sacrifices were the formulas used to appease the gods who were responsible for the violence of nature.

Human sacrifices have been practiced by many people throughout history, mostly in fertility rituals and the cult of the dead. The Old Testament tells us of the sacrifices of young children to Moloch, the god of the

Ammonites and Phoenicians. During the siege of Carthage in 307 B.C., the followers of this god burned two hundred children to death to seek his protection.

Similarly, Syrian priests sacrificed young children to their sun-god Baal on occasions of great importance. In Africa, during the nineteenth century, the Ashanti sacrificed each year 100 victims to their gods of harvest. They also killed many slaves and planted their heads on the ground during their "new yams" festival.

The burial of slaves, while they were still alive to honor dead relatives, was a common practice in Nyasaland and Uganda. The Dahomey made special elaborate sacrifices at the death of a king; and in North America, as late as 1836, the Skidi Pawnee, the Natchez, the Iroquois, the Hurons and some Indian tribes of the Pueblo region also practiced human sacrifices, but, the Aztecs began the system and made it a matter of "state policy."

While there is evidence that in some conquered areas the execution of prisoners of war diminished after consolidation, in other locations it increased to prevent subject peoples from rebelling. The reign of terror was sufficiently strong to impose a tributary system that required no military garrisons to enforce.

The Aztecs, as most people from Mesoamerica, saw themselves as insignificant tools of the gods. Since they lived at the mercy of a capricious universe, rituals and ceremonies were a necessity of life and the only way they knew of how to please their deities.

Certain questions, however, remain unanswered. Why were these people so preoccupied with death? How could a culture so advanced in arts and sciences be so obsessed by blood and sacrifices? These were people who built palaces and temples, immense open plazas, canals and lush gardens, and cities more advanced than those found in Europe at the time.

But, as the ancient Romans who enjoyed themselves at the sign of blood in the gladiator combats, and roared to approve the wanton sacrifices of Christian prisoners, the Aztecs seem fascinated by the slaughter of innocent victims and preferred this form of religious experience more than anything else.

For the Aztecs, human sacrifices had political, religious and magical consequences. These Indians made no absolute distinction between the living and the dead. They feared the outcome but believed that death was a

Figure 88   Fragment of a serpent's head representing Xiuhcoatl, the fire serpent that guided the sun. (INAH).

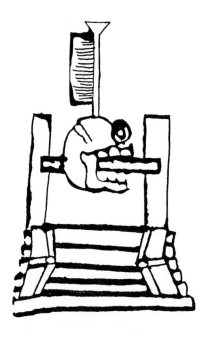

Figure 89 Head with banner on skull
rack Codex Mendocino)

continuation of life in another world. Historian J. G. Frazer calls their religious beliefs "the most monstrous on record" and adds, "no more striking illustration could be given of the disastrous consequences that may flow in practice from a purely speculative error."

A briefe Narration of the deſtruction of the Indes, by the

Spanyardes.

He Indes were diſcouered the yeere one thouſande, foure hundred, nientie two, and inhabited by the Spaniſh the yeere next after enſuing: ſo as it is about fourtie niene yeeres ſithens that the Spaniards ſome of them wēt into thoſe partes. And the firſt land that they entered to inhabite, was the great and moſt fertile Iſle of Hiſpaniola, which contayneth ſixe hundreth leagues in compaſſe. There are other great and infinite Iles rounde about and in the confines on all ſides: which wee haue ſeen the moſt peopled, and the fulleſt of their owne natiue people, as any other countrey in the worlde may be. The firme lande lying off from this Ilande two hundreth and fiftie leagues, and ſomewhat ouer at the moſt, contayneth in length on the ſeacoaſt more then tenne thouſande leagues: which are alreadie diſcouered, and dayly be diſcouered more and more, all ful of people, as an Emmote hill of Emmots. Inſomuch, as by that which ſince, vnto the yere the fourtieth and one hath beene diſcouered: It ſeemeth that God hath beſtowed in that ſame countrey, the gulphe or the greateſt portion of mankinde.

G O D created all theſe innumerable multitudes in euery ſorte, very ſimple, without ſutteltie, or craft, without malice, very obedient, and very faithfull to their naturall liege Lordes, and to the Spaniardes, whom they ſerue, very humble, very patient, very deſirous of peace making, and peacefull, without brawles and ſtruglings, without quarrelles, without ſtrife, without rancour or hatred, by no meanes deſirous of reuengement.

They are alſo people very gentle, and very tender, and of an eaſie complexion, and which can ſuſtayne no trauell, and doe die very

A   very

Figure 90   Page from Las Casas'
book about the deſtruction of the
Indies, England, 1583. (University
Microfilms).

10

Trade, Commerce and War In Ancient Mexico

The Aztecs' Economic System

One of the most important activities of the
Mesoamerican world was trade. Commercial exchanges not
only provided goods of different economic systems, but
also serve to trade ideas, concepts of organization, life
styles and cultural views. Commerce and technological
development were the dynamic forces that move the
Mesoamerican people (Robles 101).

The Aztec economic system was and important part of
the political, religious and social structures of the
state. Agriculture, manufacturing and trade provided the
principal sources of wealth while warfare and the payment
of tribute maintained the empire under the control of
Tenochtitlan.

Throughout the years, the Aztecs extended their
commercial operations to the Gulf of Mexico and the
Pacific coast. They also expanded their trade to the
Guatemalan highlands and the northern provinces of the
empire. The Nahuatl language became the official language
of trade and commerce in Mesoamerica.

The Aztecs also received a significant amount of
tribute from their vassal states. The plunder enriched
the nobility, the clergy and the upper class. In less
that a century, Tenochtitlan evolved from a small island
city-state to one of the richest urban centers in the New
World. The Aztec army maintained the security of the
state and protected the commercial routes of the empire.

The payment of tribute and the demand for sacrificial
victims created turmoil and unrest throughout the

empire. More than once, the Aztec soldiers had to march to foreign territories to suppress local revolts. The need for resources strained Tenochtitlan's ability to rule and dominate their vassals successfully. Passive resistance to Aztec authority and material exactions subverted the imperial enterprise.

Trade and Commerce in Ancient Mexico

By the middle of the fifteenth century, the Aztecs' capital had become the most important urban, political and economic center of Mesoamerica. The city developed a huge infrastructure of administrative and bureaucratic controls that regimented all phases of life. Hundreds of visitors arrived daily from all the regions of the empire, some of them from areas as far away as Guatemala.

During this period, thousands of immigrants also began to arrive in search of work. While the birth rate of the native residents remained small, in less than thirty years immigration increased the local population to more than 200,000 inhabitants (Rojas 81-84).

To support this large population the Aztecs built a well-organized trade and market system that reached all the provinces of the empire. Tlatelolco, the commercial center of Tenochtitlan, was by 1476 the most important market of the nation. People would travel long distances to reach it.

During the sixteenth century, the Spanish historian Francisco Javier Clavijero discussed Aztec trade in great detail. He wrote that the Aztecs had started their trading operations right after their arrival at Lake Texcoco. They traded fish for maize, cotton, wood, stone and lime regularly. These early commercial transactions expanded during the formative years of the empire.

The Mexican merchants soon became known for their ability to negotiate trade arrangements. They gained political power throughout Mesoamerica and served as the Aztecs commercial and diplomatic representatives. These merchants organized public markets and trade fairs. Most of these businesses operated daily, but the largest and most important of them conducted their activities once a week (Clavijero 235).

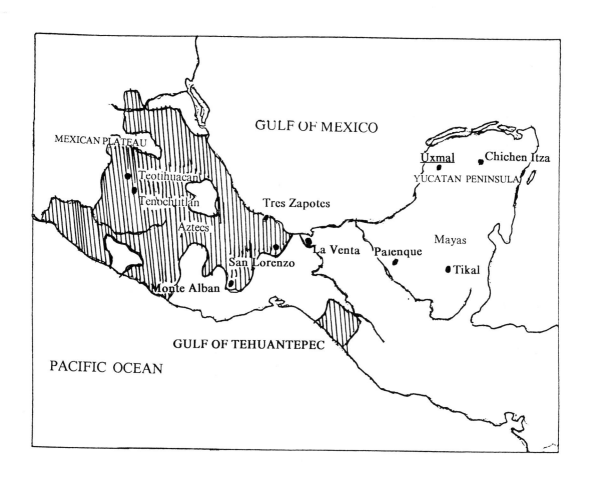

Figure 91 EXTENT OF AZTEC EMPIRE

The Market at Tlatelolco

The principal business center of the empire operated in Tlatelolco. The large marketplace, according to Hernan Cortes, was twice as big as the center square of Salamanca, Spain. The Spanish conqueror wrote that about 50,000 people traded in this market every five days. The Spanish historian Anonymous Conqueror, mentioned that between 20,000 to 25,000 people used the market daily (Cortes 143, 145).

According to the Spanish chroniclers, every section of the market area was divided according to the type of goods sold or services rendered. No one could exchange a place of business without consulting the market supervisors. There were so many goods sold in Tlatelolco that the meticulous Spanish chroniclers who visited the place could not list them.

Clavijero wrote that anything produced in the empire, or in the neighboring kingdoms, could be purchased in Tlatelolco. Even canoes filled with human waste were sold for fertilizer. Merchants also traded slaves by lot or individually (235-236).

Bernal Diaz del Castillo and Toribio de Benavente have left detailed accounts of Tlatelolco. They said that it fitted thousands of vendors and ten of thousands of customers. Motolinia writes that the market was very well organized and "in some sections they only sold bread, while in others planting seeds were traded. The sale of fowl and domestic animals was done with great effectiveness. There were many vendors. Merchandise arrived from all the corners of the empire and the prices were very low" (Motolinia 397).

Diaz del Castillo, who observed the market operations wrote: "After we have seen and consider everything, we went to the great square where a multitude of people bought and sold all type of articles; the noises and sounds of words could be heard a league away. Our soldiers, many of whom had visited Constantinople, Italy and Rome, said that they had never seen such regularity, population and organization" (173).

Other Commercial Activities

The Indian markets sold or traded all types of goods, but some of them specialized in particular commodities.

**Figure 92   Upper chamber, Temple of the Warriors,
Chichen Itza, Yucatan.**

Alcoman was famous for their meat shops. It also had a dog market where people could buy dogs for sacrifices, weddings, as food, or to accompany the death in their journey to the after world. Many people consumed small hairless dogs as a delicacy. Azcapotzalco sold a wide selection of them (Duran 180).

Customers purchased slaves for sacrifices, domestic services and farm work. Duran writes that the merchants who sold the human beings made them sing and dance in front of the public to attract potential buyers. The law required that slaves must be in good health before they could be sold to the public (Duran 181).

Cholula was the best market for luxury goods, fine feathers, and jewels. Texcoco, the intellectual capital of the empire, specialized in rich textiles, works of art and fine clothing. Texcoco, Tlaxcala, Cholula, and Huexotzinco operated in the same way as Tlatelolco. Cortes wrote that more than 30,000 people went regularly to the Tlaxcalan market. The Aztec purchased more than forty percent of the food that they consumed in these markets. The law specified the locations where merchandise could be sold (Orozco y Berra 411–417).

Rules of Trade

Every Aztec market had a group of inspectors or managers that supervised trading activities. There was a tribunal of twelve magistrates that judged the cases of merchants accused of irregular practices. Traders paid taxes for using the market facilities. In return, the government guaranteed them to protect their businesses, hear their complaints, and compensate for unavoidable losses (Clavijero 237).

The magistrates decided the prices of the commodities, set trade matters, resolved disputes between merchants, regulated market operations and punished those who violated the established codes. Inspectors of weights and measures legalized all transactions.

Integrity and efficiency in business affairs were very important. Rarely there was a robbery because the punishment for such a crime was death. Motolinia narrates the case of two women who fought in the marketplace until one stab the other lightly. The authorities arrested the woman who did the attack and condemned her to death (Clavijero 237).

Buyers and sellers used a variety of ways, including exchanges, to do their business transactions. The merchants conducted these activities very professionally. They had a general idea of the economic forces that regulate a market economy, such as supply and demand.

The Aztecs did not use currency as a medium of exchange. They used five different systems to pay for the articles they purchased. A special type of cocoa, different from the one used as beverage, served as money. They also used cotton mantles for the same purpose. The Indians also used quills of gold dust, copper and tin as mediums of exchange. Other articles used in trade were textiles, maize, and jade (Clavijero 236).

Industry and Craftsmanship

The Aztec made beautiful jewelry, so finely crafted that only a close check could discover an imperfection. The craftsmen who worked in gold and silver were mostly foreigners or descendent of the Toltecs. Their precious metals, however, had a limited financial value. The Aztecs used gold and silver to create ornaments for the merchants, the rich and the members of the nobility.

Teotihuacan and Texcoco were among the most important commercial and manufacturing centers of the Aztec empire. The products of their craftsmen were sold throughout Mesoamerica. Artists used basalt, one of the world's hardest rocks, to make religious artifacts. The Indian used obsidian extensively for weapons and cutting tools.

This mineral was one of the most important materials used by the Aztecs. The principal source of the volcanic rock was the present-day province of Hidalgo. About the use of obsidian, Thomas Y. Canby writes that a prominent American doctor equipped his surgeon with hand-flaked obsidian blades for an open-chest surgery. The blades "were sharper than the finest steel scalpels." Canby also observes that photographs of obsidian blades taken at a very high magnification show the edges of these tools to be sharper and smoother than modern steel scalpels (Canby, 333, 355).

The Pochteca

The Pochteca were the most important merchants of the

Figure 93   Yacatecuhtli, Lord Nose,
patron god of the merchants (Codex
Fejervary-Mayer)

empire. As businessmen they had considerable independence and were responsible only to the emperor and their leaders. If they committed a serious crime, they could only be prosecuted by their peers under a special legal code. The emperor selected five magistrates to prosecute these cases in the palace of Tlatelolco. The magistrates who judged them had the authority to use capital punishment (Peterson 119).

The Pochteca had very strict trading procedures. Women and minors could enter business, but children needed the consent of their parents and the approval of the state. A woman could join a business activity, but the law required that she first received the permission of her husband. These merchants utilized older people as trading agents. Contracts were part of their normal business operations and any failure to abide by them was reported promptly to the Pochteca judges for punitive action.

The Pochteca did most of their specialized business transactions under the rules of a wandering merchants' guild. This "association" had specific procedures for trading. The most important rules applied to the artisans who worked in gold and feather objects for the nobility.

Admission to the organization was restricted to the most experienced artisans and traders. The members of these guilds worshiped particular gods and performed their own religious ceremonies. They had special privileges, such as being exempted from agricultural labor (Sahagun 490-496).

Other Functions of the Pochteca

It was based on the geographical data collected by the Pochteca that the Aztecs knew the extent and dimensions of their empire. The Pochteca drew maps of the regions of Mesoamerica, conducted foreign policy for the Aztec government, and sent trading expeditions to remote places of the empire. They served as ambassadors, tax collectors, advisers and spies, and even started wars on their own when confronted with challenges within their territorial jurisdiction. Through them, the government controlled most of the foreign trade, established tributes and exerted political power and pressures on the vassal states.

The prestige of the Pochteca was so high that any

Figure 94 Merchant carrying fan, staff, and cargo of quetzal birds (Codex Fejervary-Mayer)

interference with their business operations could result in armed intervention. According to the Mexican writer Alfonso Caso, these traders were always well armed. Sometimes they provoked armed attacks to generate conflict and gain new territories or commercial concessions.

When the Pochteca returned from long journeys, their sovereign honored them with titles and treasures. But, when the Aztec's enemies discovered their spying activities they suffered horrendous deaths. Caso quotes a Nahuatl story that says "they were ambushed and slain and served in chili sauce."

Aztec influence in the Central Valley of Mexico depended considerably on the trading activities of the Pochteca. Their business expeditions often involved years of absence from Tenochtitlan or Tlatelolco. If a merchant died in a foreign land, victims of an assassination, the Aztec army punished the criminals and the inhabitants of the region. Their raids always resulted in further booty for Tenochtitlan.

The resources that the Pochteca trade provided, supplemented by manufacturing and intensive farming, brought considerable wealth to the Aztecs. Trade policies and military expansionism complemented each other for the benefit of the state (Acosta Saignes 12-24).

The Pochteca System of Operations

The Aztec merchants sought the advice of the older members of the profession before leaving on a distant trip. They discussed the purpose of the journey and asked them for their opinions. The elders normally encouraged them to continue with their plans, but to be careful when traveling in foreign territories.

For safety reasons, the Pochteca traveled by caravan, carrying with them a black ornament that represented their god Iyacateucli, the protector of trade. While the merchant was traveling, his wife and children did not wash their hair to denote sorrow for his absence. When merchants died during their long journeys, the elders of the community conveyed the news to the family and took care of the funeral arrangements.

The Pochteca acted as military leaders when they arrived to a new region. Before entering a town they usually formed protective lines on both sides of the

Figure 95 Pochteca merchants being
assaulted (Codex Mendocino)

road to defend their porters and the merchandise they carried. The formation was also a precaution against an enemy attack.

The merchants seldom traveled to the northern regions of the country, but they visited regularly the southern territories. They maintained good relationships with the provincial rulers and gave them rich presents to insure a safe passage through their lands. On their return trip, they used a different route and covered the merchandise thoroughly to prevent others from seeing it. Often, elite members of the Aztec army accompanied them, specially when the merchants carried military information.

The Aztecs did not trade by sea. On the other hand, the Maya did considerable trade by sea from the port of Xelha in Yucatan, according to investigator Jose Fernando Robles. The Pochteca commercial ventures, which had extended as far as Yucatan, probably linked with the Mayan sea-traders (Robles 101–108).

Trained porters transported most of the goods used or consumed in Tenochtitlan.   These men could carry up to 50 pounds of merchandise for great distances. In Lake Texcoco, the merchants used canoes for their commercial activities. Most of the cities and towns that surrounded the lake traded with each other. Many of them supported Tenochtitlan directly with tribute, laborers and agricultural products (Clavijero 238).

The Aztec Tributary System

The Aztec empire was a tributary state. Those who challenged their authority and loose paid a specified type of tribute. To control the sources of taxation, the Aztecs divided the empire into thirty-eight provincial regions, each with a town responsible for collecting the resources demanded by the state.

The *Matricula de Tributos*, a painted manuscript compiled after 1512, lists these towns and the amount of tribute allocated to each of them. The document also shows the quantities of goods exerted by the Aztecs from their vassal states.

R. H. Barlow grouped these tributes by region to evaluate the amount of resources consumed by the capital. A typical example was Acolhuacan in central Mexico. Among the merchandise that this city sent to the Aztec capital every year was 2,000 bundles of large white mantles;

Figure 96 Tributes paid to Tenochtitlan,
shields and war-dresses (Code
Mendocino, Bodleian Library, Oxford)

1,200 bundles of thin mantles; 400 bundles of loincloths; 400 warriors' costumes with shields; 120 bundles of women's skirts and blouses; and four wooden bins of maize, dry beans, chia and huauhti (Barlow 71).

N. Molins Fabrega, who studied the Codex Mendoza in detail, also observes that in modern terms the quantity of grain received by the Aztecs every year amounted to 7,000 tons of maize, 4,000 tons of beans, 4,000 tons of chia and 4,000 tons of huauhti. Chia was a lime-leafed sage, used for making a soft drink. Huauhti was a mosquito-egg delicacy harvested from the surface of lakes and still used today (Molins Fabrega 376).

The quantity of goods received by Tenochtitlan was beyond the needs of the population. Friedrich Katz observes that the food alone received during one year was sufficient to feed a population of 360,000 people. The number of carriers required to deliver such a large amount of food must have been enormous, considering that a porter could only carry a load of no more than 50 pounds at a time. To direct, manage, and control such a logistical support, hundreds of people must have been employed by the Aztec bureaucracy (Katz 94).

Different Interpretations

Throughout the years, the Aztecs' tribute system has been the subject of many interpretations. The Spanish chronicler Alonso de Zorita held that the pre-Columbian Indian tribute in Mexico was judicious and manageable. According to the writer, the system of taxation imposed on the people was reasonably because the government assessed it to a community as a whole and not to its individual members.

In those instances when workers could not pay the required share because of natural calamities, droughts or low agricultural yields, they received a reduction on the amount to be paid or the cancellation of the debt (Zorita 67).

For other writers, the payment of tribute placed the inhabitants of the provinces at a great disadvantage. The demand for sacrificial victims and the frequent military raids that the Aztecs conducted created distrust and hate. Even under the most favorable conditions, the onerous demands of the Aztecs impoverished the inhabitants of the empire. With no end in sight, they

Figure 97 Detail of the upper chamber wall, Temple of
the Warriors, Chichen Itza, Yucatan.

awaited silently for an opportunity to revolt.

During the recent excavations made in the *Templo Mayor*, or Great Temple, most of the artifacts discovered were manufactured in southern Mexico. Most of them related to the cult of Tlaloc. This evidence shows that the Aztecs probably obtained religious contributions and artifacts from their vassal states in addition to their regular tribute. The offerings, however, could have been gifts or "ceremonial exchanges between rulers" (Moctezuma 217).

The Matricula de Tributos

Besides consumer goods, many other articles arrived regularly to Tenochtitlan. From lumber and stone, to lime and charcoal, smaller communities contributed large quantities of raw materials to the city. This tribute did not include the rewards received by the nobles, or the amount of foodstuffs collected by the other two members of the Alliance. While the value of this additional tribute was not as high as the one paid to the government, it was an additional burden to the people (Molins Fabrega).

The *Matricula de Tributos* and the Codex Mendocino also show the extent of the commercial traffic. According to Zorita, four different groups of people paid taxes. The teccallec paid tribute to their lords instead of the government. The calpullec paid tribute to the state, did agricultural work for their master, and provided him with domestic service.

Merchants who inherited the right to do business and had the permission to do so paid tribute to the state. The tlalmaitec or mayeques were part of the land they lived in and could never leave. They planted and harvested it as sharecroppers and provided the owners with fuel, water and domestic services (Zorita 182–183).

Other Business Considerations

While the tributes paid to the state were large, those of the nobility were small. The rendering of forced domestic service by the mayeques was limited since nobles depended on slave labor for most of their personal needs. Zorita writes that Indians of the pre-Conquest period enjoyed better working conditions than those under the

**Figure 98   Pyramid and Plaza of the Moon, Teotihuacan.
Quetzalpapalotl Paalace is in the foreground.**

Spanish administration. They had sufficient food and ate at regular hours, worked in areas familiar to them, and in jobs that they were trained to do. The Spanish writer believed that the Aztec workers had a sense of purpose, were happy and healthy.

In spite of the enormous quantity of merchandise sent to the Aztec capital, there were times that hunger and starvation made their appearance in the city. Droughts, floods and other climatic changes periodically caused famine and pain in Tenochtitlan. During the middle of fifteenth century there was a great shortage of food.

Moctezuma I could not bring into the city enough of it to feed the people, though the tributary regions of the empire had extended to southern Mexico. The Aztecs offered human sacrifices to their gods to end the catastrophe. At the end, weather changes and food consignments from the coastal settlements reduced hunger and starvation. The city suffered again similar problems in 1475, 1505 and 1514 as result of earthquakes, floods and famines (Duran 241-244).

Population Imbalances

Tenochtitlan had a low birth rate and a high level of mortality. This population imbalance would have reduced, eventually, the Indian capacity to function as an organized state. If the Aztecs understood the consequences of a limited population gain, would they have endangered their productive capacity, their trade and their ability to protect themselves by the wholesale elimination of people through the practice of religious sacrifices? Even when the victims were prisoners of war, the precedence would have been dangerous and demoralizing to the people (Rojas 74-76).

On the other hand, the chroniclers wrote that the population of the city increased consistently throughout the years. While there are no reliable statistics or census information about this population gain, and the increase has been attributed to immigration, the two statements contradict each other (Rojas 75-76).

Realizing the great need that the Aztecs had for workers for agriculture and transportation, it is difficult to accept all the stories of Aztec human sacrifices that have been portrayed throughout the history of Mexico. The Aztecs sacrificed prisoners of war from other regions because that was a way of maintaining the empire under control.

Since the Aztecs ruled their empire out of fear, conducting raids for sacrificial victims was inherent to their method of political control. The Aztecs even used their blood-thirsty gods to convince others that they were the "selected ones," that any threat to their system would be punished severely by the deities of the universe that protected them.

There was no unemployment in the Aztec state and especially in Tenochtitlan. The emperor had a very low esteem for those who refused to work. The system assigned a task to every individual, including the nobles.

The Aztecs did very little agricultural work in Tenochtitlan and the city acted in the whole as any modern business and trade metropolis. Most of the people were specialists in production and distribution, religious matters, politics and craftsmanship. Other professionals included physicians, scribes, soothsayers, artists, prostitutes and merchants (Rojas 120).

War As An Instrument of the State

The Aztec empire was also a military theocracy. The merchants and the members of the upper class were more militaristic in orientation than other Indian groups of Mesoamerica. The nobility and the rich landlords used force to control the lands given to them by the emperor. They exacted tribute from the soil as if it was from a conquered territory (Murphy 30).

The nobles acted as absentee landlords, interested only in the tribute collected from the tenants. Their philosophy of land ownership paralleled the system begun by the government in the provinces. The rules that they devised to control property created the appropriate conditions for revolt and violence.

The Aztec empire, as Robert F. Murphy notes, was not a centralized system of government but an aggregation of states ruled by Tenochtitlan under a system of uneasy and limited controls. The members of this confederation served the interests of the Aztecs out of fear. Military activity, therefore, was essential to prevent uprisings, force the payment of tribute, protect the imperial system and defend the structures of land ownership (Murphy 30).

Historian Ross Hassig writes that the Aztec empire "was based on a pervasive and dominating influence rather than on territorial control." He attributes the development of this type of imperialism to the inability of the Aztecs to create an adequate technology (Hassig 17).

Hassig writes that Tenochtitlán did not have and efficient transportation system. The Indians had no way to storage and preserve large quantities of food, or the means to insure a continuous supply at a low cost. During many years, climatic changes devastated their agricultural system. Since that time, the production of sufficient food to supply the growing population of the city had been unreliable.

Thus, with survival at stake, the answer was in a military-theocratic system, supported by constant warfare, that could produce the essential supplies needed on a regular and systematic way. The creation of a tributary empire managed by force and terror was the Aztec solution to their particular problem.

Hassig analyzes further the Aztec option by saying that the Mexica had a limited interest in conquering and administering large territories. Their principal object was to extract large quantities of goods from them with limited expenses. Their approach of leaving the vassal government in local hands, therefore, was the logical decision for their form of imperialism (Hassig 17-19).

Under this system, the Aztecs reduced the threat of rebellion and permitted the army to continue further imperial expansion. It also satisfied the requirement of exercising political control through fear and "extracting goods at local expense, by requiring tributaries to both produce and transport goods without recompense" (Hassig 17).

War and the Tributary System

The Aztec army engaged in military raids and armed confrontations because Tenochtitlan required a constant flow of raw materials and luxury goods that could not be produced locally. Indian carriers brought to Tenochtitlan most of the essential provisions needed by the population.

The Aztecs' law required that all men, beginning at age fifteen, be prepared to join the army. Those who

Figure 99 **Type of tribute paid to the Aztecs. (Codex Mendoza)**

served as soldiers were not paid, but received from the government land grants, food, clothing and personal slaves. The Aztec rulers themselves usually led the army into war. The Calpulli of each town provided contingents of armed soldiers during conflicts.

The priests and tribal elders did most of the military planning, and organization for war because the gods dictated to them the way of success. They selected the proper time for starting hostilities using their knowledge of the calendar. Dressed in special costumes, the priests convened the warriors by dancing in the streets while holding shields and lances in their arms. They assembled the warriors by sounding war drums and singing war chants. The warriors responded by wearing their military attires and brandishing their weapons in front of the religious temples.

Before going into battle, the Aztecs performed many religious ceremonies to assure the help of their gods. They performed auto sacrifices, such as perforating their ears, tongues, and limbs to offer blood; cutting their flesh; and making human sacrifices. Hassig explains that astrology, the supernatural and magic were interwoven with Aztec warfare (Hassig 9).

Preparations for War

Before the army was to march, small groups of scouts went ahead to study the enemy defenses and make sure that the warriors would not be ambushed when they began to march. The priests kept a vigil throughout the period of conflict and performed daily rites to assist the soldiers. Priests also carried images of the war gods into battle and fought behind the military leaders as common soldiers. (Hassig 9).

The military units did not march to war together, but maintained a distance of a day's march between them. Attacks were suddenly and unannounced; surprise being the principle tactic of war. The Aztecs attacked their enemies with great strength and valor, their faces and bodies painted with a variety of colors to impress the enemy. Their chieftains used coats of quilted cotton, tall head dresses and shields of various kinds.

The Aztec army did not use special uniforms. Shoulder adornments, haircuts and other symbols of prestige indicated rank and achievement. For defense, the warriors

Figure 100 Aztec warrior armed with
atlatl, or spear-thrower

wore a padded cotton vest. Weapons included bows, arrows, lances, and slings. For close combat, the Aztecs used swords made with sharp bits of obsidian embedded along the length of the weapon. The Indians also used spears, hatchets and clubs. Every town had its own tlacochcalco or "house of darts" where the army stored its weapons.

Military Organization

As a modern army, the Aztec military units had engineers, cooks, healers, musicians and porters that carry war supplies and extra weapons. Food and supplies were obtained from the people of the lands and villages through which the warriors passed. The military units consisted of natives of Tenochtitlan and auxiliaries from other provinces that were loyal to the Aztecs.

The object of war was not to destroy the enemy or even his ability to make war, but to take prisoners and force the payment of tribute. The Aztecs also conducted military raids to punish those who refused to comply with their imperial instructions. As has been said, the Aztecs allowed their enemies to continue ruling their country if they accepted the hegemony of Tenochtitlan. The tribute exacted from defeated adversaries consisted of food, luxury goods, raw materials, precious stones, metals, and a variety of other products.

An army recruit shaved their heads except for a tuft of hair at his back. This adornment could be removed after the young warrior had taken one captive in battle. After the capture of four enemy soldiers, the young warrior was permitted to cut his hair as a professional officer. A warrior who captured a prisoner without any help displayed a patterned cloak and a different hair style.

Shoulder ornaments showed the number of captives a warrior had taken in combat. Military officers carried feathered standards to battle. Their body ornaments indicated the number of battles fought and the amount of captives taken in war. The use of jaguar skins denoted officers of higher rank.

A Way of Life

The Aztec lower classes dressed very simple. Men used a loin cloth that was tied in the front and back. Women

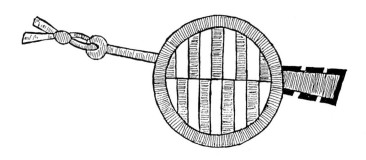

Figure 101 Nahua war -club and
shield

wore long skirts. The poor Indians utilized maguey fibers to make their loin cloth, but the nobility used embroidered cotton. Women dressed with plain skirts except during festivals. For the upper parts, they wear huipiles, a simple blouse made from a rectangular piece of cloth with holes for the head and arms.

The rich people wear elaborated capes or tunics as symbols of prestige and power. These cloaks consisted of rectangular pieces of cloth finely elaborated with gold and jewelry. The cloaks of the rich were woven with borders of rich fur or feathers.

The priests and warriors used long tunics. The ceremonial dress of an Aztec warrior was very elaborate. It indicated rank, military talent and ability to fight in battle. The ceremonial dresses of the priests were also highly elaborated.

Soldiers, priests and members of the aristocratic class wore sandals, but the majority of the people did not wear shoes. Priests had special hairstyles and warriors wore pigtails of special hair tufts to indicate their status.

The most popular accessories used by the Aztecs with their personal clothing were fans, feather adornments, beads, necklaces of bells, chest ornaments, pendant and gold bands. Poor people wore similar ornaments but substituted precious stones with glass or shells. One of the customs of the Aztecs was the wearing of ear and lip plugs. Gold rods and precious stones were also worn in the nose.

The Indians obtained most of their gems by trade. Expert craftsmen used copper tools, water and sand to cut and polish jade, turquoise, and rock crystal. The Aztecs highly prized feathers from rare birds. They were used to decorate costumes, dresses, ceremonial masks, and smaller items such as fans.

Aztec pottery was of utilitarian quality. It was more secular in purpose than the other Indian arts. Pottery, like weaving, was usually done by the women of the community. The Aztecs produced it usually in their homes during their spare time. Clay figurines contained about ten percent sand to make them porous so they would not crack when fired. The clay utensils also contained some de-greasing or grease removing substance. Most of the fine, highly decorated pottery was used during funerals and placed near the death. Much of it was painted red,

Figure 102 Stone relief of a Maya warrior, Chichen Itza, Yucatan.

Figure 103 Stone relief of a Maya nobleman, Chichen Itza, Yucatan.

yellow, white or black.

The Indians did excellent ceramics and the quality of their molds was extraordinary. Many craftsmen would use a slip on their pottery to allow decorations. Polychromatic ware was painted with geometric designs and covered with lacquer to provide a polished surface.

The principal center for distribution of manufactures was the market of Tlatelolco. Workers produced low quality utility ceramics in great quantities and sold them during market holidays. The nobles owned most of the fine ceramic shops and their employees received their livelihood from them. The professional artisans owned their businesses and often worked on commission. The principal luxury crafts were made or gold, silver and feathers. These goods were manufactured in very small quantities and sold to the nobility and the Pochteca.

**Figure 104 Brazier. Templo Mayor , Tenochtitlan.
(INAH)**

11

Agriculture and Art In the Aztec World

The Problem With Agriculture

   The land where the Aztecs lived is a valley located in
central Mexico about seven thousand feet above sea level.
Surrounded by high peaks and mountain ranges, some of
which reach a maximum elevation of 18,000 feet, the
central Valley of Mexico is fertile during the rainy
season, but barren and inhospitable during the rest of
the year. The wet season begins in May and ends in
October. During this time the soil receives about eighty
percent of its moisture. The rain is so frequent during
the summer months that floods are always a constant
threat to the area.
   Between November and March, the region suffers
occasional low temperatures and high winds that frost the
soil and damage the vegetation. While the climate is
mild, rainfall is sometimes insufficient for intensive
agriculture. A minor upsetting of the balance between wet
and dry conditions can have disastrous consequences to
agriculture.
   Similar weather affected the pre-Hispanic farmer that
lived in the region. Often the maize crops that he raised
did not do as well as expected. Agricultural yields were
always low, specially when the farmers lost their crops
to floods and winter freezes. According to Spanish
historian Juan Torquemada, between 1376 and 1427 the
Aztecs preferred to live by hunting, fishing, building
canoes and collecting war tributes than by farming.
   The topography, poor soil and periodic droughts also
affected the growing season. Since there were no beasts

of burden, the tilling and fertilization of the soil was very inefficient. While the Aztecs used some animal and plant fertilizer, they had limited success in raising bumper grain crops.

The Aztecs even reduced the size of their farms, shortened the planting season and artificially irrigated the land to increase productivity. They also built large granaries for the storage of surplus grain and had large nurseries of botanical gardens devoted to growing and studying different kinds of plants.

Other land management techniques included land drainage, crop rotation and intercropping. The Indians periodically increased the yield of the land by skillful methods of soil and moisture conservation. The lack of a plow culture also affected the Indian's ability to sustain a high agricultural yield. They tilled the soil with wooden shovels, hoes and coas, a kind of digging stick.

Soil erosion, altitude and limited topsoil further reduced the availability of good farmland. Where the terrain was gentle and leveled, the Aztecs built earth and maguey terraces to control the thinning of the soil. They also used dikes, canal irrigation and swamp reclamation techniques to protect their crops and increase productivity. In spite of these efforts, the Aztecs had difficulties in supporting the huge population of Tenochtitlan, estimated then at over 200,000 people.

An Urban Society

The small communities that surrounded Tenochtitlan produced most of the agricultural products required by the city. The city itself produced very little food. Contrary to established beliefs, most residents of this urban center were not peasants. Recent investigations show that, "the growing population of Tenochtitlan-Tlatelolco was composed of full-time occupational specialists, not peasant farmers" (Porter 424-425).

The few people who worked in agriculture within the city limits used *chinampas* to produce their crops. These farmers extended their operations to the surrounding areas of Lake Texcoco since the land available in the city was limited. Sahagun mentions that most of these farmers cultivated small crops of vegetables and trees, and Cortes wrote that he saw small orchards inside the

Figure 105 Office of a provincial governor
of Tenanco and a rampart on four rocks
(Codex Mendocino)

city (Rojas 133).

Since Tenochtitlan was an urban center dedicated primarily to rule a vast empire, the interest of the city dwellers was manufacturing, commerce, and the public administration of the resources of the land. Most of the residents were specialized technicians, artists, craftsmen, merchants, warriors, teachers, priests and government officials. The large amount of people that rushed to the market of Tlatelolco to buy food every five days (up to 60,000), denotes the consumer characteristics of the urban population (Rojas 15).

To resolve the food shortage, the Aztecs imposed a tributary system on their vassal states that provided the city with the necessary raw materials and an over abundance of food. The system also increased the wealth of the nobility, the members of government, and the merchant class.

The Aztecs maintained this tributary system through sheer terror. They constantly conducted military raids on their enemies and rebellious vassal states. In the long term, this system created dissatisfaction, hate and hostility toward the rulers of the empire.

The Aztecs never considered that their dependence on food from their vassal states would be someday one of the motives for their ultimate defeat. Rojas observes that the Spanish blockade of Tenochtitlan prevented the supply of the city. Since there was not enough land to raise crops the Aztecs died of starvation. The shortages of food, dreaded since the famines of the preceding years, ended the Aztec will to resist.

The Division of the Land

In the early stages of their civilization, the Aztecs had very limited agricultural land. Thus, they changed the traditional land patterns of their neighbors to a system of public ownership. The Calpulli, the social and political unit of the Aztecs, became the principal landlord. The leaders assigned each head of family a plot for cultivation according to set rules that included the payment of tribute to the rulers, nobles, and priests.

The farmers divided the harvest among the residents of the Calpulli and paid the required tribute to the government. Those who received a grant of land could retain it until death. If a land recipient moved to another Calpulli, he lost the entitlement. An interesting feature of this system was that only nobles could own individually plots of land.

The Aztecs were industrious people, but many were poor. Throughout their history, the peasant remained at the bottom of the economic ladder. The farmer had little incentives to produce surplus crops. Nothing could induce him to do more than what was required. The result was that the Aztecs could never resolve the problem of food shortages and must depend on continuous tribute to compensate for their limitations.

Swamp Reclamation

An impressive agricultural achievement of the Aztecs was the chinampa system, or swamp reclamation. This form of agriculture consisted of digging draining ditches, building dikes to control flooding and constructing land platforms from lake mud, debris and vegetation. The Aztecs packed these artificial islands with thick entwined stems and poured over them a mat of rich mud dredged from the bottom of the lakes. Heavy wooden poles, buried below the lake floor, held the frame in place. The Indians planted grasses and weeds on the wet soil to maintain the platform together. This type of wetland reclamation is still being used in Mexico today.

In the past this type of agriculture has been credit exclusively to the Aztecs. Apparently, the Maya also practiced this type of farming. In 1978 an aerial survey of the Passion River in Guatemala, conducted by the Jet Propulsion Laboratory of Pasadena, California, showed an extensive network of canals. Scientists discovered that they were "deep ditches from which the rich sediments had been scooped to make agricultural plots." These archaeological finds clearly suggest that the Maya also practiced the chinampa system of agriculture hundreds of years before the Aztecs.

The Maya were experts in the cultivation of areas unsuitable for farming. The Indians of Yucatan resolved the problem of water by creating *chultunes*, or cisterns, that provided enough rainwater for their immediate needs. The Aztecs learned the system of chinampa agriculture and retention of rainwater from the Toltecs, who in turn obtained them from the Teotihuacanos (Barrera

Figure 106   Coyolxauhqui, Goddess of the Moon. (INAH)

Figure 107   Serpent head motif, Chichen Itza, Yucatan

Rubio 71).

Linda Schele and David Freidel recently wrote that the Maya and the Teotihuacanos had for hundreds of years long term commercial trade. Besides the exchange of exotic goods and luxury items, the two cultures also traded philosophical and cultural ideas. Most importantly: "The result, however, was the establishment of an international network of trade along which moved material goods and ideas" (Schele and Freidel 159-164). It is natural to assume that the Aztec agricultural knowledge came from the Teotihuacano-Maya relationship and their Toltecs predecessors.

The Importance of Maize

The cultivation of maize formed an important part of the life of the Aztecs. Out of a wild plant not even known today, the Mesoamerican Indian developed a variety of grain so well adapted to different climates that now it is one of the most harvested cereal crops in the world. The Aztecs produced it in such a scale that it became their most important source of food.

Recent investigations show that the domestication of corn may have occurred simultaneously in different areas of the Western Hemisphere. Scientists have found samples of hybrid corn in South America that are, at least five thousands' years old. While archaeologists do not know when the domestication of corn took place, estimates show that the native Americans cultivated maize five to six thousand years ago. Teocintl, a plant that had tiny cornlike ears, may have been the original maize.

Unlike many plants, Indian maize is totally unable to survive in the wild. Corn is a warm-weather plant that requires high temperatures during the growing season. It requires abundant sunshine for maximum yields and fails to grow normally in the shade or during extended periods of cloudy weather. Freezing temperatures injure maize when they occur at any time during the growing season.

In ancient Mexico the Aztecs grew most of the corn in small patches of few acres and their yields were low. Corn does not require much rain or a rich soil. The crops, however, were dependent for their existence upon the care and attention of man.

These characteristics of maize were not completely understood by the Indians, who attributed them to the

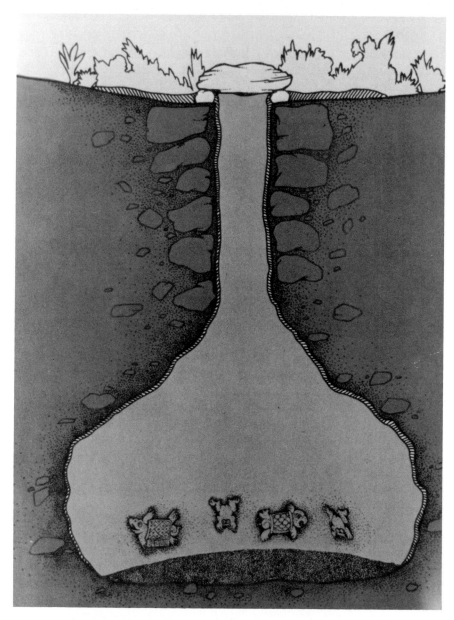

Figure 108 Underground bottle-shaped cistern used for water storage. (INAH, Merida)

caprices of their gods. The priests and wise men regulated the planting and harvesting of maize using the Indian calendar and their superstitions. They sacrificed human beings before the planting season to appease the gods and insure an abundance of rain. They also blessed the seeds of corn to insure a good harvest. During harvest time, the Indians ate special maize cakes to celebrate the end of the planting and harvesting season.

Land distribution, wealth, and political stability were related to the cultivation of maize. An adequate supply of the grain made possible social progress and the increase of population and resources. While the Aztecs also developed other crops, including squash, beans, yams, peppers and cacao, maize was the principal staple of their diet.

It was partly because of the convenience of cultivating corn in central Mexico that the Aztecs moved to the shores of Lake Texcoco. Today, about half the Mexican working class are farmers. Those who are descendent of the original native races still cultivate the soil in the same way and get about the same results. Using corn as the main ingredient, the Aztecs perfected an excellent and tasty cuisine hundred of years before the arrival of the Spaniards.

Food "fit for a king."

The use of maize, beans, and exotic vegetables, gave the Aztecs a rich, well-balanced and spicy diet. Corn, tomatoes, chocolate, squashes, avocados and tropical fruits, enhanced by the consumption of fish and fowl, complemented their basic food requirements. Wild turkeys, ducks, game and small hairless dogs were the main sources of meat. The Indians also ate a great variety of insects and aquatic life such as frogs, fresh water shrimps, white worms, tadpoles, snails, water-fly eggs, crabs, iguanas and algae.

As the international authority on Latin American cooking Susan Bensusan has written: "Much Mexican cooking is based on the ancient Indian cooking of the Aztecs . . .The `tortilla,' a flat pancake of unleavened corn, is the bread of the people. It also can be used as plate, spoon, snack, sandwich, and is the base for many dishes throughout the country." Many dishes that the Indian prepared are today part of the traditional cuisine

**Figure 109 Brazier with face of Tlaloc, the Rain-God.
(INAH, Merida).**

of Mexico and of the American southwest (Bensusan 8-9).

The Aztecs made their tortillas by grinding the maize on a flat-surfaced stone mortar using a mauler called a mano. The corn had been previously soaked in water containing lime that took off the outer skin of the kernels and gave the cakes a chalky taste. The ground fine paste was then shaped into unleavened pancakes and cooked over a comal, or ceramic griddle, over a hearth of stones. The Aztecs also used maize to prepare tamales, a meat filled dish cooked in corn husks and eaten with tomatoes and chili peppers.

The Aztecs used maize in many other forms. They toasted a paste of ground corn and mixed it with honey to make pinolli. In this form, the corn lasted for many days and could be used by warriors during their military campaigns. Mixed with water, it became a nourishing refreshment.

The Indians ate their first meal at midmorning. It usually consisted of porridge sweetened with honey or spiced with red peppers. The nobles and wealthy people drank chocolate with honey and vanilla. At midday the Indians ate a meal usually based on corn, beans, peppers, tamales and a variety of vegetables. They normally drank plain water with their food.

The upper class families usually complemented this average diet with delicacies brought from the tropical regions of Mexico. The food was boiled, steamed or basted since the Indians had no cooking fat or oil. The poor ate sparingly and usually the second meal of the day was the last one. The upper class normally had luscious banquets during the evening hours, when they smoked tobacco and consumed large quantities of food (Soustelle 154).

When Cortés visited Moctezuma II, the Indians gave him a royal banquet that surprised even the Spaniards. Diaz del Castillo wrote that there were more than "three hundred different types of dishes, warmed over live coals, all fit for a king. And for the emperor's personal staff, the palace's cooks prepared more than one thousand dishes" (167).

Other Important Agricultural Products

Another important plant cultivated by the Aztecs was maguey, also known as century plant or Agave Americana. This plant takes many years to bloom and its flower stalk

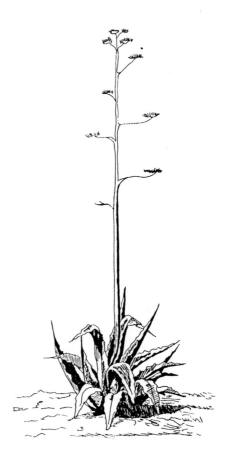

Figure 110 *Maguey,* or Mexican agave plant

may reach forty feet when fully grown. About 150 different types of maguey grow in the Mexican highlands.

The Aztecs used maguey for many purposes. From the dark-green leaves that reach a length of fifteen feet when fully grown, the Indians obtained fibers for cordage and thread. They made sandals, shields, slings, blankets and clothing from the plant's dried filaments and lye for soap from the ashes of the burned leaves. Women used the narrow parts of the plant to storage dried maize.

The Indians crush, soak and beat the dried leaves to form a thin layer of parchment that served as paper. They also used the dried leaves to thatch the roof of their houses. The thorns turned into pins and needles and the roots were cooked and eaten. Juices from the plant served to cure muscular illnesses and lighten pain.

The Aztecs made pulque from the fermented sap of maguey. To make the alcoholic beverage, they collected the sap (aguamiel) from a cavity that they made at the base of a four to six years old plant, leaving only the rind that formed a natural basin. Three or four months later, the cavity wall and the surrounding leaf bases were scraped, after which the first sap was drawn. The cavity refilled two or three times daily, for several days until the plant died. The sap was allowed to ferment until it turned into pulque.

According to the chroniclers of the Conquest the method of gathering the sap was very primitive. The Indians placed the small end of a gourd into the liquid and extracted it from the plant by sucking the opposite end. They transferred the liquid to a receptacle that they carried across their backs.

The Indians also made mescal, or wine, from the maguey. To make this beverage, they crushed the leaves of the plant and put the pulp inside a container of water until it fermented. The process produced a tasty liquor that was used during celebrations. Finally, the heavy leaves of maguey served to fence the small plots of land that the Indians received from the Calpulli.

Indian Clothing and Personal Attire

The Aztecs also cultivated cotton, which they used for making blankets, cloth and rich garments. They spun and wove it so fine that the finished product could be compared with silk. In the Aztec world, clothing

Figure 111   A recently married woman
is spinning yarn (Codex Mendocino)

indicated social status and one could know the social position of an individual just by the type of garments that he or she was wearing.

Peasants could not use cotton garments with border trims or embroidery, since the material and the style were reserved for the use of the nobility. Those who attained a high position in the society could wear elaborate clothing and jewelry. Personal attire also had religious implications. Priests wore the clothing associated with the cult of a specific deity (Munoz Camargo 138-139).

The dress of the peasants was very simple, plain and short. The men used loin cloths made of maguey fiber tied in the front and back. Women wore plain skirts and a simple blouse made from a rectangular piece of cloth with holes for the head and arms. This dress, called a huipilli, varied from region to region. Some were highly decorated while others were very plain. Most of the poor people went barefooted, although soldiers, priests, and members of the aristocracy wore leather sandals. The peasants imitated the aristocracy by wearing a variety of ornaments made from shells and natural things such as flowers and seeds.

The nobility and the rich used loin cloths of embroidered cotton. They also had elaborated capes and tunics decorated with gold jewelry and borders of rich fur and feathers. Priests and warriors dressed with long, colorful tunics and ornate headdresses. Their decorations indicated rank and honors received in the battlefield.

Sahagun writes that the "upper class" wore rich and costly garments adorned with intricate embroidery; some being of white cloth with elaborate designs in needlework. Accessories consisted of fans, beads, necklaces, chest ornaments, pendant, and gold bands. The nobility admired jade and feathers and their use led the Aztecs to extend their trade in search of feathers and luxury articles. "Their trade in feathers also caused several species of tropical birds to become nearly extinct (Peterson 218).

The bird that provided the most expensive and valuable feathers was the Quetzal, a sacred animal for the Aztecs. The Indians trapped it and plucked the plumes very carefully, because if the animal died the trapper faced the death penalty. The released birds grew back their tails after the next molt.

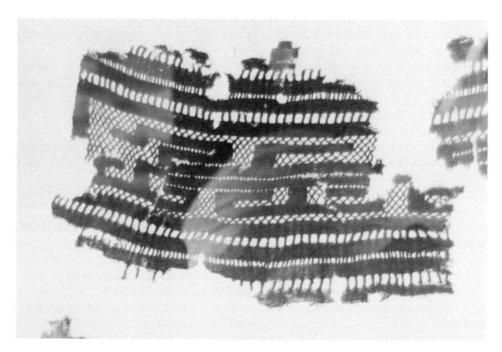

Figure 112 A segment of a Maya textile found in the
Sacred Well of Chichen Itza, Yucatan. (INAH, Merida).

Figure 113 Seat in the form of a jaguar. (INAH,
Merida).

The Aztecs portrayed their god Quetzalcoatl with quetzal plumes, and the emperor wore a beautiful headdress of quetzal feathers. Today, Guatemalan peasants kill these birds and parade their dead bodies through the streets to assure another year of good health. In spite of protective laws, there is an illicit trade of quetzal feathers that encourage poaching.

The Aztec nobility also had an obsession with jewelry. They obtained most jewels from merchants who sought the entire territory for the best quality. Jade, turquoise, pearls, amethysts and rock crystals were high prized by the Aztecs. The nobility used them set in gold to decorate the costumes and dresses that they used in festivals and ceremonies (Clavijero 268).

Men cut their hair according to their social status. Priests had special hairstyles and warriors wore pigtails. Other men cut their hair short, leaving a strip across their forehead. Women grew their hair long and loose, confined only by a band around their heads. Most of the Indians did not grow beards or mustaches. Fray Diego de Landa writes that mothers burned the children's faces with hot towels to prevent the hair to growth (Landa 35). In some rare instances, older people grew small white beards as a sign of wisdom (Peterson 224).

It was customary for the Indians to wear lip and ear studs as ornaments. Warriors who had distinguished themselves in battle wore metal disks in their lower lips. The nobility used ornaments of copper with gold pendant and precious stones. Military officers wore feather decorations and face paint applied in a variety of designs. Women seldom used make-up or ornaments on their faces, but they cleanse their bodies daily by taking repeated baths (Landa 35).

Use of Color Pigmentation

The Aztecs used many colors, pigments and dyes to beautify their bodies, decorate buildings and religious shrines, highlight art on pottery, and dye textiles. Colors had religious symbolism and deities were identified by them. The Aztecs also used colors to show direction: black meant North, blue indicated South, red was East and blue was West.

Red, blue, yellow, gray and black were used to identify

Figure 114 Nahua Pottery

social status. To the Aztecs, the color red represented blood; black related to war and young warriors painted themselves with this color to denote bravery. Prisoners were painted yellow before they were taken to the sacrificial stone. Green was the color of royalty because it was the color of the plumes of the quetzal (Peterson 222).

Coloring materials came from a variety of sources. Scarlet was obtained from the female cochineal beetle that lived in the cactus plantations. The insect was carefully tended by special workers because it was very fragile. The Aztecs used the pigment to dye the delicate garments of the nobility.

Achiote, the fruit of the annatto tree, was crushed into a paste and mixed with grease to form a yellow-red pigment. The Indians applied the dye to the fabrics during the spinning process. Achiote was also used to add color to food, dye the hair and provide protection against the insects and the sun.

The color blue was mostly used by the nobility because it was very expensive. To obtain the dye the Indians crushed the leaves of the indigo plant and spread urine over it to release a colorless substance that turned blue when exposed to air. They obtained a purple dye from mollusks and red and black pigments from bark chips. Herbs, roots and iron oxide provided an array of browns, yellows, blacks and purples that the Indians used to paint murals and beautify pottery (Peterson 223).

Pottery, Ceramics and Craftsmanship

Historian Hugh Thomas observes that, "by coincidental development to which, perhaps, inadequate attention has been paid, pottery was also invented in America" (Thomas 48). This achievement occurred without the invention of the potter's wheel. While the Aztec heritage in the manufacture of pottery was, at least, three thousand years old, their efforts in this area were not as spectacular as those of other Mesoamerican Indians who did elaborate sculptures, fine painted vases, and magnificent works of art.

Pottery was mostly utilitarian in nature. The Aztecs did not create pottery for religious purposes, but for regular daily use. Most of the utensils, containers and figurines made of pottery were done by the women of the

Figure 115 Nahoa pottery vessels

community, although there were some professional potters who made fine, highly decorated utensils for funeral purposes.

The finest earth ware was brought from Cholula, where the older artistic traditions of the Toltecs had been continued for years. Their pottery was infinitely superior to the Aztec clay workers. These professional Indian potters were specialists and the quality of their molds was extraordinary.

They painted much of their work red, yellow, white or black and decorated polychromatic ware with geometric designs and lacquer. Their clay figurines contained many innovations, such as adding sand to the molds to make them porous. Clay utensils also contained various chemical agents to simplify cleaning.

The Aztec artisans made articles of gold, copper, bronze and tin of exceptional quality. Their metallic implements, however, did not eliminate the use of obsidian blades and other hard stones. The Spaniards who visited Mexico wrote that they saw barbers shaving men with obsidian razors.

More recently, a prominent American doctor equipped his surgeon with hand-flaked obsidian knives for an open-chest surgery. The blades "were sharper than the finest steel scalpels," according to Thomas Y. Candy. He also writes that photographs of obsidian blades taken at a very high magnification show the edges of these tools to be sharper and smoother than modern steel scalpels (Canby 333, 355).

Other Artistic Expressions

Mesoamerican traditions influenced considerably Aztec art. There is little difficulty, however, in comparing carvings and sculptures made during their time and those belonging to an earlier period. The Aztec artistic expression is simpler, direct, more primitive and mechanical.

There was no doubt of the intention of the Aztec artist. He expressed his feelings with a sense of arrogance and superiority. He used basalt, one of the world's hardest rocks, with a technique unknown before. To decorate knives, masks, shields, and architectural decorations, the Aztec artists used inlaid mosaics of unprecedented quality.

Figure 116 Nahua cinerary clay urns

The Aztecs coated their temples and buildings with a form of cement that provided a base for decoration and painting. Although many original wall paintings have been lost, those that survived show a high level of originality and artistic quality.

The ruins of Cacaxtla discovered in 1975 are a masterpiece of artistic balance. The well-preserved and detailed drawings and paintings show ancient priests and battle scenes, one of them is fifty-six feet long. Sections of palaces and temples with magnificent murals are still being excavated. Other surviving works of Aztec art include the statue of Coatlicue, the Calendar Stone, and the Monument to Tizoc, all of them presently located in the National Museum of Anthropology in Mexico City.

Leon Portilla tells us that the Aztecs believed that artists were born, not made. In the Aztec society, they were highly respected. The artists devised the headdresses of the warriors and government officials; the fans, robes, and clothing of the nobility; and the decorations of the temples and places of worship.

They wrote poems about nature and love, used flowers profusely, and experimented with a variety of color combinations. Traditionally, the Aztecs loved flowers and perfumes. Men carried bouquets of flowers and sweet-smelling herbs to their wives. For the people, the painter, singer, sculptor, poet and engineer were "deified hearts, visionaries who, having truth themselves, were empowered to create divine things" (Leon Portilla 169-171).

Most of the artists, craftsmen, weavers, potters, gold workers and scribes that lived in the Aztec capital were descendants of the Toltecs and did their work with pride. The few remaining Aztec texts mention the artistic genius of the Toltecs with respect and admiration. "Everything that is marvelous, beautiful and deserving appreciation," read these descriptions, "was made by the Toltecs "(Leon Portilla 161).

Music and Dance in the Aztec World

Music, song and dance played a major role in Aztec life, specially during weddings and religious ceremonies. The Aztecs used these arts mostly to honor and appease their gods, express their faith and satisfy their religious fervor. Music and dance played an important

Figure 117 **Tlaloc ceramic vessel, Templo Mayor, Tenochtitlan. (INAH)**

part in religious ceremonies, rites and incantations. Professional entertainers also played music to the nobility. This was probably the only time when music was used for secular activities and social entertainment.

Most of the Aztec religious ceremonies, according to Sahagun, were accompanied by songs, dances and musical performances. Samuel Marti writes that "Pre- Columbian music reached a level of development comparable, perhaps superior, to the contemporary cultures of Europe and Asian origin" (Marti 6).

Weddings were important occasions and normally the celebrations were accompanied by music. The ceremonies began during the evenings when the parents of the bride carried her to the groom's home. The tradition called for the young girl to ride on the back of an old woman, while family members with lighted torches illuminated the way. The bride and groom kneeled before a hearth and knotted their tunics to formalize the ceremony. The married couple then burned incense and prayed to specific gods for four days. The event was celebrated with music and food.

The extensive number of musical instruments found in archaeological excavations show the importance of this art to the Aztecs. Instruments were mostly made of clay and included flutes, drums, whistles, rattles, xylophones, shell trumpets and bells. There were no string instruments or written music and the players improvised their tunes during a performance.

Marti observes that some Aztec flutes could produce three or four sounds simultaneously. The use of these types of instruments showed that the Aztecs were familiar with the idea of pure harmony, two hundred years before the development of polyphony in Western Europe (6).

Jeronimo de Mendieta explains that the Aztecs used two different types of drums, one high and thicker than a man's body and the other smaller and more versatile to use. The larger drums were about forty inches in height and eighteen in diameter. They had a tanned deer skin at the mouth that resounded very efficiently. The other drums were tuned to a lower scale and produced two different sounds. They were played with rubber tipped sticks or the palm of the hand (Marti 9-16).

Diaz del Castillo narrates that during the battle for Tenochtitlan, the Aztecs charged the Spanish soldiers repeatedly when they heard the sound of a huge drum that had been placed at the top of the main pyramid. The tones could be heard throughout the valley and every time the drum sounded it spread terror among the Spaniards (Diaz del Castillo 250).

Musicians used two trumpets simultaneously to improve the quality of sound. Most of these musical instruments were made of shells, but there also were instruments of clay that produced the first four tones of a musical scale. Flutes were tubular in form and could play a variety of music since they had from two to six finger-holes. The principal type was characterized by a long air duct modify to conform with the shape of the tube.

Another type of flute made by the Aztecs is called the Flute of Tezcatlipoca because it was mostly used during ceremonial rites. Its shrilling high-pitched sound was readily recognized by the people as a religious call to their war god. Torquemada writes in his *Monarquia Indiana* that warriors who heard the sound of this small flute responded by asking Tezcatlipoca for strength and courage against the enemy.

Figure 118 MIxtec lord "11-Grass. " (Codex Nuttall).

12

Man, Science and Destiny

The Transformation of a God

The Aztecs forged their vision of life during their long period of migration. Many of their basic views about man's destiny emerged then. As conflicts developed with the sedentary tribes that lived in the path of their journey, they adjusted their lives and expectations to the new environment. They also accepted the traditions, beliefs and deities of other people when it became necessary for their survival.

During this time, the Aztecs speculated about the origins of the universe, the mystery of life and death, the comprehension of the unknown, and the destiny of mankind. They developed a fatalistic attitude toward life because they expected to die as result of earthquakes, starvation and drought.

Years before their elders had told them that nothing could prevent the end of the human race. Cataclysmic forces had previously destroyed the world four different times and mankind could expect that the present age also will perish at the completion of a fifty-two year cycle. The only thing that man could do was to dedicate his live to Huitzilopochtli, in the expectation that he may change the scheme of things.

This indoctrination compelled the Aztecs to live in a world of uncertainty and to experience terrifying moments when the forces of nature battered their towns and villages. They reacted with fright and fear when they faced the unknown, and created magic, a bloody religion and a powerful priesthood to protect them from evil.

Figure 119 Mixtec lord prepared for combat . (Codex Nuttall).

Religion was, therefore, the most important feature of the Aztec culture. The worship of their gods was essential to their way of life. According to the Mexican scholar Miguel Leon-Portilla, the Aztecs imagined religion as an ultimate truth with divine and human purposes.

Aztec legends recounted how Huitzilopochtli directed the humble fishing tribe to central Mexico to begin a new life as a young and powerful military state. Under his divine guidance, the Aztecs began an aggressive path of conquest and empire building. The custodial god directed their efforts, but in the process he changed from an original water-deity into the god of the rising sun.

This change came about gradually, but the transformation had been completed when the Aztecs left Tula. As a sun-god, Huitzilopochtli demanded bloody sacrifices and the slaughtering of human beings to sustain his strength against the forces of evil.

A Fusion of Ideas

As the Aztecs progressed from a wandering tribe to an urban society, their martial ideas blended with the rich cultural heritage of the classic world of Mesoamerica. A world of strange mythological conceptions and beliefs emerged out of this cultural fusion. As the chosen people of Tonatiuh, the Sun-God, the Aztecs believed that their supreme responsibility was to fulfill the needs of the Giver of Life.

For them, the forces of life were locked in eternal combat with the forces of evil. In the Mexican world, the universe was a product of the eternal combat between Quetzalcoatl and Tezcatlipoca. The beneficial hero of art and agriculture constantly battled the god of night, who arrayed in a tiger skin, protected the wizards, the wicked and the oracle of death.

It has been observed that the overriding theme of Aztec religious philosophy was sacrificial warfare. Huitzilopochtli, the god of war, and other Mexican deities, demanded a continuous flow of human blood to satisfy their desires. To fulfill this obligation, the Aztecs sacrificed slaves and captives that they captured in war. Those who die on the sacrificial stone or in the battlefield received the reward of virtue.

Priests became the most important members of the state

since they alone could explain natural phenomena and the changes that occurred in society. The priests that directed the main religious functions were relatives of the monarch or members of the nobility. Those who had other responsibilities came from the ranks of the Calpulli. The hierarchy of priests grew considerably and when Cortes arrived to Mexico there were thousands of religious officials in society.

The Wise Men

The Aztecs held the tlamatinime, or wise men, in awesome regard. According to Leon Portilla, a sharp distinction must be made between priests and wise men. The tlamatinime were the counselors, teachers, psychologists, moralists and philosophers of the Aztec society. They were interpreters of the codices, the keepers of the historical past and the soothsayers of the somber future.

They practiced religion on an intellectual plane and examined the fundamental idea of nature from a metaphysical perspective. They developed a modern outlook of philosophy despite their strong beliefs in predestination. For the tlamatinime knowledge and education was poetry, philosophy was art, and truth was intuitive.

While the priests dedicated their lives to the cult of religion, the tlamatinime attempted to resolve human problems in a logical way. They attempted to rationalize myths on an intellectual plane without committing heresy. They also speculated about the meaning of life and death and the creation of the universe. In a way, their beliefs were not too distant from the philosophy of Zoroaster, the Persian prophet who in the sixth century B.C., accepted a universal struggle between the forces of light and darkness.

As teachers, the tlamatinime instilled in their students the values of patience, honesty and kindness. They taught their pupils to "assume a face, to place a mirror before them," so that they could become wise and prudent in their relationships with others. They attempted to bestow people with wisdom so that they could comprehend life better and live a happier existence. The wise men believed that the origin of man was in Ometeotl, the life-giving power of god. Yet, the universe developed

Figure 120 Aztec war-dress and headgear. (Codex Mendoza)

as it did through the struggle between good and evil (Leon Portilla 125-127).

The wise men were also astronomers, experts in the chronology of time, custodians of knowledge, and the protectors of tradition and public morals. Through "flower and song" the wise men gave Ometeotl a dual and ubiquitous characteristic. For Leon-Portilla, the Aztec world was a mixture of humanism and barbarism.

The Aztec Vision of Time

Every Aztec knew the meaning of the important signs of his life. The calendrical symbols for the date of birth, entrance to school and date of marriage were significant because they represented destiny. Since nature operated in cycles and everything had a beginning and an end, it was necessary to know one's place in the scheme of things, to foretell the future in the best possible way.

In spite of this fatalistic attitude toward life, the Aztecs hoped that the gods had not foreordained things in a way that they could not be changed. As a result, they practiced self discipline and worked hard. They built temples and ceremonial centers out of scale with practical needs, and offered sacrificial victims to the gods in an attempt to alter their fate.

As a mystic-agrarian society, the Aztecs used the calendar to foretell destiny, to schedule the planting season, conduct business, make war, and find out the most favorable opportunity for religious rituals. They used two different systems to measure years: the tonalpohualli, a count of 260 days, and the xiuhpohualli, a calendar of 365 days.

They used the first system to do rituals and conduct religious ceremonies. It consisted of twenty months of thirteen days each, with such names as Miquiztli (Death), Mazatl (Deer), Tochtli (Rabbit), Atl (Water), Itzcuintli (Dog), Ozomatli (Monkey), and Malinalli (Grass). In this calendar, each day had a different number and the combination of days and months named the religious periods as 1-Mazatl, 2-Rabbit, 3-Deer, and so forth.

The xiuhpohualli, or solar calendar, divided the year into eighteen months of twenty days each for a total of 360 days. The Aztecs called the remaining five days of the period the *nemontemi* or time of danger and death. The Aztecs inherited much of their knowledge of

Figure 121 Patecatl, god of pulque, with the sign "2-Rabbit." (INAH)

Figure 122 Office of resident governors
of Atzacan (Codex Mondocino)

recording time from the Maya and the Toltecs. They knew that the Maya had been observing the heavens for a long time and had developed a system so perfect that it was possible for them to distinguish without duplication any given day in thousands of years.

The Aztecs made many changes to their calendar when they met the Toltecs.   They adopted the Toltecs fifty-two year cycle, formed by the combination of the solar year and the 260-day ritual calendar, and begun to count their periods from the spring equinox. The Aztecs, as most Mesoamerican people, had an obsession with time. This interest may have been the result of their belief that the world was going to end at the completion of a fifty-two year cycle.

Before the Aztecs made changes to the calendar, it had three forms. In the first calendar the year consisted of 365 complete days commencing with the winter solstice; since it was s sidereal year 1461 years had to pass before it again began with the winter solstice. On noticing this discrepancy, the Aztecs changed the first day of the cycle to the summer solstice by interpolating a day at the end of four years.

The Aztec calendar of years and months and the astronomical observations based on a complex system of days and hours were so accurate that their year was fixed at 365.2420 days, which is only two ten-thousands of a day shorter than modern calculations.

The Sun Stone

In 1790, a group of workers who were repairing the foundations of the Plaza Mayor discovered the famous Sun Stone, commonly known as the Aztec Calendar. The monument was moved to the west side of the Cathedral where it remained for almost one hundred years. The National Museum of Anthropology finally rescued it in 1885.

The stone, a monolith of basalt measuring 11.7 feet in diameter and weighing 24.5 tons, was carved in 1479 during the reign of the emperor Axayacatl. The Aztecs erected it as a monument in the Main Temple. In 1521 the Spaniards knocked it down. Between 1561 and 1569 the Archbishop Antonio de Montufar ordered that it be buried because he believed that it was a sacrificial stone.

The center of the monolith contains the face of Tonatiuh, the sun-god, with a mask of fire. A sacrificial knife protrudes from his mouth like a tongue. Over his forehead are the symbols representing the renewal of life after a fifty-two year cycle. Tonatiuh has a small collar that shows the six parts of the sacred time cycle.

Four rays representing the cardinal points radiate from the center, with a variety of projections that include two tigers' paws holding human hearts. On the edge of the stone two serpents encircle the relief, their tails meeting at the date of creation.

The carvings relate to the beginning and end of the Aztec world. The dates when the four previous worlds perished are included around the center. Encircling them is a group of symbols representing day-signs.

The Aztecs never used the monolith as a calendar. It was carved to honor the sun-god, his many manifestations, and the human sacrifices related to his cult. The massive carving also depicts the Aztec cosmological views of the universe and represents the Aztecs' level of advancement in art and mathematics. Today it is the most popular Mexican monument in the National Museum of Anthropology.

Architecture and Urbanization

The artistic discipline and organizational abilities of the Toltecs influenced the architectural design and city planning ideas of the Aztecs. These Indians borrowed the techniques and refinements of their predecessors, but in the process they developed their own artistic style. It had such beauty and strength that it amazed even the conquering Spaniards.

While no major buildings of Tenochtitlan escaped the brutal destruction of the conquerors, and only fragmentary remains of the ancient site are left, the descriptions of the city by the Spanish themselves acknowledge the extent and splendor of the city. During that time, Tenochtitlan was one of the most beautiful cities in the world, and the largest urban center of ancient Mexico.

In building Tenochtitlan, the Aztecs succeeded in fusing the most diverse architectural designs of the Indian world "into one of the most fantastic artistic amalgams that Mesoamerican produced, especially in the field of stone sculpture." The Aztecs built their urban structures with care and taste and whitewashed them with

**Figure 123   Maya corbeled arch, Palace of the
Governors, Uxmal, Yucatan.**

a coat of cement. The buildings were one story high and had no windows (Gendrop 110).

The Aztecs used their buildings for granaries, schools, warehouses, arsenals and living quarters. The Spanish chroniclers wrote that one of these buildings was so large that it served as the home for three hundred Spanish soldiers and thirty horses. The Indian palaces were spacious and well-constructed with beams and rafters of cedar and other aromatic woods.

The Aztec structures had beautiful patios adorned with flowers and a lavish vegetation. The palace of Moctezuma had zoological and botanical gardens, museums, libraries, a bird sanctuary, orchards, fountains and an abundance of trees. According to Sahagun, drifting clouds of butterflies could be seen flying in the palace grounds.

A ceremonial precinct of beautiful buildings and palaces surrounded by a serpent wall occupied the center of the Tenochtitlan. It contained a plaza that measured about 1,085 feet by 930 feet. A twin pyramidal temple dedicated to the gods Huitzilopochtli and Tlaloc stood in the middle of the square.

Temples and Pyramids

The Aztecs built their stepped temples and pyramids of hewn stone over a core of earth, rock and debris. Researchers have found that often the rubble and artifacts located inside these pyramids are older than the facing. The Aztecs applied cement made from lime and charcoal to the exterior of the structures to decorate and preserve them. They painted the white stucco with brilliant colors and geometric designs.

The Aztecs followed the Mesoamerican tradition of reconstructing their pyramids every fifty-two year. They rebuilt them by building over the previous base. The Teotihuacanos used a similar technique, but they added to the final structures a *talud and tablero system* of stepped cornices and vertical walls. This arrangement provided protection against wind erosion and gave the pyramid added beauty and a base for religious decorations. The Aztec pyramids had exterior stairs without banisters.

Historian John Berger believes that the buildings, monuments and insular character of the city gave the residents a false sense of security. When the Aztecs

Figure 124   Maya frieze representing a snake head. Palace of the Governors, Uxmal.

Figure 125 Nunnery Quadrangle, Uxmal, Yucatan.

compared the beauty and organization of the city with the landscape of the valley they believed their stronghold was impregnable and no one could succeed in invading or destroying it (Berger 206).

Astronomical Observations

The Mesoamerican Indians observed and studied the universe hundreds of years before the arrival of the Spaniards. In April 1982, a group of astronomers and historians met in Lower California to evaluate the progress of astronomy in ancient Mesoamerica. Sponsored by the University of Mexico, the conference studied the pre-Hispanic and modern periods of astronomy in Mexico (Moreno Corral 7-10, Leon-Portilla 11-16).

In the discussions that followed, many new facts relating to the scientific advancement of the Mesoamerican Indians were considered. Among them was their use of magnetic forces, such as the compass, years before the Chinese discovered them (Carson 753-760).

The Mesoamerican Indians were never conditioned to the Christian beliefs that limited scientific progress in Europe. Without these restrictions and unfamiliar with the Aristotelian logic and cosmology, they developed a different approach to scientific investigation. Adding to their knowledge the works of others, they studied the behavior of the natural forces and made direct observations of scientific phenomena.

There were several astronomical observatories and cities in Mesoamerica that were oriented according to specific astronomical calculations. The Great Temple of Tenochtitlan, for example, had a 17-degree deviation from an East-West orientation, which indicates the special importance that the Aztecs gave to the sunset. The temple was also used for astronomical observations, and even the city played a part in the scientific inquiry of the Aztecs (Manrique Castaneda 28).

The pyramid known as *El Castillo*, located in Chichen Itza, is a good example of the astronomical and mathematical genius of the ancient Mesoamerican Indians. Apparently, it was build as part of an astronomical system that included the famous *El Caracol* observatory. The pyramid has four stairways of 91 steps each, with another step toward the upper platform. Together they

Figure 126 Hieroglyphic representation of solar eclipse

add to 365, which was the number of days in the Toltec year.

The pyramid has nine corners on each side, which adds to eighteen, also the number of months in the Toltec year. Each facade of the structure has fifty-two sections of *tableros*, or rectangular sculptured panels, that represented the number of years of the Toltec time cycle.

The monument also contains many other astronomical oriented features, such as the "serpent of light" that descends from the top of the structure at particular times. *El Castillo* was constructed by the Toltecs, the same people that taught astronomy, mathematics and the calendar to the Aztecs.

The observatory of *El Caracol* in Chichen Itza also played an important role in the scientific inquiry of the Toltecs. The upper chamber apertures of this structure are precisely oriented to the setting of the sun, the moon and the planet Venus during different times of the year.

Eclipses played an important role in the religious beliefs of the Aztecs. The Indians were terrified by them. They believed that the tzitzimime came to earth during that time to eat the people. If the eclipse lasted for a long time, the horrendous and feared visitors would dominate the world.

The Aztec learned from the Toltecs the exact place in the horizon where the planets, the sun and the moon will appear and disappear every day. Using their hands as a sextant to measure the movements of the stars, they also calculated with precision the exact time the sun would rise and set. They even worked correctly the orbital period of Mars and the synodical and sidereal periods of Venus.

The tlamatinime understood eclipses, solstices, and equinoxes. This knowledge was essential to them since the salvation of mankind depended on the correct interpretation of the scientific facts and the demands of the gods. One of their concerns was to explain correctly the movement of the Pleiades in the constellation Taurus.

According to Aztecs' beliefs, the journey of that star cluster across the sky every fifty-two year determined the survival or the end of mankind. Besides the Pleiades, Aztec astronomers also could identify other constellations, such as Tezcatlipoca (Big Bear), Citlatxanecuilli (Little Bear), Colotl (Scorpio), and

Manalhuaztli (Taurus).

Science and Technology

In mathematics they adopted the concept of zero from other Mesoamerican groups, and applied it to a vigesimal system of nineteen numbers and a zero. The Aztecs used their mathematical knowledge with great effectiveness, but never got the success of the Maya. That ancient race is now considered as the forerunner of scientific discipline in Mesoamerica. Their system of writing describes historical events; religious, social and business activities; scientific matters and everyday affairs. New research also shows that Mayan hieroglyphics contain genealogical descriptions, military affairs and business transactions.

While the Aztecs understood the principle of the wheel and built toys with them, they did not use this invention for transportation. It would have been difficult for them to move vehicles in mountainous terrain without draft animals to pull the loads.

From the military point of view, it is unlikely the superior weapons, tactics and firepower of the Europeans defeated the Aztec armies. While the Spanish horses created a pathological fear among the Indians, the Spanish muskets were rudimentary weapons.

In close combat conditions, the Spanish lances and swords were easily matched by the Indians' numerical strength. Besides, the Aztecs had many professional trained soldiers that could fight as well as the Europeans, While the Indian allies contributed significantly to the Aztec defeat, the Aztecs' soldiers had more experience and were better organized.

Thus, there must have been other reasons for their military defeat at the hands of Cortes. Probably, the same island-fortress defense mechanism that protected them for two hundred years against their enemies contributed to their defeat. Surrounded by the Spaniards, with no help from the outside, lacking adequate food and water, and unable to supply their forces, the Aztecs were doomed from the moment the Spaniards began the assault of Tenochtitlan.

The epidemic of smallpox and other infectious diseases that spread throughout the capital city also lowered their morale and reduced their fighting abilities.

Figure 127 The Sun and the Morning Star. (Codex Bodleian

Abandoned by their gods and facing a stubborn enemy, the Aztecs had no other recourse but to surrender their forces to an unknown fate.

The Practice of Medicine

The Aztecs considered medicine as an important human and religious necessity. Indian healers, called ticitl in Nahuatl, used a variety of treatments and orthodox methods to cure diseases. Among them were infusions, hot and cold baths, blood letting, purges, use of powered minerals and even surgery. They had a great understanding of the curative power of plants, herbs and roots, and periodically tested them to decide their effectiveness.

The physicians saw wounds with human hair and mended broken bones with massage, bandages and home remedies. They also cured infections and reduced high fevers with potions made from herbs and roots. According to the Spanish chroniclers, the standards that the Aztec physician had to meet were not very different from their own.

Indian cures were very effective. In 1570 the private physician of King Philip II, the renown Francisco Hernandez, went to Mexico to study Indian medicine. For seven years he collected information about Aztec medical practices. When he returned to Spain he published the results of his investigation. His book contained information about more than one thousand two-hundred native medicinal plants and a praise for the effectiveness of Aztec medicine. He had worked very close with Indian physicians during an epidemic in 1576.

Dental health was very important to the Aztecs. They cleaned their teeth several times a day with salt and powdered charcoal. The use of lime in the soaking of corn also helped them to maintain their teeth clean. They had treatments for toothaches, broken teeth, and mouth infections. Teeth could be extracted or sharpened depending of the desires of the individual.

Besides folk medicine, the Aztecs also used magic and ritualistic cures since they believed that certain diseases were the work of angry gods. The Indians considered Tlaloc responsible for skin problems, leprosy, and ulcers; Xochipille for venereal diseases. To cure these illnesses the healer did incantations, witchcraft and magic. The wearing of amulets was a good protection

Figure 128   Maya architectural design, Uxmal.

Figure 129   Maya Puuc architectural designs in mosaic form, Uxmal, Yucatan .

against illness.

The Aztecs used hallucinogens such as peyote to talk with their gods during religious ceremonies. Psilocybin, the principal chemical component of the drug, gave them a sense of euphoria, loss of the sense of distance and a sense of well-being that they identified with divine intervention.

The Aztec Educational System

The Aztecs had a great interest in education. They wanted to develop a youth with broad minds and many abilities. The schools emphasized rhetoric, music, the chronology of time, religion, the military arts and astrology. Parents taught their children self-restraint, honesty, the meaning of law, and the expectations of life.

Children were encouraged to love the land, to be grateful to their gods, to enjoy work, to share with others and to respect the forces of nature. Girls were taught to be clean and beautiful, to protect their families, and to share the pleasures of sex because "it was the way in which the gods planted men on this earth" (Diaz Infante 42).

The Codex Mendocino illustrates the training that the children received at home until age fifteen. It describes the tasks, punishments, and food rations given to the children. At age three, children received half a maize cake; at four a whole cake. At this early age they brought water to the home as part of their responsibilities.

By five, children carried small loads of wood or grass for kindling, and girls learned how to use the spindle. At six, children did menial task and received one and one-half maize cake per day. As the child grew older, he was given additional responsibilities. At thirteen boys were taught how to sail canoes, while girls learned to grind maize, cook and do house chores. At that age the children received two tortillas a day. These corn cakes were at least a foot in diameter. With beans, vegetables and game they provided a nourishing diet.

Children who disobeyed their parents were pricked with maguey spikes or bounded with ropes. Lazy children were beaten with a stick. Punishments were harsher as the children grew older. They included the forceful

Figure 130 Thirteenth-year old being taught
to grind corn (Codex Mendocino)

inhalation of smoke, laying all day on damp grounds, or working for many hours.

When male children reached the age of fifteen they married and were given the choice of going to a religious or military school. Those who wanted to be warriors went to the *house of youth*," or the Telpuchcalli. There they learned the economic life of society and the martial arts. The Telpochcalli corresponded to a military school. It was under the protection of the god Tezcatlipoca and priests and warriors directed its activities.

The Calmecac taught the youth government, administration and priestly responsibilities. It was mostly a school for the elite, but exceptional students from the lower class also could be admitted. The students learned philosophy, art and the power of creation. They studied writing, science, religion, government and the memorization of hymns. Contemplating the heavens and "the orderly motions of the stars," were also requirements for the students of the Calmecac. Leon Portilla writes that the teachers conditioned the youth to believe that the Aztecs were a nation with a mission.

The students who completed a satisfactory program joined the priesthood, the government or the military elite. The course of study was severe because it included fasting, participation in religious rites, and the study of astrology. Young girls were accepted in the Calmecac if they showed a special vocation for the priesthood.

Writing and Literature

When Hernan Cortes entered the Valley of Mexico there were one hundred seventy-five different languages and dialects being spoken in Mesoamerica. The language of the Aztecs, however, was the principal unifying linguistic system of the area. It was preferred for business, trade, political affairs, and religious communications.

The Aztecs lacked an alphabet, but the limitation did not stop them for developing writing, literature, poetry, science, rhetoric and philosophy. Their pictographic writing, while containing phonetic principles, consisted mostly of symbols and was not flexible enough to record legends, poetry and other literature. The Aztecs projected their ideas and expressions even when their form of writing could not record abstractions (Caso, Archaeology 948).

Figure 131 A Maya deformed cranial skeleton. The Maya considered elongated heads a mark of beauty.

Figure 132 Another example of cranial deformity.

The Aztecs memorized legends, poetry, speeches, and other forms of literature. Since education was not compulsory, and many children were never taught how to read or to write, family members committed most of the available knowledge to memory. Their ability to recall past events and sections of Aztec literature and history was very high. The Spanish chronicler Fray Bernardino de Sahagun had no difficulty in writing his famous *Historia General de las Cosas de Nueva Espana* from the information remembered by the Indians.

The Aztecs' literary works are known today as result of the efforts of the Mexican anthropologist Angel Maria Garibay K., a Nahuatl scholar who wrote the *Historia de la Literatura Nahuatl*. His work in the religious poetry of the Aztecs is of great literary value to modern scholars.

Some Aztec's manuscripts contain *rebus writing*, that is, the use of a picture whose sound suggests another word. Most of the glyphs or characters used by the Aztecs in their writing were miniature pictures that described incidents. For numerals, they used a vigesimal system. They wrote the numbers one to nineteen with dots. Twenty was written as a small flag and the multiplication of twenty by twenty was recorded as a fir tree. Other numerals included a bag or pouch to denote increments of twenty.

In the marketplace the Aztecs sold merchandise by quantity and number of units. The basic unit of measurement was the span of one man's hand. Other measurements included the distance from the ground to the height of a person's reach.

Sports and Games

The nobility played ball games before large audiences. The common people were allowed to participate as spectators. The game was played by using a solid rubber ball in a long court enclosed by high walls. Goal rings were located on the side walls. Play was violent and players were frequently bruised or seriously injured during a game. Under the sponsorship of the priests, ritualistic games were played on special occasions.

A popular board game was the patolli, a game similar to backgammon. It was played by all the social classes and consisted of a board shaped as a cross and divided in

Figure 133   Maya head modification.   (INAH,   Merida).

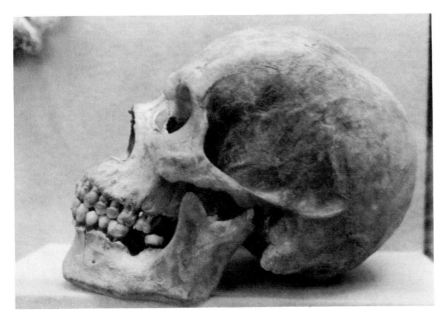

Figure 134   Deformed Maya skull.   (INAH,   Merida).

fifty-two spaces. Four players played the game simultaneously using marked dry beans. The participants moved colored pieces across the board with each throw of the "dice." The player who returned to his square first was the winner. People gambled on this game and invented ways to get lucky.

The *volador* was a spectacular entertainment practiced by the Aztecs and other Mesoamerican Indians. It consisted of a high flying act where four men suspended by ropes, and dressed as falcons with percussion instruments attached to them, jumped from a rotating platform at a given signal. With their weight, they rotated the platform and "flew" around the pole thirteen times before touching the ground.

Their gyrations formed a complete cycle that represented fifty-two years. Before the ceremony began, a fifth man stood on top of the pole and played an instrument to invoke the gods' acceptance of the event. The *voladores* represented solar birds and the arrival of rain (Jordan 86).

Hunting was a pastime and a necessity. The white-tailed deer was one of the preferred preys. The wealthy people hunted quails and pigeons using blowpipes that fired small pellets to kill the birds. Fishermen used spears and arrows very effectively to catch wild animals and fish.

Figure 135 Sculpture of Rain-God Tlaloc. (INAH)

13

The Search for Truth

As Others See Them

The information that is available about ancient Mesoamerica is overwhelming. The published and unpublished material that exist in English and Spanish alone will take a lifetime of reading. European and North American historians have always been interested in Mexico. The editors of Venture wrote in 1967: "No people have ever suffered so much agonizing analysis as the Mexicans. They have been admired, envied, damned, imitated, satirized and serenaded. What, one asks, is so compelling about these people? The answer, perhaps, is in their history" (13).

About the Aztecs, Gene S. Stuart wrote: "They came from obscurity, lifting themselves from misery to might, surviving calamitous misfortunes, enduring the most extreme hardships to prevail in the worst of times against their enemies." Perhaps that statement explains, better than anything else, the reasons for Western interest in the Mexican culture (Stuart 36).

The Aztec society was a microcosm of ancient America. These Indians were the dominant force in Mesoamerica when Cortes arrived on the shores of Mexico. Their empire represented a compendium of thousands of years of earlier native accomplishments.

Since the colonization of Mexico by the Spaniards many stories have been written about the role the Aztecs played in Mexican history. Ignorance of Indian traditions and customs resulted in poor judgments and misconceptions. For years well-known writers portrait

Figure 136   Colossal Snake Head, Templo Mayor.
(INAH)

Figure 137   Detail of the Feathered Serpent. Pyramid of
Quetzalcoatl, Teotihuacan.

the Aztecs as savages who piled the skulls of sacrificial victims near religious temples. Many people accepted, without questions, the views of the earlier chroniclers. They hastily conceived the idea that the Spaniards were mesmerized by the sight of blood and death when they entered the Aztec cities. For others, nightmare visions of the grotesque, the fantastic, and the terrifying abounded in the Aztec culture.

Images of blood-thirsty priests tearing human hearts from beating chests were accepted as a mark of the Aztec world. The practice of cannibalism, especially of younger children, was imprinted in the mind of many people. Stories of skull racks containing up to 136,000 human heads were accepted as part of the "historical literature of ancient Mexico."

Those who wrote about the Aztec society keep asking: "Why were these people so preoccupied with death? How could a culture so advanced in the arts and science be so obsessed with blood and sacrifice? "Animalistic, fatalistic and magical ideas probably ruled supreme," they concluded.

More Imaginative Tales

Well-known writers wrote extravagant claims about the Aztecs. An article that appeared recently reads: "Dedicating their Great Temple in 1487, they sacrificed between 10,600 and 80,400 people, depending on different sources; at least we know that the ritual killings continued without pause, four at a time, from sun up to sun down for four days. The whole city stank" (McDowell 727).

About that incident, William H. Prescott said: "The prisoners formed a procession nearly two miles long. The ceremony consumed several days, and seventy thousand captives are said to have perished at the shrine of this terrible deity."

The Spanish historian Juan Torquemada stated the correct number of victims most precisely at 72,344. The Mexican chronicler Fernando Alba Ixtlilxochitl placed the number at 80,400 (Prescott 76). None of these writers were eye witnesses to the event, or had seen reliable evidence about the exact numbers of victims that died that day.

Some writers have called this society as a "cannibal

empire." Others have observed that the Aztec obsession with human sacrifices and death was the result of their preoccupation with religion and fate. The Aztec rain god had to be appeased; the sun god had to be protected during his nightly passage through the underworld. Priests sacrificed victims to satisfy the insatiable appetite of these gods for human hearts and to insure their acceptance of human weaknesses. Author Burr Cartwright Brundage writes: "The story of the Aztecs, whatever else it may be, it is a tale of midnight murders, intrigues, and wild revenges " (xv).

Very few people have ever stop to ask: "Was all this true? Could it have been possible to kill thousands of victims without affecting the welfare of the state?" Were ritual sacrifices the only thing that these Indians ever knew? Are the narratives of the Spanish friars and soldiers reliable sources of information?

About the sacrifices at the Great Temple, Frank S. Onderdonk once wrote: "Such a thing is hardly creditable. Working twelve hours a day and allowing one victim for every five minutes, it would have required a year and a half to complete the bloody job. What would they have done with eighty thousand corpses? Probably three thousand would be a conservative estimate. Even this number was sufficient to bring a terrible pestilence upon the city" (16).

The transportation, security and disposal problems would have been monumental. Not even the assassination teams of Nazi Germany, with their effective methods of collective extermination, could have done the job using only obsidian or flint knives.

The Chroniclers of the Past

Often the imagination of the early Spanish writers ran ahead of their common sense. The "father of Aztec chronology," the respectable Spanish Friar Bernardino de Sahagun, even joined the feast of allegorical descriptions. He described the ritual to Tlaloc during the month of Atlcahualo, or February, with an intensity that only those who specialize in writing television melodramas can understand.

He wrote that the ritual began on the second day of February. On that day the Aztecs celebrated a festival in honor of the gods of rain. For the celebration, they

319

Figure 138 The Nunnery Annex, Chichen Itza, Yucatan.

Figure 139 El Caracol, a Maya astronomical observatory in Chichen Itza, Yucatan.

bought many infants, choosing especially those who had two twisted tufts of hair on their heads.

The priests adorned the little children with precious jewels, colorful feathers, blankets and sandals. They put paper wings on their shoulders, painted their cheeks with oil and draw white circles on their faces. Accompanied by musicians that played flutes and trumpets, they took the victims to a hill in rich decorated litters.

Upon reaching the slope of a mountain, the priests rested. During the night, they watched the infants continuously to insure that they did not fall asleep. If the infants cried the priests rejoiced, for that meant there was going to be abundant rain for the next planting season. Next day the priests sacrificed the children to Tlaloc by removing their young hearts. Then they cooked the small body parts and ate them.

A large quantity of children, the author writes, died in this manner every year. The priests did the rituals in seven different places. Sahagun even ended the story by soliciting from God swift punishment for those who did this type of work for the devil. In his view, only Satan could have devised such a horrendous crime (Sahagun 100-101).

Incredible as this tale may seem, it has been told and retold countless of times. No one has ever questioned the truth of the story, nor the passiveness of parents and children to the performance of the ritual. Did the parents willingly accept the sacrifice of their children? Where did the priests get the western idea of wings for the infants, to make them look like angels? Did the loving parents allow their children to be sacrificed so easily? Why would they let the children die when was so easy to cut the "twisted tufts of hair?" The Sahagun informants probably attempted to impress the friar with a story that would justify the Spanish destruction of the Aztec temples and religious centers.

While the story of the children's sacrifice to the rain god Tlaloc may be doubted, the belief in him may have been extended to the present. A statue of Tlaloc made by the Aztecs stands today at the entrance of the National Museum of Anthropology in Mexico City. The monument was found in the town of Coatlinchan, thirty miles from the Mexican capital.

On April 16, 1964, the directors of the museum moved

the statue to its present location. The journey began under difficult circumstances and it was not until nightfall that the workers reached the center of the city. Twenty-five thousand people gathered in the Zocalo to greet the arrival of the rain-god. That evening a severe thunderstorm drenched the crowd with one of the most severe thunder showers ever recorded in Mexico. There had been no rain for several months because the region had been in the middle of an extraordinary dry season.

Literary Inconsistency

Another problem that makes the search for truth difficult is literary inconsistency. At the beginning of this century, Mexican writers expressed themselves with a high level of emotional nationalism. Their works on Indian life had a pro-Aztec tone. Manuel Orozco y Berra and Alfredo Chavero converted the native Aztec-Nahua culture into something more than a classic Mesoamerican civilization. For Orozco, Tenochtitlan is Rome and Texcoco is Athens. This lack of objectivity and historical impartiality tarnished the truth.

Perhaps a good example of the negative results of these views is the eradication of Hernan Cortes from the historical discussion, and the glorification of Cuauhtemoc as the sole hero of Tenochtitlan. Many of those who explored the Mesoamerican past did not state the facts of history as they really occurred, or twisted the observations of others to fit their particular needs.

Until recently, the literature of the sixteenth century was the major source of information about the Aztec race. The situation changed somewhat in 1978 with the location of the ruins of the Great Temple. The archaeological discovery brought to the surface a new treasure of scientific information. Archaeologists have found more than 3,000 artifacts in the ruins of the pyramid. The wealth of information that became available modified many of our earlier views. The Great Temple now stands as the center of religious, social and commercial activities of Tenochtitlan and the Aztec empire.

The Codices

There are many important sources of information

Figure 140   Ball Court, Uxmal.

Figure 141   Corbeled arch, The Nunnery Quadrangle,
Uxmal, Yucatan.

available for the study of the Aztecs. The most important are the original Nahuatl sources known as codices, and the writings of the first missionaries, explorers, and chroniclers of the Conquest.

That event inspired many writers to record the eyewitness accounts and testimonies of those who participated in it. The early chroniclers gathered the information directly from both Spaniards and Indians alike and their works are considered authentic. The missionary friars who recorded the sources left a considerable volume of documentation in chronicles, reports, accounts, and histories. With very few exceptions, they represented the Spanish side of the story (Leon-Portilla 150).

Many early investigators attempted to justify the destruction of the Nahua race because the Indians were evil worshipers. Others pretended to explain the origins of these tribes in relation the biblical story. Fray Diego Duran wrote that the Nahua descended from the Lost Tribes of Israel.

Among those who left their imprints in the Aztec literature were Father Jose de Acosta, Fray Francisco de Aguilar and Fray Diego Duran. Others were Fray Andres de Olmos, Fray Toribio de Benavente (Motolinia), Fray Bernardino de Sahagun, and Fray Bartolome de Las Casas.

The most important of the early documents are the accounts of the natives themselves. They contain their views on tradition, religion and the creation, and are written mostly in Nahuatl. Others present the Indian version of the Conquest. These Indian works are similar to the studies conducted today by scientists who investigate the ethnological characteristics of native populations throughout the world.

Other accounts describe the Aztec society, structures of government and the imperial tributary system. Some contain statistical facts and philosophical views. The Indians prepared the manuscripts on deerskins or paper made from maguey fibers. They used hieroglyphic writing to record the information and folded the finished manuscripts into screens or accordions (Duran 38).

The Spanish conquerors found many Indian codices in the Calmecac and the Telpochcalli, the Aztecs' educational academies. As has already been said, Christian priests destroyed most of them, thinking that they contained symbols of Indian superstition. Several original documents survived the destruction and today are preserved in Europe (Prescott 89-91).

Among the most important ones are the Codex Borgia, the Codex Borbonicus, the Codex Bologna or Cospiano, and the Codex Fejervary-Mayer. These documents illustrate the richness of the Aztec culture. They contain calendrical matters, tax reports, military maps, and information on the economic, educational, and religious activities of the Aztecs. The Spaniards accompanied many of these codices with short explanations and notations.

Importance of the Basic Sources

The importance of these documents were discussed during a Symposium on Mesoamerican Archaeology held by the University of Cambridge in 1972. The scholars who attended the seminar determined that these codices are among the most valuable surviving manuscripts of the Aztec society.

The Codex Borgia describes most of the astronomical observations of the Aztecs. In 1831 Viscount Edward Kingsborough reproduced the manuscript and in 1848 the Duke of Loubat financed its reproduction. During the nineteenth century the German scholar Edward Seler studied the Codex and concluded that the document was Zapotec. Recent investigations made by the Mexican anthropologist Alfonso Caso suggest that it is of Aztec origin (Leon-Portilla 198)

The original manuscript is now in the Ethnological Museum of the Vatican Library in Rome. Formerly, it belonged to the Giustiniani family of Florence. Its owners did not protect it properly and their young children set it on fire. Fortunately, the manuscript had been written on deerskin and its pictorial material did not receive serious damage (Prescott 91). Seler's commentaries on the document "contain studies of permanent value that has not been possible to supersede which form the solid basis for subsequent investigations" (Keen 448-449).

The Codex Borbonicus contains information on philosophy and religion. Part of this manuscript is a tonalamatl, or sacred book of divination, which describes the Indian's superstitious practices. The document also discusses witchcraft and the liturgy used during funeral processions. In 1899 the French antiquarian E. T. Hamy

Figure 142 Chac-mool, or reclining figure, of Toltec origin. (INAH, Merida)

Figure 143 Thousand Columns Hall, Temple of the Warriors, Chichen Itza, Yucatan.

published this work in Paris. The original manuscript is now in the Chamber of Deputies Library in Paris.

Another of the Indian codices that describe the fundamental ideas of Aztec religion is the Codex Bologna or Cospiano. It is now located in the Library of the University of Bologna in Italy. The manuscript contains information on astronomy, the weather, the seasons, and agronomy. This Codex also provides views on the religious beliefs that influenced the Aztec idea of time. The Mexican anthropologist Alfonso Caso believes the origin of this document to be in the Puebla-Tlaxcala region because its style "is identical with that of the paintings that decorate the altars of Tizatlan in Tlaxcala" (Caso 11).

The myth of creation, the destruction of mankind, and other allegoric descriptions from Aztec mythology are the principal themes of the Codex Fejervary-Mayer, and early Mexican manuscript located now in England. The document contains details of the Aztecs communal life and their system of government. The American anthropologist Celia Nuttall studied this manuscript in 1886 with the Codices Borgia and Vaticanus-Rios. She published the results of her investigations in the *Proceedings of the American Association for the Advancement of Science*.

Nuttall observed that the Aztecs practiced communal living in their society. She advanced the theory that the Aztec calendar and the sacrificial stones were records of "communal property and of equal division of contributions." In 1901 the Duke of Loubat published an edition of this work in Paris (Nuttall 325-327).

The Painted Manuscripts

Besides the original texts, there are several written and painted manuscripts prepared by Franciscan and Dominican friars. Among then are the Codex Ramirez (or the *Historia de los mexicanos por sus pinturas*), the Codex Mendocino, and the *Matricula de tributos*. The last ones are taxation documents of the Aztec state.

The Spanish chroniclers used the narratives of Indian elders for their works. Many of these post-Columbian manuscripts and most of the supplemental explanatory writing prepared by the clergymen were never published as result of the censure established by the Inquisition. The *Cantares mexicanos* are perhaps the oldest of these

327

written accounts.

This work, prepared by Aztec poets few years after the Spanish destruction of Tenochtitlan, describes the psychological impact of their defeat by the Spaniards. The poems reflect the emotional views of the Aztecs and the hopelessness of their life. The original manuscript of the *Cantares mexicanos* did not survive, but a copy was made from the original and is now in the National Library of Mexico. The American scholar Daniel G. Brinton published twenty-eight of the poems in Philadelphia in 1887. In 1904 the Mexican anthropologist Antonio Penafiel published a photoengraved edition of the work.

Manuscript 22, entitled *Unos anales históricos de la nacion mexicana*, is a rare document describing the Aztec view of the destruction of their empire. This work, located in the National Library in Paris, is an important source of historical information and a document of great literary value. It was prepared by natives of Tlatelolco in 1528.

According to the Mexican anthropologist Miguel Leon-Portilla, "the most remarkable thing about this document is the fact that its Indian authors somehow learned the correct use of the Latin alphabet . . .to write out some of their past events, above all their account of the Conquest (Leon-Portilla, 154-155).

Huehuetlatolli, or *Platicas de los viejos* (Conversations with the Elderly), is a group of documents on moral behavior addressed to the Aztec students. In 1600 the Spanish priest Juan P. Bautista published these platicas in both Nahuatl and Spanish. In 1875 Fray Andres de Olmos included several of them in his book *Arte para aprender la lengua mexicana*.

In 1943 Angel Maria Garibay also published several of these documents to accompany an article written for the Mexican journal Tlalocan. The original documents are now in the National Library of Mexico and in the Library of Congress in Washington, D. C.

The *Anales de Cuauhtitlán*, or Codex Chimalpopoca, is a group of Indian texts written in Nahuatl and Spanish before 1570 by the Franciscan friar Pedro Ponce. Compiled with the help of anonymous writers, it consists of original native sources, eyewitness accounts and testimonies of individuals who participated in the Conquest. The original documents once belonged to the Mexican historian Fernando de Alva Ixtlilxochitl.

Figure 144 Punishment of a disobedient
child. Maguey spikes are being inserted
into his flesh (Codex Mendocino)

Between 1880-1884, the Mexican writer Faustino G. Chimalpopoca translated and published them. The Mexican historian Primo F. Velazquez also published the texts in 1945 under the title Codex Chimalpopoca (Barlow 559-560).

The Codex Mendoza

Another important document that is available for the study of the Aztec civilization is the Codex Mendocino or Mendoza. This work contains descriptions of the Aztec social, religious and political institutions. It is divided into three parts containing the civil history of Tenochtitlan, data on the imperial tributary system, and information concerning the socioeconomic structures of the empire.

The manuscript also describes the Indian systems of law, education, and religion. It gives some knowledge on the organization of the Aztec empire, and provides facts about the business and commercial activities of the people.

The Viceroy of New Spain Antonio de Mendoza ordered the preparation of this document, which was published in France in 1625. Since 1925 it has been published in Europe and North America several times.

The Codex Vaticanus-Rios contains historical information from the Conquest to the year 1553. It also describes in great detail the religious practices and beliefs of the Aztecs. In 1877 the Mexican anthropologist Gumersindo Mendoza studied this Codex and concluded that the manuscript depicted "the formation of suns and worlds out of the chaotic play of atoms and molecules."

Mendoza believed that the Aztec culture was well developed at the time of the Spanish arrival (Keen, La Imagen, 426). According to Alfonso Caso, the first section of the Codex Vaticanus-Rios is apparently a copy of a pre-Hispanic text. In 1831 Lord Kingsborough reproduced it in his Antiquities, and in 1900 the Duke of Loubat published it.

The Codex Telleriano Remensis, contains many references to the Aztec religion. This manuscript describes the Aztec pantheon and the religious rites practiced by the Indians. The manuscript details the cult of the sun-god, their belief in predestination, and the sacrificial rites done by the priests.

Figure 145 Mask representing the face of Chaac, god of rain. Kabah, Yucatan . (INAH)

Figure 146 Detailed view of the "Iglesia," Chichen Itza, Yucatan.

The text is incomplete and much of the original work has been lost. The information that remains complement the record presented in the Codex Vaticanus-Rios. The text is in the Manuscript Division of the National Library in Paris. Lord Kingsborough published it on his Antiquities of Mexico.

The Work of Sahagun

The Spanish language version of the Codex Matritense, which is in part material that Fray Bernardino de Sahagun used for the *Historia general de las cosas de Nueva Espana*, is a work of special interest. Sahagun began to compile this work in 1547 in Mexico. He used the narratives of Indian elders to do the historical task. Later, he published sections of his manuscript under the title *Augurios, astrologia y calendarios de los Aztecas* (Leon Portilla, Aztec Thought 185-187).

The twelfth book covers Aztec region, literature, arts, medicine, botany, zoology and personal skills. It is important because of its authenticity. He did not accept individual testimonies when he was preparing his compilation, but questioned well-known Indian elders to insure that the information given to him was correct. His informants were mostly "the sons of high ranking nobles, undoubtedly former students of the Calmecac" (Leon-Portilla, Aztec Thought 185).

The evidence that Sahagun compiled was so authentic that in 1577 the Spanish government ordered its destruction because it reflected the extent of the Nahua culture in a positive way. The Church believed that the writings could revive the ancient beliefs and the prohibited religious practices.

Sahagun kept a copy of his texts in spite of the Royal Order. These manuscripts are now preserved as the Codex Matritense in the Royal Academy of History in Madrid. There is another copy of these works in the Nahuatl and Spanish languages in the Laurentian Library of Florence, Italy. It is called the Codex Florentine (Portilla, Aztec Thought 186-187).

Between 1905 and 1907, the Mexican scholar Francisco del Paso Troncoso published most of the material contained in the Codex Matritense, making it available to scholars for the first time.

The writings of Sahagun and other Spanish chroniclers

Figure 147 Small basket found at the Great Temple. (INAH)

IXTAB, DIOSA DEL SUICIDIO

Figure 148 Ixtab, Maya Goddess of Suicide. (INAH, Merida)

and historians who came to the New World after the Conquest, as well as the original Nahuatl sources described, are the most important sources available for a detailed study of the Aztec civilization. The importance of these early works to Mexican history cannot be overemphasized. Their translation and publication during the last fifty years have simplified the study of ancient Mexico.

The Letters of Cortes

The first letters that Cortés wrote to Charles V between 1520 and 1526 are invaluable records of his experiences during the Conquest. Commonly known as the *Cartas de Relación*, the manuscripts are located in the Imperial Library of Vienna. The original of the first letter was lost without being officially published.

The German printer John Cromberger published the second letter in Seville in 1522, more than two years after Cortés wrote it. Soon its contents were known throughout Europe. Probably, it is the most interesting one since it describes Tenochtitlan and the Aztec world first hand. It describes in great detail the Aztec cultural and political achievements.

The third letter is longer than the preceding one and includes Cortes' activities in Mexico between 1520 and 1522. The fourth letter, published in 1525, concerns the post-Conquest activities of the Spaniards. These letters provide the reader with valuable information about the Conquest of Mexico.

Another important source is the Relacion de Texcoco, an Indian view of the destruction of Texcoco by the Spaniards. Written by Juan Bautista Pomar, a mestizo writer of the sixteenth century, the Relación was not published until the nineteenth century.

Similarly, the *Historia Eclesiástica Indiana*, written in 1597 by the Franciscan friar Jeronimo de Mendieta, is a defense of the Indians and an indictment of the Spaniards who enslaved them. Mendieta became an expert in native Indian languages and fought the ecclesiastical authorities to protect the Indians. He praised the Aztec civilization, especially their educational, legal and governmental institutions. The priest wrote that the Indians lived better during their period than under the Spanish administration. His enemies succeeded in preventing the publication of his book. It was finally published in 1870 by the Mexican scholar Joaquin Garcia Icazbalceta (Keen 134-135).

In 1552 Francisco López de Gómara wrote his famous *Historia de las Indias*, or *Historia de la Conquista de Mexico*, as it is more generally known. The author was Cortes' private secretary and chaplain. The book became the best biography of the Conqueror and was promptly suppressed by the authorities.

It is a celebration of the heroism of the Spaniards, and as such, placed the European adventure as a struggle between good and evil. Gomara included in his narrative many descriptions of the Aztecs' history, society and religion, extracted primarily from Motolinia's Memorials.

Fray Toribio de Benavente, better known as Motolinia, wrote in 1541 the *Historia de los indios de la Nueva Espana*, and the following year drafted the *Memorials*, "a rich store of ethnographic material, obtained from Indian informants and picture writings" (Keen 111). The work is very impartial and a magnificent source of information about Aztec religion.

The *Historia verdadera de la Conquista de Nueva España* was written half a century after the Conquest by Bernal Diaz del Castillo, one of the conquerors. The writer was high impressed by the beauty of Tenochtitlan and writes about it as a soldier enchanted by a world he has never seen before. It is different in the sense that the author had no religious dogmatism to sell or an academic theory to propound.

The Archivo General de la Nacion

There are many more works that can be consulted by those interested in studying further the lost world of the Aztec Indians. Other valuable documentation is in the Archivo General de la Nacion in Mexico City. The official repository of Mexican historical documents contains thousands of copies of government reports, questionnaires, statistical data and other important documents. Written mostly in Spanish, they are found under such titles as Indians, Land Grants, Inquisition, Tributes, and *Mercedes* (Favors).

The colonial manuscripts are assembled in more than 25,000 volumes of unbound *legajos* (bundles) according to general or topical content. These bundles are part of

**Figure 149   Sculpture of the Mexican goddess Xilonen
from Veracruz. ((INAH)**

130 *ramos* (divisions) of unequal extent of some 4,000 volumes each. The *Correspondencia de Virreyes* alone, an important source for the study of the Indian civilizations, comprises 442 volumes.

The National Library in the Mexican capital also has valuable documentary collections on the subject. Nahuatl texts on Christian doctrine predominate among the colonial manuscripts found in the Library. Roberto Moreno cataloged most of this material in 1965-1966 and published the information in the Library's official research bulletin (Moreno 35-116).

Many Mexican historical records have been photographed by the Universities of Texas and Tulane. The reproduced copies of these documents are located in the Latin American libraries of both universities in Austin and New Orleans.

Problems of Historical Research

Selecting adequate sources for the study of the Aztec civilization is often a problem. The vast and richness of early colonial sources provide almost unlimited research opportunities for the student of Mesoamerican civilizations. But the wealth of documentation also creates serious scholastic difficulties.

As has been indicated, the pictorial manuscripts, or codices, are the most original sources for the study of the Aztec civilization. Painted in signs or glyphs, they are mostly from the early colonial period. The information on these codices includes "lives of individuals, historical events, chronicle histories, cartographic-chronological histories, cartographic documents, lawsuits, fiscal and economic documents, and ethnological data on acculturation, land tenure, rules governing inheritance patterns, and the evolution of costume, furniture, architecture, and painting" (Robertson 125).

Many of these documents, or authorized copies, are located in the National Library of Anthropology in Mexico City. This library also has an adequate collection of information for the study of the Aztec civilization from other sources. These documents are secured and can be viewed only by special permission.

Plundering of the Past

During recent years, there has been considerable interest in the Mesoamerican culture. In foreign countries, exhibitions of historical records and artifacts have attracted thousands of visitors. Every year, hundreds more visit the architectural wonders of past civilizations. This interest also has created serious negative effects. The plundering of ancient graves and the stealing of ancient records is big business. Despite strict measures, looters and culture thieves continue the depredation of ancient archeological sites.

The trade of stolen artifacts and documents is destroying the knowledge about the past. The looters destroy precisely the kind of information that professional archaeologists must gather to study the importance of a particular find. Archaeological theft is being promoted by the illegal purchases made by museums and private collectors.

On Christmas Eve, 1985, thieves entered the National Museum of Anthropology of Mexico and stole 124 pre-Columbian artifacts. Most of the objects were later recovered from the man that masterminded the theft. But the result of the incident will affect all of those who desire to investigate the heritage of the ancient races that occupied Mexico before the arrival of Cortes. Tight government controls of all antiquities, including documents, now restricts scholarship and a researcher's ability to complete his work.

Perhaps in the long run solutions will be found to resolve the problem. But as long as the danger of looting exists, historical investigation will suffer and with it the advancement of modern civilization.

Figure 150 The "Iglesia," or Church. Chichen Itza, Yucatan.

14

The Mexican Experience

Tales of Wonder and Mystery

Historians have always recognized the Spanish conquerors that came to America as arrogant, romantic, and extremely devoted to their Christian faith. They also have portrayed them as courageous, tenacious and loyal to their king. Their primitive behavior accepted pain, suffering and the shearing of blood without concern. Medieval romanticism gave them a thirst for adventure and a passion for the unknown.

For years, tales of monsters, princesses, and enchantments conditioned their minds. Missionaries, sailors and merchants often told them about the existence of mysterious regions, such as *Mare Tenebrosum*, that hid everything from sight. This ocean, according to the tales, was the end of the earth and the abode of creatures beyond the thought of man.

Others believed that Cathay in China was a magnificent city of emperors who dressed in jeweled robes and lived in golden palaces. India and Cipangu, or Japan, had "rose colored pearls" and gold "abundant beyond measure." The Moluccas had perfumes and species unknown to the Western World.

The most important potentate of these regions was Prester John, a Christian king of unprecedented wealth. So convincing were many of these stories that legend interweaved with reality. For years, the Popes sent missionaries to the Far East to search for Prester John.

The Spanish conquistadors were also the product of years of war, anguish and history. They had seen their land occupied for hundreds of years by Iberians,

Tartessians, Celts, Phoenicians, Carthaginians, Romans and later by Moslems from Northern Africa. These invaders left behind a culture of violence, austerity and duress where success meant everything and failure was intolerable.

The Spaniards also inherited from the Roman civilization an emphasis for land ownership and urban living. They acquired from that race a Spartan exaltation of kings. From the Visigoths who invaded the Spanish peninsula they learned the art of war and the organization of military castes.

A Clash of Centuries

The Moorish invasion of Spain brought a religious reaction and a subsequent war of *Reconquista* that lasted for eight hundred years. The fall of Granada, the last Moorish bastion occurred in 1492, the same year of the discovery of America, and barely twenty-seven years before the arrival of Cortes to Mexico.

During the Moorish campaigns the Spaniards developed a special attachment to Christianity. The two most notorious institutions of the Spanish state, the Inquisition and the *Santa Hermandad*, were founded to terrorize the people into religious submission.

The Inquisition fought racial and religious diversity. It maintained the purity of the Catholic faith and proclaimed one nation, one king, and one empire. It had both the powers of church and state and succeeded in expelling the Jews and Moors from the country (Kamen 156-157).

It was during the Reconquista that the Spaniards developed their military character, exaltation for the warrior class, aggressiveness and a crusading religious spirit. They formed military organizations such as the Orders of Calatrava, Alcantara and Santiago to support the Crown. These attributes served them well during the conquest of Spanish America, especially when they fought against the numerically superior forces of the Aztecs.

In A.D. 1050 Portugal separated from Spain and the Spaniards began to fight among themselves. Anarchy and civil war almost stopped the Reconquista. The Christian Church intervened and established peace among the warring factions; in the process it helped to defeat the Moslems. During this time, the Spanish language became the predominant system of expression in the Iberian peninsula. The famous historical epic *El Cid Campeador* appeared in Spanish in 1085

An Empire is Born

The Spanish society that emerged from this turbulence had a great martial spirit, a crusading religious zeal, unusual personal honor, a powerful monarchy, and practiced individualism beyond reason. It was a society consumed by religious fever and the desire to expand Spain's national boundaries.

During these years, Spain made great strides in military technology, commerce, and navigation. The power of the Spanish monarchs grew considerably. Machiavelli wrote that Ferdinand, the King of Spain, undertook great enterprises and maintained his army with "the money of the Church and the people." Under the pretext of religion, he also resorted to pious cruelty. He drove the Moors out of Spain, despoiled them, attacked Africa, and undertook a bloody military campaign against the Italian states and the kingdom of France (Machiavelli 110).

Thus, with calculated foresight, Ferdinand and Isabella transformed their medieval kingdom into one of the greatest empires in history. After 1492 the country changed its national character to bourgeoisie mercantilism. The merchant class assumed control of the country's direction while the nobility lost its political influence. These changes initiated "the expansion of Europe."

As historian J. H. Parry has observed, "The foundations of European dominance were prepared in the fifteenth century, and firmly laid in the sixteenth and seventeenth. In those centuries sea-faring Europeans visited almost every part of the world." Subsequent generations retained that dominance in Latin America, Africa, and Asia. Not until the twentieth century the balance of political power changed from Europe to America (Parry 5).

Effects of the Discovery of America

As has been observed, the discovery of America in 1492 changed the world. The results of the great discoveries

Figure 151 Queen of Uxmal. Part of the façade of the
Magician's Pyramid in Uxmal, Yucatan.

were far reaching. In less than fifty years, the Spaniards took possession of most of the lands bordering on the Gulf of Mexico. The historical epic unleashed a clash of cultures never to be seen in this planet again. The Columbian enterprise permitted the expansion of Europe and the continuation of Spain's crusade for Christianity.

After the voyages of Columbus, Spain transformed the Western Hemisphere into a new European frontier. To dominate the native races, the Spaniards applied in America the same techniques used for the conquest of the Moslem world. The colonization of the Western Hemisphere became the final step in the consolidation and reorganization of the Iberian nation.

The Spaniards came to America for a variety of reasons. Among them were the spirit of adventure, the desire for wealth and the ambition to participate in colonial plunder. Other settlers came to colonize the region, seek land and exploit the mines and natural resources of the continent. Some came with an earnest desire to convert the natives to Christianity, but the majority came to secure riches, glory and fame.

Most of the conquistadors were disinherited second sons of aristocratic families with limited education and no family responsibilities. Very few were professional soldiers, but had lived for many years in a military environment and knew how to fight well.

The Spanish Conquest of the Western Hemisphere was a risky business. Those who came to America paid for and directed their own expeditions. Private lenders financed many of the explorations. They signed contracts with the government that allocated one-fifth of the profits to the Crown. Successful conquerors, such as Hernan Cortes, received later impressive titles and a social recognition from the Emperor.

Many of the settlers that came to America had illusions of grandeur and expected to own large sections of productive land without knowing how to manage it. As a result, the earlier attempts to colonize the West Indies were a disaster. But, the adventurers had a determined spirit and adapted readily to the new conditions and new realities.

The exploration and colonization of the Western Hemisphere was a very dangerous work. The mortality rate among the Spaniards was very high, mostly the result of fighting and sickness. Thousands died in battles, or as result of starvation and disease.

The new experiences in the Western Hemisphere revitalized the crusading spirit to the Catholic Church. Faith became an important instrument in the conversion of the Indians. The friars set up missions, built hospitals and churches in which to worship. For their efforts, the Spanish priests received land, prestige, authority and special privileges.

The Mesoamerican Indian

When the Spanish explorers first landed in America, they found that many of the Indian tribes had advanced only slightly beyond the Stone Age. Others, as we have seen, had a much larger civilization. The Indians who lived in Mesoamerica had many traits and characteristics that made them different from other cultural group, except for the Incas of Peru.

Many of these natives lived in city-states and urban centers that had pyramids, markets, schools, aqueducts, and ceremonial centers. They had organized governments, social classes, and legal systems that surprised even the conquerors who destroyed them. These societies had knowledge of writing, mathematics and astronomy; and could keep track of time in a very accurate calendar.

Leon Portilla described those who lived in the central valley of Mexico as high civilized, with magnificent cities, organized commerce, a knowledge of medicine, and a complex religion. They also wrote beautiful poetry and literature, and had a structured system of education.

The social and cultural progress made by these Indians were, in broad outlines, similar to that of Europe, but occurred at different times and in different forms. Compared with the Old World story, "the evolution of man and culture in aboriginal America was greatly compressed. There is no telling what might have happened had the course of history been different" (Titiev 174-75).

The Aztec World

Among the primitive or civilized societies that the Europeans found in Mesoamerica, it was the Aztecs who fascinated most the Spaniards who conquered Mexico. These Indians had a complex society where religion and trade

Figure 152   Temple of the Jaguars, Chichen Itza, Yucatan.

became the catalysts for social evolution.

Rigid codes of law structured their society and everyone had to obey them. Special courts dealt severely with crimes of the nobility, and often the judges punished the aristocrats with stronger penalties that those imposed on the poor. Theft, black magic, incest, homosexuality and adultery received the death penalty. Homicide, even of a slave, also brought capital punishment.

With a system that was highly militaristic, the Aztecs developed a society that demanded conformity, loyalty and full participation in the affairs of the state. Commerce played an important role in the economic development. Communal rules permitted the sharing of farm products and the farming of corn alongside roads for the hungry and the poor.

Aztec influence depended mostly on their ability to force others to pay tribute. The merchants organized guild systems; conducted foreign policy; sent expeditions to remote places; served as businessmen, tax collectors and spies; and even started wars on their own when confronted with challenges to their territorial jurisdiction. Through them, the government controlled most of the trade and exerted power over the vassal states.

Religion, war and militarism formed the basis of Indian life. The Aztecs used war for defense, revenge, and economic motives. Their religious beliefs also compelled them to fight their enemies constantly to gather sacrificial victims for their ceremonies. War and religion also influenced communal life, education and ethical conduct. The ritual was a dominating influence in the Aztec society. The Aztecs convinced the people that their rulers were divine and had supernatural powers.

Cultural Beliefs

Life, death and the survival of their world were the most important concerns of the Indians of central Mexico. For them the nature and form of death determined the fate of the soul, and the spirit suffered pain or attained happiness in the other world depending upon how the victim died.

The Aztecs believed that there had been four

historical ages and each had been destroyed by a cataclysm. The age where they lived was also going to be destroyed by earthquakes and famines. To prevent the fifth destruction and give renewed energy to the sun, the giver of life, they conducted human sacrifices.

In two respects the Aztec beliefs were no different from those of the conquerors. Both societies were extremely religious and fatalistic. Aztecs and Spaniards attempted to force their religious beliefs on others. When we compare modern beliefs with old Aztec ideas, the similarity is remarkably clear.

The Aztecs build monuments and structures out of scale with typical human need because they served as a place for their religious rituals, and as a spiritual center for their ideological ways. They attempted by all possible means to prevent the destruction of their world by sustaining the perpetual life of the sun through human sacrifices.

At the end, their world was destroyed not by the feared natural cataclysm predicted by their wise men, but by the sword of Hernan Cortes. The conqueror's ability to conduct psychological warfare and persuade others to fight for him made the task of conquering the Aztecs much easier. Cortes' management of the superstitious beliefs of the Aztecs, the use of his superior weapons, and the introduction of infectious diseases cast the final die in the history of the Aztec state.

The Aztecs, proud conquerors themselves for two hundred years, could not defend their empire because a more advanced technological race rendered their ancient system obsolete. Cuauhtemoc, the last Emperor, fought bravely to stop the march of time, but he failed. His heroic deed of patriotism is honored today in Mexico.

The End of an Era

It was not long after Cortes discovered Mexico that the Mesoamerican ways of life began to collapse. Their imperial controls, tributary system and demand for sacrificial victims, made enemies of those who pretended to be loyal vassal states. These tribes welcomed the opportunity to join Cortes during his siege of Tenochtitlan.

The saga of the Aztec nation against and European power was to be repeated often in the nineteenth century, when the imperial powers of Europe sought colonies in Africa, the Middle East and Asia. While the colonial expansion of Europe was not as violent as the confrontation between Aztec and Spaniard, the results were the same. The stronger, industrialized nations always defeated the agrarian, weaker ones. Historians now believe that this clash of cultures will repeat itself where there is greed and mankind chooses to establish new foundations.

The exploration, colonization and settlement of Mesoamerica were not an easy task. Spain had a limited population and could not colonize every area of the region with the same intensity as they in central Mexico. As a result, most of the native inhabitants of the region continued their ancient customs, traditions and way of life, modified slightly by the appearance of the Catholic faith in their mist.

Mexico and Central America provided an unlimited area for the deeds of adventurers, a magnificent laboratory for religious and social activists, and a profitable field for missionaries. It also became a treasure of incalculable value to the Spanish government, which seized the richness of the land without questioning its ownership.

Spanish Settlement of Mexico

Emigration to Mexico did not assume a high proportion during the first decades after the Conquest. Those family groups that settled in the country were small in numbers. Thus, adventurers and people with little respect of the Indian traditions came to America to make fortunes and enjoy the fruits of the discovery.

Cross-breeding between Spaniards and Indian women became commonplace. The interchange produced the mestizo race that has been the racial landmark of Mexico since the sixteenth century. Subsequent marriages between Europeans and native women contributed in the long term to establish friendly relations between the two races.

In the cities of America, sporadic settlements of eager, enterprising urban residents sow the seeds of a Mediterranean culture that superimposed its values over those of the Indian. Their interest in city life and refinement probably prevented the further slaughtering of the Indians.

Figure 153   Maya painted pottery. (INAH, Merida)

Figure 154   Maya painted pottery. (INAH, Merida).

In the countryside, the Spaniards continued to use until 1555 the old Aztec's tributary system. In that year a new measure was placed into effect to collect taxes based on the colonial records kept by the Church. This system remained in effect for many during the colonial period. Periodically, the Spaniards conducted head counts to adjust the tax payments. Such counts were designed to redistribute the assessments more fairly, but they usually resulted in greater suffering for the Indians.

The judges sent to conduct the counts were transported, fed, housed, and pampered at the expense of the Indian communities. The payments of these expenses were especially difficult for people who could ill afford such costs. Because they expended none of their money, the judges relished such service and accordingly extended their stay. The Spanish tributary system caused extreme hardship, dislocated families, decimated whole towns, prompted many suicides, and impoverished the Indian race.

Zorita's arguments should be used carefully because often he portrait the Indian life in romantic terms. His *Brief Relation of the Lords of New Spain* has been often criticized for its negative views about the treatment of the Indians. Critics of Zorita believe that he overdrew the gap between Spanish colonial administrative theory and practice.

Nevertheless, Zorita was a Spanish jurist who was concerned with the plight of the Indians. He probably believed that the severity of the Spanish abuse could only be corrected by describing the Indians in their most favorable light. In this respect, the Spanish scholar was in a distinct minority in the Spanish community. He sacrificed some objectivity to gain positive results.

The Spanish Justification

The Spaniards believed that they were serving God and their king when they subjugated the Indian empire. This is mentioned repeatedly in the letters that Cortes sent to the king of Spain. He implored the Aztecs to become servants of His Majesty, the King of Castille, to change their religious ways, and to accept Christianity.

Many of those who came to Mexico to convert the Indians to Christianity believed that by saving them from

The Spaniards undermined the authority of the Indian lords by appointing them as governors and government agents. The peasantry vilified them for collaborating with their enemy. Often, the peasants accused innocent leaders of wrongdoing to force them out of office. Many of them left their responsibilities under humiliating conditions.

The Agony of the Survivors

The *encomenderos* caused poverty and hunger to the native communities by demanding excessive amounts of tribute, treasure and personal services. They also inflicted unprecedented cruelties on the Indians themselves and dehumanized their life style beyond reason. These cruelties, compounded by the frequent plagues and the constant threat of punishment decimated the Indian population of Mexico to about one third of the original size.

Zorita also wrote that the Spanish administrative management and labor system contributed to the extermination of the Indians, the dismantling of their cities, and the destruction of their crops and farmlands. The construction of large masonry buildings, roads and water systems reduced the strength of the workers already weakened by disease and malnutrition. The Spaniards forced many of the Indian workers to work in places far away from their homes and families.

The local Spanish officials and the encomenderos generally circumvented or ignored the government edicts that attempted to reduce the worst abuses. When the Crown stipulated that no Indians could be forced to work in the mines, the Spaniards in Mexico simply dispatched them to "sweep out" the shafts.

The Burden of a Defeated People

The Spanish officials assessed taxes directly to the Indians instead of demanding them from the community, as had been required previously. This system was new to the Indians and caused considerable disruption to their lives since each had to share a part of the full burden. No allowances were made for illness or other incapacity, or for the destruction of agricultural crops by natural calamities.

In the countryside, the Spaniards continued to use until 1555 the old Aztec's tributary system. In that year a new measure was placed into effect to collect taxes based on the colonial records kept by the Church. This system remained in effect for many during the colonial period. Periodically, the Spaniards conducted head counts to adjust the tax payments. Such counts were designed to redistribute the assessments more fairly, but they usually resulted in greater suffering for the Indians.

The judges sent to conduct the counts were transported, fed, housed, and pampered at the expense of the Indian communities. The payment of these expenses were especially difficult for people who could ill afford such costs. Because they expended none of their money, the judges relished such service and accordingly extended their stay. The Spanish tributary system caused extreme hardship, dislocated families, decimated whole towns, prompted many suicides, and impoverished the Indian race.

Zorita's arguments should be used carefully because often he portrait the Indian life in romantic terms. His Brief Relation of the Lords of New Spain has been often criticized for been too negative in the treatment of the Spanish authorities. Critics of Zorita believe that he overdrew the gap between Spanish colonial administrative theory and practice.

Nevertheless, Zorita was a Spanish jurist who was concerned with the plight of the Indians. He probably believed that the severity of the Spanish abuse could only be corrected by describing the Indians in their most favorable light. In this respect, the Spanish scholar was in a distinct minority in the Spanish community. He sacrificed some objectivity to gain positive results.

The Spanish Justification

The Spaniards believed that they were serving God and their king when they subjugated the Indian empire. This is mentioned repeatedly in the letters that Cortes sent to the king of Spain. He implored the Aztecs to become servants of His Majesty, the King of Castille, to change their religious ways, and to accept Christianity.

Many of those who came to Mexico to convert the Indians to Christianity believed that by saving them from

Figure 155   Funeral mask with turquoise, serpentine, and shell incrustations. (INAH).

Figure 156   Maya ceramic vessel. (INAH, Merida)

evil they would guarantee their own salvation. Spanish religious fanaticism could not permit thousands of victims being sacrificed every year, nor accept the cruel, idolatrous worship of the Indians. The Spaniards saw the violent practices of the Aztecs as uncivilized and vulgar; they never considered they own cruel and ruthless practices during the destruction of the Indian states.

The Spaniards were very frank about admitting that they came to the New World in search of gold and glory. They were for the most part very observant of life, customs, cultures, nature, and land that they found. When possible, they would compare it to something that was familiar to them. Otherwise, they described the action or event as best they could do. They seldom neglected to explain something just because they did not understand it.

The Spaniards' activities in central Mexico caused a clash of cultures that was very different from what took place in other regions of North America. In Mexico, the totally dissimilar cultures of the Indians and the Spanish set up strict caste differences that still exists today.

The Columbian Exchange

Many Spanish historians and chroniclers of the sixteenth century wrote that the population of Tenochtitlan on the eve of the Conquest was close to 200,000 people, making it the largest city in the Western Hemisphere. That population was reduced to about 40,000 people within few years after the Spanish victory.

S. F. Cook, and W. Borah, after making an analytical investigation of the precolonial records, estimated the Indian population of central Mexico to be about 25.3 million before the Conquest. One- third of the Indians, or 8.5 million, died during the subsequent three years of the Spanish administration. By 1605, the native population of Mexico had been reduced to one million people, perhaps the greatest catastrophic destruction of human life in the history of the world (Sanchez-Albornoz 41).

Fray Bartolome Las Casas, who studied the Spanish genocide, attributed the population losses to the cruelty, systematic killing and excessive overwork forced by the Spaniards. He writes: "There were so many cruelties, killings and destruction of human life; there was so much looting, violence and tyranny, that everything that we have narrated pale in comparison with what the Spaniards did" (Las Casas 100).

Contemporary writers believed that epidemics caused the major population decline. According to them, these epidemics occurred at regular times. Disease is now recognized at being the prime cause for the destruction of Tenochtitlan and for the reduction of the Indian population. Near half the population of that great city died of an outbreak of smallpox.

Historian Alfred W. Crosby, in discussing the first smallpox epidemics, observes that the isolation of the New World had weakened the Indians' resistance to disease. As a result, the smallpox germs brought by the Europeans decimated the native populations and created serious demographic imbalances.

Other Factors to be Considered

Other factors that had been mentioned to explain the Indian population losses are military encounters and deliberate acts of murder by Spanish soldiers. The wanton assassinations and the systematic terrorizing of the people made up for the military disadvantage of the Spaniards.

Las Casas writes the Europeans used those tactics to ensure success in their settlement efforts. Ill-treatment, suicides, drops in fertility rates, rebellions, and starvation also contributed to the decline of the Indian population.

But if the Cook and Borah estimates are correct, could these factors together explain the loss of 24.3 million lives in less than a century? Since there are no statistical records of this period that can be used to explain the population imbalances all conjectures must be studied carefully.

In view of the type of weapons used, the difficulty of mountain warfare, and the number of military forces involved, war can be discounted as a major reason for the decline of the Indian societies. While epidemics were a major cause of destruction of human life at the beginning, natural adaptability during subsequent generations probably reduced the original impact of contagious diseases.

Other factors that had been previously mentioned also contributed to the destruction of the Indians, but there is no factual evidence to categorize their specific impact. The fact remains that while there were enormous population losses in Mexico after the Spanish invasion, there is no acceptable historical evidence to explain the problem of population decline in that country (Sanchez-Albornoz).

Changes in Economic Life

European brought a wealth of domestic animals that changed the social and economic life of the Indians. The introduction of useful plants, such as wheat, barley, oats, and rye, sugar cane and coffee from Europe and Africa changed Indian agriculture. On the other hand, such products as maize, potatoes, beans and manioc also changed the European agrarian system (Crosby 170-172).

Farm animals were first exported across the ocean from one hemisphere to another without considering the damaging effects to the ecology. The results of this exchange devastated some natural biological systems, while in others it improved the productive capacity of the land.

Since initially Europe received a limited amount of agricultural products from the Western Hemisphere, the exchange caused less harm to that continent than to America. During the first century and a half after the discovery little in the way of agricultural goods was sent to Europe. Even the quantity of West Indian sugar sent to the Europeans was small; the use of sugar itself was very limited because of the cost.

Centuries passed before the usefulness of western products such as the potato were discovered. Many other products that later became known as "colonial luxuries" were not known. Not until the seventeenth century did the life style of the Europeans favored the use of products from the Western Hemisphere.

Results of the Columbian Exchange

Crosby describes the Columbian Exchange with a pessimistic note: "No one can remember what the pre-Columbian flora was like. . . the flora and fauna of the

New World have been reduced and specialized by man. The Columbian Exchange, has left us with not a richer but more impoverished genetic pool" (Crosby 219).

What really affected Europe was the introduction of precious metals from America. There are no accurate records about the amount of gold and silver extracted from the Western Hemisphere, but the quantities were considerably. In 1548 the Spaniards discovered new silver mines in Zacatecas and Guanajuato. With those of Potosi in South America, the new found wealth affected considerably the stability of the European financial markets. The use of mercury to extract silver produced so much of it that the metal lost most of its value. The depreciation caused the financial ruin of many European merchants.

Richard Humble writes that by 1650 an awesome 1181 tons of gold and 16,000 tons of silver had been taken to Spain. This great quantity of bullion unsettled the European markets. It created inflation and food shortages. Prices fixed in terms of certain weights of gold and silver advanced rapidly, for to increase the total supply of money results in large scale inflation.

The constant supply of precious metals increased the prices of essential commodities. This problem had a depressing effect on the incomes derived from interest and rent. The effects of the fall in the value of money and the general advance in the price of commodities were felt in all directions and that state of affairs continued in Europe for almost a century.

Resurgence of the National Consciousness

Within a hundred years after the invasion of Mexico, there was not a region in Mesoamerica that had not been influenced by the Spaniards. In most of the cases, the contacts between Indian and European were not productive. The Spaniards established a master-vassal relationship that permeated throughout the colonial society and remained unchanged until the triumph of the Mexican independence movement.

During the succeeding colonial administrations, the descendants of the proud Indian race occupied the bottom of the social and economic ladder. The Spanish colonists transferred their feudalistic land practices to America. In Mexico, the oppression of the peasants became ordinary. He either tilled the soil as a sharecropper, worked in the mines and forests of a landowner, or starved to death. The decadent Spanish aristocracy of the eighteenth century attempted to revitalize itself with the sweat and tears of the Mexican peasant.

Mexican independence did not help much either. As Eric R. Wolf explains, "the oppression of the campesino communities continued without hindrance." Mexican native proprietors quickly took over the land holdings of the Spaniards and the Church and retained them in a semi-feudalistic system, just as their predecessors had previously done. The effects of that system still permeate throughout the peasant society of Mexico. The Indians are among the poorest groups in that country (Wolf and Hansen 228).

With the success of the Mexican Revolution in 1910, a national consciousness based on Indian values slowly developed in the nation. To be a mestizo was considered then as a racial improvement. The Mexican philosopher Jose Vasconcelos called the racial response a "cosmic race." *Mestizaje* became a national symbol and a political force. As Sanchez-Albordoz explains: "By rejecting the predominance of anyone particular racial group and asserting the mestizo nature of Latin-American peoples and their culture, the interplay of ethnic groups became a focal point in the historical process . . ." (Sanchez-Albordoz 2).

The Mexican Revolution intensified itself with these values, and soon after its success *indigenismo*, or Indianism, became part of the nationalistic consciousness and spirit of modern Mexico. The rebirth of Mexican nationalism has been centered primarily on the cultural traditions inherited from the Aztecs. While the present Nahuatl-speaking Mexicans are less than two percent of the population, and there are no more than one million descendants of the Nahua tribes, Mexican pride is based on their cultural heritage.

Dances, musical compositions, literary works, handicrafts, and many other expressions of Mexican arts and culture based on Aztec themes have proliferated in that country. As the late professor Fernando Horcasitas wrote: "The mass has been said in Nahuatl; the National Anthem has been translated and sung; a movie, Yanco, has been filmed in Nahuatl; and political speeches in commemoration of the death of Cuauhtemoc have been delivered in that language."

The study of their historical roots has provided the Mexican people with a sense of national in their Indian heritage. They have found that a common background unifies them with the Mesoamerican past. The hundreds of Nahua and Aztec descendants that live in the central valley of Mexico today view that past with increasing dignity and self-respect.

The same thing can be said of those who have migrated to the American Southwest, and who will become American citizens soon or later. To understand them, it is essential that we study their values, their traditions, and their ancient heritage. They are members of a proud race. They feel that it is important for them to share their rich cultural traditions with those who are contributing to the development of the American society.

In spite of the great gulf that separates pre-Columbian thought from the modern world, the culture and traditions that the Aztecs established five centuries ago shines down to our own day. Their message is still meaningful to those who will take the time to study their civilization and the essence of their way.

SELECTED BIBLIOGRAPHY

ACHENBACK, JOEL. "Debating Columbus in the New World." *The Washington Post National Weekly Edition*. The Washington Post, (October, 1991).

ACOSTA SAIGNES, MIGUEL. "Los pochteca." *Acta Antropológica*, Vol. 1, no. 1, (1945).

"Anales de Antropología e Historia, 1976-1977." *Instituto Nacional de Antropología e Historia*, Mexico, (1977).

ALVA IXTLILXOCHITL, FERNANDO DE. *Obras Históricas*. Universidad Nacional Autónoma de Mexico, Mexico, (1965).

ANTON, FERDINAND AND FREDERICK J. DOCKSTADER. *Pre-Columbian Art and Later Indian Tribal Arts*. Harry N. Abrams, Inc., New York, (n.d.).

BANDELIER, ADOLPH F. *On the Art of War and Mode of Welfare of the Ancient Mexicans*. Peabody Museum Tenth Annual Report, Vol. 2, Cambridge, (1877).

BARLOW, ROBERT H. *The Extent of the Empire of the Culhua-Mexica*. Ibero Americana Series, No. 28, University of Calif, (1949).

BARLOW, ROBERT. "La Fundación de la Triple Alianza (1427-1433)."*Anales del Instituto National de Antropología e Historia*, UNAM, Mexico, Vol 3, (1947-48).

BARRERA-RUBIO, ALFREDO. "Patrón de Asentamiento en el Area de Uxmal, Yucatán, Mexico." *Memoria del Congreso Interno*, UNAM, (1979).

BAUDOT, GEORGES and TZVETAN TODOROV. *Relatos Aztecas de la Conquista. Editorial Grijalba, Mexico,* (1990).

BEALS, RALPH L. and HARRY HOIJER. *Anthropology*. MacMillan Co., New York, (1971).

BERNAL, IGNACIO. *Mexico Before Cortez*. Anchor Books, New York, (1975).

BENSUSAN, SUSAN. *Latin American Cooking*. Galahad Books, Great Britain, (1974).

BEUTELSPACHER, CARLOS R. *Las Mariposas entre los Antiguos Mexicanos*. Fondo de Cultura Económica, Mexico, (1988).

BIERHORST, JOHN. *The Mythology of Mexico and Central America*. William Morrow and Co., Inc., New York, (1989).

BORAH, WOODROW, and S.F. COOK. *The Aboriginal Population of Central Mexico on the Eve of the Spanish Conquest*. University of California, Berkeley, (1963).

BOTURINI BENADUCI, LORENZO. *Idea de una Nueva Historia General de la América Septentrional*. Editorial Porrúa, Mexico, (1986).

BOURNE, EDWARD G. *Spain in America 1450-1580*. Barnes and Noble, New York, (1904).

BRAUDEL, FERNAND. *The Structures of Everyday Life, Vol. 1*. Harper and Row, Publishers, New York, (1979).

BRAY, WARWICK. *Everyday Life of the Aztecs*. B. T. Bats, Ltd., Great Britain, (1968).

BRUNDAGE, BURR CARTWRIGHT. A *Rain of Darts: The Mexica Aztecs*. University of Texas Press, Austin, (1972).

BRUUM, GEOFFREY and H.S. COMMAGER. *Europe and América Since 1492*. Houghton Mifflin Co., New York, (1954).

CABRAL del HOYO, ROBERTO. A *Thumbnail History of Mexico*. The Comite Norteamericano Pro-Mexico, Mexico, (1964).

CAMUSSO, LORENZO. *The Voyages of Columbus*. Dorset Press, New York, (1991).

CANBY, THOMAS. "Search for the First Americans." *National Geographic*, Vol 156, no. 3, (1979).

CARRASCO, DAVID. *Religión of Mesoamérica*. Harper and Row, San Francisco, (1990).

CARLSON, J.B. "Lodestone Compass: Chinese or Olmec Primacy." *Science*, Vol. 189, (1975).

CASO, ALFONSO. *El Pueblo del Sol*. Fondo de Cultura Económica, Mexico, (1985).

CASO, ALFONSO. "La Correlación de los Años Azteca y Cristiano" *Revista Mexicana de Estudios Antropológicos*, Vol.3, no.1., Mexico, (1939).

CASO, ALFONSO. "Instituciones Indígenas Precortesianas: Métodos y Resultados de la Política Indigenista de Mexico." *Memorias del Instituto National Indigenista*, Vol. 4, Mexico, (1954).

CHASE, STUART. *Mexico: A Study of Two Americas*. The Macmillan Co., New York, (1935).

CHAVERO, D. ALFREDO. *Mexico A Través de los Siglos*. Editorial Cumbre, Mexico, (1980).

CHEVALIER, FRANCOIS. *Land and Society in Colonial Mexico: The Great Hacienda*. University of California Press, Los Angeles, (1963).

CLAVIJERO, FRANCISCO J. *Historia Antigua de Mexico*, Editorial Porrua, Mexico, (1987).

CLENDINNEN, INGA. *Aztecs*. Cambridge University Press, Cambridge, (1991).

COE, MICHAEL, et.al. *Atlas of Ancient America*. Facts on File, New York, (1988).

COLON CRISTOBAL. *Diario. Relaciones de Viajes*. Editorial Sarpe, Madrid, (1965).

CORTES, HERNAN. *Cartas de Relación*. Editorial Porrúa, Mexico, (1985).

CROSBY, ALFRED W. JR. *The Columbian Exchange: Biological and Cultural Consequences of 1492*. Greenwood Press, Conn.,(1972).

DAVIES, NIGEL. *The Aztec Empire*. University of Oklahoma Press, Norman, (1987).

DIAZ DEL CASTILLO, BERNAL. *Historia de la Conquista de Nueva España*. Editorial Porrúa, Mexico, (1974).

DIAZ INFANTE, FERNANDO. *La Educación de los Aztecas*. Panorama Editorial, Mexico, (1985).

DOR-NER, ZVI. *Columbus and the Age of Discovery*. William Morrow and Co., New York, (1991).

DUFFY, JAMES. *Portugal in Africa*. Penguin Books, Baltimore, (1962).

DURAN DIEGO, FRAY. *Historia de las Indias de Nueva España*. Editorial Porrúa, Mexico, (1984).

FAGAN, BRIAN. *The Adventure of Archaeology*. National Geographic Society, Washington, (1976).

FELL, BARRY. *America B.C.* The New York Times Book Co., New York, (1977).

GENDROP, PAUL. *Compendio de Arte Prehispánico*. Editorial Trillas, Mexico, (1987).

GILLMOR, FRANCES. *Flute of the Smoking Mirror*. University of New Mexico Press, (1949).

GREENLEAF, RICHARD E. and MICHAEL C. MEYER. *Research in Mexican History*. University of Nebraska Press, Lincoln, (1973).

HANKE, LEWIS. *The Spanish Struggle for Justice in the Conquest of America*. Little, Brown & Co., Boston, (1965).

HART, HENRY H. *Marco Polo*. University of Oklahoma Press, Norman, (1967).

HASSIG, ROSS. *Aztec Warfare*. University of Oklahoma Press, Norman, (1988).

HERRING, HUBERT. A *History of Latin America*. Alfred A. Knopf, New York, (1968).

HIGHWATER, JAMAKE. *Arts of the Indian Americas*. Harper & Row, New York, (1983).

JIMENEZ MORENO, WIGBERTO. "Tula y los Toltecas Según las Fuentes Históricas." *Revista Mexicana de Estudios Antropológicos*, Vol 5, Mexico, (1941).

JORDAN, BARBRA D. "Mesoamérica vista a través de la etnografía/etnología." *XIX Mesa Redonda de la Sociedad Mexicana de Antropología*, UNAM, Mexico, (1990).

JORDAN, TERRY and LESER ROWNTREE. *The Human Mosaic*. Canfield Press, San Francisco, (1976).

JUDGE, JOSEPH. "Our Search for the True Columbus Landfall." *National Geographic*, Vol. 170, no. 5, Washington, (1976).

KAMEN, HENRY. *Spanish Inquisition*. New Amererican Library, New York, (1965).

KANDELL, JONATHAN. *La Capital*. Henry Holt and Co., New York, (1988).

KATZ, FRIEDRICK. "Situación Social y Económica de los Aztecas durante los siglos XV y XVI." *Instituto de Investigaciones Históricas*, UNAM, Mexico, (1966).

KEEN, BENJAMIN. *La Imagen Azteca*. Fondo de Cultura Económica, Mexico, (1984).

KIRKPATRICK, F.A. *The Spanish Conquistadores*. The World Publishing Co., Cleveland. (1946).

KRICKEBERG, WALTER. *Las Antiguas Culturas Mexicanas*. Fondo de Cultura Económica, Mexico, (1961).

LA FAY, HOWARD and DAVID A. HARVEY. "The Maya, Children of Time." *National Geographic*, Vol. 148, no. 6, Washington, (1975).

LANDA, DIEGO DE, FRAY. *Relación de las Cosas de Yucatán*. Editorial Porrúa, S. A., Mexico, (1986).

LAS CASAS, BARTOLOME DE. *Brevísima Relación de la Destrucción de las Indias*. Ediciones Cátedra, Spain, (1984).

LEON-PORTILLA, MIGUEL. *Los Antiguos Mexicanos*. Fondo de Cultura Económica, Mexico, (1961).

LEON-PORTILLA, MIGUEL. *Aztec Thought and Culture: The Ancient Nahualt Mind*. University of Oklahoma Press, Norman,(1963).

LOPEZ DE GOMARA, FRANCISCO. *Historia de la Conquista de México*. Editorial Porrúa, S.A. Mexico, (1988).

MANRIQUE CASTANEDA, LEONARDO. *El Eclipse en el Mundo Prehispánico*. Instituto Nacional de Antropología e Historia, Mexico, (1991).

MAQUIAVELLI, NICCOLO. *The Prince*. New American Library, (1962).

MARTI, SAMUEL. *Music Before Columbus*. Ediciones Euroamericanas, Mexico, (1978).

MCDOWELL, BART, et. al. "The Aztecs." *National Geographic*, Vol. 158, no. 6, Washington, (1980).

MARTINEZ, JOSE L. *Nezahualcoyotl, Vida y Obra*. Fondo de Cultura Económica, Mexico. (1972).

MOCTEZUMA, EDUARDO M. *The Great Temple of the Aztecs*. Thomas and Hudson, London, (1988).

MOLINS-FABREGA, N. "El Códice Mendocino y la economía de Tenochtitlán." *Revista Mexicana de Estudios Antropológicos*, (1955).

MORENO CORRAL, MARCO A. *Historia de la Astronomía en Mexico*. Fondo de Cultura Económica, Mexico, (1986).

MORISON, SAMUEL E. *Admiral of the Ocean Sea*. Little, Brown and Company, Boston, 1942

MORLEY, SYLVANUS G. "Yucatán, Home of the Gifted Maya." *National Geographic*, Vol. 70, no. 5, Washington, (1936).

MOTOLINIA TORIBIO, FRAY. *Historia de los Indios de la Nueva España*. Editorial Porrúa, Mexico, (1984).

MUNOZ CAMARGO, DIEGO. *Historia de Tlaxcala*. Editorial Innovación, Mexico, (1978).

MURPHY, ROBERT F. "Cultural Change." *Biennial Review of Anthropology*, Stanford University Press, (1967).

MUSER, CURT. *Facts and Artifacts of Ancient Middle America*. E.P. Dutton, New York, (1978).

NICHOLSON, H.B. "The Mesoamerican Pictorial Manuscripts: Research, Past and Present." *Proceedings of the 34th International Congress of Americanists*. Vienna, (1962).

ONDERDONK, FRANK S. *A Glimpse at Mexico*. Board of Missions Church, Nashville, (1930).

PARRY, J.H. *The Establishment of the European Hegemony: 1415-1715*. Harper & Row, New York, (1966).

PETERSON, FREDRICK A. *Ancient Mexico*. G.P. Putnam's Sons, New York, (1961).

PIHO, VIRVE. "Reconstrucción histórica del albarradón antiguo de los indios." *III Congreso Interno Mexico Antiguo*, Vol 41. Instituto Nacional de Antropología e Historia, Mexico, (1991).

PIÑA CHAN, ROMAN. *Quetzalcoatl Serpiente Emplumada*. Fondo de Cultura Económica, Mexico, (1977).

PIÑA CHAN, BARBA D., et.al. *III Congreso Interno Mexico Antiguo*. Instituto Nacional de Antropología e Historia, Mexico, 1991)

PORTER, MURIEL. *The Aztec, Maya and their Predecessors*. Academic Press, (1981).

PRESCOTT, WILLIAM H. *History of the Conquest of Mexico, Vol.1*, David McKay, Publisher, Philadelphia, (1891).

RADIN, PAUL. *The Sources and Authenticity of the History of the Ancient Mexicans*. University of California, (1920).

RIBEIRO, DARCY. *The Americas and Civilization*. E.P. Dutton & Co., Inc., New York, (1972).

RICE, DON S. "The New Archaeology." *The Wilson Quarterly*, Vol. 9, no. 2, Washington, (1985).

RILEY, JAMES. "Conditions for Discovery." *The World and I*, Vol. 6, no. 12, (1991).

ROBERTSON, DONALD. "Research in the Colonial Period." *Research in Mexican History*. University of Nebraska Press, (1973).

ROJAS, JOSE LUIS DE. *Mexico Tenochtitlán*. Fondo de Cultura Económica, Mexico, (1988).

ROJAS RABIELA, TERESA and WILLIAM SANDERS. *Historia de la agricultura- Época prehispánica siglo XVI*. Instituto Nacional de Antropología e Historia, Mexico, (1985).

ROYAL, ROBERT. "Columbus as a Dead White European Male." *The World and I*, Vol. 6, no. 12, (1991).

SABLOFF, JEREMY A. *The New Archaeology and the Ancient Maya*. Scientific American Library, New York, (1990).

SAHAGUN, BERNARDINO DE. *Historia General de las Cosas de Nueva España.*Editorial Porrúa, Mexico, (1975).

SANCHEZ-ALBORNOZ, CLAUDIO. "España y el Islam." *Revista de Occidente*, Vol. 70, no. 7, (1929).

SANCHEZ-ALBORNOZ, NICOLAS. *The Population of Latin America* University of California Press, Berkeley, (1974).

SCHELE, LINDA and DAVID FREIDEL. A *Forest of Kings*. William Morrow and Co., Inc., New York, (1990).

SIMPSON, LESLEY B. *Many Mexicos*. University of California Press, (1964).

SOLIS, ANTONIO DE. *Historia de la Conquista de Mexico*. Editorial Porrúa, Mexico, (1985).

SOUSTELLE, JACQUES. *El Universo de Los Aztecas*. Fondo de Cultura Económica, Mexico, (1986).

SOUSTELLE, JACQUES. *The Daily Life of the Aztecs on the Eve of the Spanish Conquest*. The Macmillian Company. New York, (1962).

STUART, GENE S. *The Mightly Aztecs*. National Geographic Society, Washington, (1981).

TITIEV, Mischa. *Cultural Antropology*. Holt, Rinehart and Winston, Nerw York, (1949)

THOMAS, HUGH. A *History of the World*. Harper Colophon Books, (1982).

TOYNBEE, ARNOLD J. A *Study of History*. Oxford University Press New York, (1947).

VAILLANT, GEORGE C. *La Civilización Azteca*. Fondo de Cultura Económica, Mexico. (1944).

VAN ZANTWIJK, RUDOLPH. *The Aztec Arrangement*. University of Oklahoma Press, Norman, (1985).

VEGA, FRANCISCO. *Los Aztecas*. Multipub, Barcelona, (1983).

VON HAGEN, VICTOR M. *Aztec: Man and Tribe*. New American Library, New York, (1958).

WILKERSON, S. JEFFREY. "Following Cortés: Path to Conquest." *National Geographic*, Vol. 162, No. 10, Washington, (1984).

WINN, PETER. "A Forest of Kings - A Review." *History Book Review*, (1990).

WOLF, ERIC R. and E. C. HANSEN. *The Human Condition in Latin America*. Oxford University Press, (1972).

WOOD, PETER. *The Spanish Main*. Time-Life Books, New York, (1979).

ZAPATA, ALONZO, GUALBERTO. *Guía de Chichen Itza*. Mexico, (1989).

ZORITA, ALONSO DE. *Life and Labor in Ancient Mexico: The Brief and Summary Relation of the Lords of New Spain*. Rutgers University Press, New Jersey, (1963).

GENERAL INDEX

AGE OF EXPLORATIONS

Generally, 12

Erickson, pre-Columbian exploration of North America by, 12
Eric the Red, pre-columbian North America travels by, 12
Labrador, pre-Columbian visits of Vikings to, 12
Newfoundland, pre-Columbian visits of Vikings to, 12
Northeastern U.S., pre-Columbian visit of Vikings to, 12
Nova Scotia, pre-Columbian visit by Vikings to, 12
Royal Society of Copenhagen, report of early American travels by, 12
Vikings, pre-Columbian travels to America by, 12

AGONY OF THE SURVIVORS IN FORMER AZTEC EMPIRE

Generally, 353

Cruel Spanish practices, decimation of Indian population by, 353
Encomenderous, demanding of excessive tribute (taxes) under system, 353
Forced labor, use of by Spaniards, 353
Mines, forced labor in, 353
Spanish management system, damage to Indians caused by, 353

AGRICULTURE PROBLEMS IN THE AZTEC WORLD

Generally, 262, 262

Beasts of burden, absence of in Aztec farming, 261
Canal irrigation, use to increase crop production, 262
Crop rotation techniques, use by Aztec farmers, 262
Digging sticks, use in cultivation of crops, 262
Dikes, protection of crops by, 262
Droughts, effect on crop yields, 262
Dry season, period covered by, 262
Elevation of farmlands, 262
Fertilizers, use by Aztec farmers, 262
Floods, damage to crops caused by, 262
Frost, damage to crops caused by, 261
Granaries, use by Aztecs to store grains, 262
Hoes, use in crop cultivation, 262
Intercropping techniques used by the Aztecs, 262
Irrigation, use by Aztec farmers, 262
Land drainage techniques used by Aztec farmers, 262
Maize (corn), substandard nature of co crops, 261
Nursery botanical gardens, use by Atecs, 262
Plow, effect of absence in Aztec farming, 262
Poor soil, effect on crop yields, 261

AGRICULTURE PROBLEMS IN THE AZTEC WORLD (Cont'd)

ARCHITECTURE AND URBANIZATION

Generally, 297, 299

Arsenals, use of buildings for, 299
Beam construction, use by Aztecs, 299
Bird sanctuary at palace of Montezuma, 299
Botanical garden at palace of Montezuma, 299
Cement, use by Aztecs in building construction, 297, 299
Diverse architecture designs in Aztec capitol, 297
Fountains at palace of Montezuma, 299
Grain storage, use of buildings for, 299
Libraries, presence of in palace of Montezuma, 299
Living quarters, use of buildings for, 299
Major Aztec buildings, destruction of by Spaniards, 297
Museums, presence of in palace of Montezuma, 299
Origin of Aztec architecture, 297
Patio construction by Aztecs, 299
Rafter construction, use by Aztecs, 299
Schoolhouse, use of buildings for, 299
Types of wood used in Aztec construction, 299
Warehouse, use of buildings for, 299
Whitewashing of buildings by Aztecs, 297, 299
Windowless construction, use by Aztecs, 299
Zoological garden in palace of Montezuma, 299

ARCHIVO de la NACION

Generally, 336, 338

As official respositiry of Mexican Historical Documents, 336
Data contained in the Archivo, 336
Location of Archivo, 336, 338
National Library of Mexico, data contained in, 338
Tulane University a data resource on Aztec history, 338
Unbounded volumes, number in Archivo, 336
University of Texas as data resource for Aztec history, 338

GENERAL INDEX

ARTISTIC EXPRESSIONS

Generally, 281, 283

Architectural decorations, use by Aztec artists, 281
Arrogance, expression by Aztec artists, 281
Artists, status in Aztec society, 283
Cacaxtla ruins, art treasurers contained in, 283
Cement, use in building decorations, 283
Hard-rock technique, use by Aztec artists, 281
Knife decoration by Aztec artists, 282
Mask decoration by Aztec artists, 282
Mesoamerica traditions, influence on Aztecs by, 282
National Museum of Anthropology, art treasury contained in, 282
Poems written by artists, contents of, 282
Shield decoration by Aztec artists, 282

ASTRONOMICAL OBSERVATIONS BY MESOAMERICANS

Generally, 301, 303, 304

Aristotelian logic, freedom of Indians from, 301
Christian beliefs, freedom of Indians from, 301
Classical cosmology knowledge, Indian's lack of knowledge about, 301
Compass, early use of by Mesoamericans, 301
Eclipse, religious significance of, 303
El Caracol, scientific observations made by, 303
El Castillo pyramid, astronomical importance of, 301, 303
Great Temple of Tenochtitlan, significance of 17-degree deviation, 301
Magnetic force, knowledge about by Mesoamericans, 301
Moon, measurement of location by Aztecs, 303
Pyramid El Castillo, astronomical significance of, 301
Pyramid stairways, astronomical significance of, 303
Scientific investigations, different type developed by Indians, 301
Sun, charting of movements by Aztecs, 301, 303
Sunset, use of hand to determine, 303

AZTEC CIVIL AND CRIMINAL LAWS

Generally, 185

Adultery, death penalty imposed for, 185
Aristocratic class, harsher punishment meted out to, 185
Burning of hair of adulterer, 185
Child crimes, death punishment imposed for, 185
Gender-cross dressing, severe punishment for, 185
Perjury, severe punishment for, 185
Private execution afforded aristocratic class, 185
Stoning to death, use as punishment tool, 185
Strangulation, death by means of, 185
Tar/feather, use as punishment tool, 185

AZTEC CRIMINAL JUSTICE SYSTEM

Generally, 190, 191, 193

Adulterers, execution of by burning alive, 191
Appellate jurisdiction in Aztec judicial system, 193
Amputation of limbs as form of Aztec punishment, 19
Aztec judicial system, structure of, 191, 193
Banishment as a form of Aztec punishment, 191
Cashless society, operation of, 190
Death-row holding cells for condemned prisoners, 190
Enslavement as a form of punishment, 190
Humanitarian treatment, absence of in Aztec system, 190
Judges, qualification of, 191
Method of selection of Aztec judges, 191, 193
Mutilation as form of Aztec punishment, 191
Nature of punishment under Aztec system, 190, 191
Property destruction as form of Aztec punishment, 191
Rehabilitation services, absence of in Aztec system, 190
Restitution, use in Aztec judicial system, 191
Sadistic execution of prisoners, 190, 191
Seating of law officers in Aztec court proceedings, 193
Severe punishment under Aztec system, 190, 191
Shearing of hair as form of punishment under Aztec system, 191
Solitary confinement of death-row prisoners, 190
Stoning executions, use of by Aztecs, 191
Strangulation execution, use of by Aztecs, 191
Swift justice under Aztec judicial system, 190
Trial courts, procedures before, 191

AZTEC ECONOMIC SYSTEM

Generally, 231, 232

Agriculture, importance in Aztec society, 231
Commercial operations, areas controlled by Aztecs, 231
Commercial routes, protection of by Aztec army, 231
Foreign invasions by Aztec army, suppression of revolts by, 232
Tribute from conquered people, importance to Aztec economy, 231
Warfare, effect on Aztec economic system, 231, 232
Wealth, method of eating, 231

AZTEC EDUCATIONAL SYSTEM

Generally, 308, 310

Areas stressed in Aztec educational system, 308
Art, teaching of in Aztec schools, 310
Child's age, type of instruction determined by, 303, 310
Disobedient child, punishment meted to, 308, 310
Early childhood at home, 308
Girls, type of education received by, 308, 310
Lazy children, punishment meted to, 308, 310
Male children, mandatory marriage at age 15, 310
Parents, teaching of children by, 308
Philosophy, teaching of to children, 310
Priesthood education, 310
Sex education given to girls, 308
Subjects studied in Aztec educational system, 310
Warriors, training given to, 301

AZTEC HOMELAND

Generally, 63

Area-size of Aztec homeland, 63
Conservative classes, control exercised on Mexico, 63
Foreign capitalism, Mexico's fight against, 63
Location of Aztec homeland, 63
Mexico Indians, duration of stay there, 63
Present racial classifications of Mexico's residents, 63
Racial mixing in Mexico, extent of, 63

AZTEC WORLD

Generally, 346, 348

Adultery, death penalty imposed for, 348
Aristocrat criminal offenders, added punishment meted to, 348
Aztec rulers, divine character of, 348
Black magic, death penalty imposed for, 348
Communal practices carried on by the Aztecs, 348
Conformity behavior patterns demanded by Aztecs, 348
Crime, severe punishment for committing, 348
Foreign policy conducted by merchants, 348
Homosexuality, death penalty imposed for, 348
Human sacrifice, attempted survival based on, 349
Incest, death penalty imposed for, 348
Law code, existence in Aztec Empire, 348
Merchants, performance of state functions by, 348
Militaristic Aztec society, existence of, 348
Poor criminal offenders, lesser punishment meted to, 348
Religion, effect in Aztec Empire, 348
Revenge, wars based on, 348
Slave-killing, death penalty imposed for, 348
Special courts, existence of in Aztec Empire, 348
Spie work conducted by merchants, 348
Supernatural powers, Aztec rulers previewed as having, 348
Theft, death penalty imposed for, 348
Tribute (ta), system, extent of, 348
Wars, starting of by merchants, 348

AZTLANS (PLACE OF THE HERONS)

Generally, 112, 113

Aubin, location of Aztlan by, 113
Bancroft, location of Aztlan by, 113
Chavijero, location of Aztlan by, 113
de Acosta, location of Aztlan by, 113
de Bourbourgh, location of Aztlan by, 113
de Mendieta, location of Aztlan by, 113
Languistic similarities between Indian groups, 113
Moreno's opinion about the origin of the Aztecs, 112, 113
Mythical birthplace of Aztecs, Aztlan as, 113
Nahuati language, speaking of by Aztecs, 113
Ramirez, location of Aztlan by, 113
Tezozomoc, location of Aztlan by, 113
von Hunboldt, location of Aztlan by, 113

BARBARIAN INVASIONS

Generally, 126

Agricultural groups, invasion of Tula by, 126
Chichemec invasions, intensity of, 126

BASIC SOURCE IMPORTANCE

Generally, 325, 327

Aztec astronomical observations, description of, 325
Cambridge Symposium, discussion of condices in, 325
Myth of creation, discussion of by Fejervary-Mayer, 327
Nuttall, observations about Aztec history made by, 327
Philosophy information, Aztec documents containing, 325
Religious information, Condex Borbonicus containing, 325
Vatican Library, original document stored in, 325

BEGINNING OF AZTEC EMPIRE

Generally, 136

Dwellings, types of projects engaged in by Aztecs, 136
Hostile Indian states, threat posed to Aztecs by, 136
Incorporation of Tlatelolco into Aztec Empire, 136
Market places, erection of by Nahua group, 136
Mexico-Tenochtitlan, origin of name, 136
Nuhua, building of city by, 136
Poor agricultural land, selection of by Aztecs, 136
Swamps, selection of by Aztecs, 136
Temple building by Aztecs, types build, 136
Trading centers, development of by Tenochtitlns, 136
Undesirable territory, initial selection of by Aztecs, 136

GENERAL INDEX

BEGINNING PF THE END

Generally, 27, 29

Blankets, gifts to Spaniards by Aztecs, 27
Calvery charge, Aztecs impressed by, 27
Cannon firing, Aztecs impressed by, 27
Food supplies, furnishing of by Aztecs to Spaniards, 27
Garment gifts to Spaniards by Aztecs, 27
Gold gift, weight of, 27
Gold necklace, gift of by Aztecs to Spaniards, 27
Huts, building by Aztecs for Spanish invaders, 27
Indian officials, greeting of Cortes by, 27, 29
Montezuma's illness, curtailment of greeting plans by, 29
Garment gifts by Aztecs to Spaniards, 27
Pictographic sketches of Spaniards, sending of Aztec ruler, 27
Silver gift, weight of, 27
Spanish arrival, Aztec's reaction to, 27, 29
Spanish military strength, display of, 27
Superstitious beliefs of Montezuma, impairming of judgement by, 27
Turquoise mask gifts, 27
Unarmed solders, number greeting Cortes, 27
Unapposed landing of Cortes, 27

BOTURINI'S DESCRIPTION OF JOURNEY

Generally, 118-120

Alcoholic beverages, manufacture of by Aztecs, 120
Atlicalaquia, moving of Aztecs to, 118
Aztec warriors, gaining of freedom by fighting, 120
Barbarians, destruction of city by, 118
Capture of Aztecs, slave status resulting from, 120
Chapultepec, settlement of Aztecs in, 120
Coatepec, semi-permanent established in, 118
Huitzilopochtli, killing of sister by, 118
Human sacrifices, continued practice of, 120
Mayhem, Aztecs' practice of, 120
Prisoners of war, use in sacrifice rites, 120
Salt, availability of to Aztecs, 120

GENERAL INDEX

CENTER OF CULTURE IN AZTEC EMPIRE

Generally, 139, 141

Academy of Music, existence of in Aztec society, 139
Artistic performances, prior approval needed from Academy of Music, 138
Art galleries, existence of in King's palace, 141
Art treasures, destruction of by Spaniards, 141
Bathing facilities, erection of by Aztec king, 141
Chronicles of Aztec kings, burning of by Spaniards, 141
Conference rooms, existence of in king's palace, 141
Financial reports, burning of by Spaniards, 141
Golden throne, ruling of Aztecs king from, 141
Indian education, expansion of by Academy of Music, 139, 141
Irrigation waterways, building of by Aztecs, 141
King's garden, collection of plants in, 141
Library literature, destruction of by Spaniards, 141
Military compaign data, destruction of by Spaniards, 141
Museums, existance of in king's palace, 141
Nahuatl language purity, controlling of by Academy of Music, 139
Nezahualcoyotl (poet-king), development of Aztec culture by, 139
Nezahualcoyotl's palace, size of, 141
Patios, existence of in king's palace, 141
Royal Aztec Archives, burning of by Spaniards, 141
Supervision of teacher's work by Academy of Music, 141
Teacher qualifications, approval by Academy of Music, 141
Texcoco as interlectual center of Aztec Empire, 139½
Wives, number possessed by Aztec king, 141

CHANGES IN COMMON LAW PRACTICES

Generally, 183, 185

Bestiality, death penalty imposed for, 183
Black magic practices, death penalty imposed for, 183
Body-quartering executions by Aztecs, 183
Changes in Aztec Code, 183
Crime-victim's wife, pardon power of, 183
Executed criminal, confiscation of wealth belonging to, 183
Family of executed criminal, selling into slavery resulting from, 183
High treason, death penalty imposed for, 183
Highway crimes, death penalty imposed for, 183
Homesexuality, death penalty imposed for, 183
Impersonation of an official, death penalty imposed for, 183
Incest, death penalty imposed for, 183
Marketplace thief, death penalty imposed on, 183
Marriage between relatives, death penalty imposed for, 183
Merciless executions by Aztecs, 183

CHRONICLERS OF THE PAST

Generally, 319, 321, 322

CLASH OF CENTURIES

Generally, 342, 343

CLASSIC PERIOD

Generally, 94, 96

CLIMATIC CONDITIONS IN MEXICO

Generally, 75, 77

Altitude, importance of in Mexican weather patterns, 75
Erratic rainfall patterns, disadvantage of, 75
Frost in highlands, existence of, 75
Lakes, scarcity of in Mexico, 75
Mountain barriers, reduction of humidity by, 75
Rainfall shortage, human sacrifice used to remedy, 75, 77
Rivers, scarcity of in Mexico, 75
Tropical Conditions, existance of in Mexico, 75

CODICES

Generally, 322, 324, 325

Aztec academies, discovery of Condices in, 324
Calendrical matter, Condex containing, 325
Codex Barbonicus, importance of, 325
Codex Bologna, importance of, 325
Codex Borgia, importance of, 325
Codices, discovery of by Spaniards, 324
Destruction of Indians, justification for, 324
Educational activity, Codex containing, 324
Hieroglyphic writing, use by Indians, 324
Historical information, methods for gathering, 324
Lost Tribes of Isreal, Indians as, 324
Survival of Codices from Spanish destruction, 324, 325
Tax/tributary system, description of, 324

GENERAL INDEX

COLONIZATION/EXPLORATION OF THE NEW AMERICA

Generally, 17-19

COLUMBUS/CHRISTOPHER

Generally, 13-15

GENERAL INDEX

COLUMBUS' NEW WORLD DISCOVERY

Generally, 15, 16

Accidential discovery of America by Columbus, 15
African slavery, extention into Western Hemisphere, 2, 15
Ancient societies, destruction of by Columbus, 15
Christianity expansion, Columbus' effort in achieving, 2
Cities, destruction of by Spaniards, 4
Civilization, Columbus' effort to bring to America, 2
Colonization of America by Columbus, 4
Columbus' diary, contents of, 4
Extermination of people by Spaniards, 4
Ecological disaster, America's discovery as causing, 2, 4
European civilization, enrichment of by discovery of
America, 2
Intention of Columbus' voyage, 2
Mass extermination of people, America's discovery resulting
in, 4
Mutiny, threat posed by, 15
Plunder of lands by Spaniards, 4
Riley, description of Columbus' voyage by, 2
Risk involved in voyage, 2, 4
Spanish aggrandizement as basis for voyage, 2

COMMERCIAL CONTEST BETWEEN EUROPEAN AND EASTERN COUNTRIES

Generally, 6

Art, presence in Palestine during Crusades, 6
Crusades, effect on discovery of America, 6
European/Middle-East trade, increase of knowledge based on,
6
Genoese merchants, trading with Palestine by, 6
Italian traders, expansion of trade to Eastern sites by, 6
Literature, presence during Crusades, 6
Luxury of Palestine, observation of by Crusade soldiers, 6
Medications/remedies, presence during Crusades, 6
Muslin luxury, observation of by Crusade soldiers, 6
Venetian merchants, trading with Palestine by, 6

COMPROMISE FOR SURVIVAL (AZTECS)

Generally, 138

Allied aggression of Aztecs,nature of, 138
Aztecs' first three (3) rulers, names of, 138
Aztec-Tlatelolco truce, establishment of, 138
Herring, description of Aztec unification by, 138
Mendoza, showing of drawings by, 138
Mercenaries, Aztecs serving as, 138
Skilled workers, types present in Tenochtitlan, 138
Spoils of war, sharing of by Aztecs, 138
Tepanec-Aztec alliance, destruction of Culhuacan by, 138
Texcoco, destruction, effect on Aztec aggression, 138
Tributes, payment by Aztecs to masters, 138
Trophies, awarding of for captured prisoners, 138

CONDEX MENDOZA

Generally, 330, 332

Condex Vaticanus-Rios, historical information contained in, 330
Educational system, description of, 330
National Library of Paris, location of Condex in, 332
Political system of Aztecs, description of, 330
Reference contained in Condex, 330
Religious life of Aztecs, description of, 330
Social life of Aztecs, description of, 330
Spanish Viceroy, documents prepared for, 330
System of laws, description of, 330

CORDOBA'S ENTERPRISE

Generally, 22, 24

Cape Catoche, visit to by Cordoba, 22
Daytime sailing practice of Cordoba, 24
Death of Cordoba, 24
Gold stories, effect of Cordoba's search, 24
Maize (corn) fields, stories about, 24
Mayan civilization, discovery of by Spaniards, 22
Mayans, confrontation with Cordova's invaders, 22
Native houses, stories about, 24
Number of men in Cordoba forces, 22
Number of ships in Cordoba's command, 22
Return to Cuba by Cordoba, 24
Rich Indian cities, stories about, 24
Silver, stories about, 24
Water shortage, difficulty caused to Cordoba, 24
Yucatan Peninsula, discovery of by Cordova, 22

CORTES, HERMAN

Generally, 25, 26

Background of Cortes, 25
Business ventures of Cortes, 25
Experience of Cortes' sailing crew, 25
Financial arrangement by Cortes, type made, 22
Mayor of Santiago, appointment of Cortes as, 25
Military conquest operations, participation in, 25
Political views of Cortes, 25
Rehabilitation of Cortes, 25
Sailing supplies, purchase of by Cortes, 25
Smuggling of Cortes aboard ship, reason for, 26

CORTES' LETTERS

Generally, 335, 336

Aztec culture, description in letters, 335
Contents of Cortes' letters, 335
Cromberger, publishing of letters by, 335
de Gomera, suppression of book written by, 336
de Mendieta, criticism of Spaniards by, 335
Location of Cortes' letters, 335
Motolinia, description of Indian life by, 336
Texcoco, destruction of, 335

CULTURAL BELIEFS IN AZTEC EMPIRE

Generally, 348, 349

After life, Aztec's belief in, 348
Cortes, destruction of Aztec Empire by, 349
Fatalistic element of Aztec beliefs, 349
Form of death, fate of soul determined by, 348
Four historical ages, Aztec's beliefs in, 348, 349
Historical ages, destruction of by cataclysm, 348, 349
Infectious diseases, effect of Aztec downfall, 349
Superior military weapons, effect of Aztec downfall, 349
Superstition, effect of Aztec downfall, 349

GENERAL INDEX

DROUGHTS AND WEATHER CHANGES

Generally, 116

Aztlan, nature of place, 116
Aztecs' reason for leaving Aztlan, speculation about, 116
Barbarian invasion, destruction of Toltec Empire by, 116
Davies, study weather conditions in former Aztlan by, 116
Toltec writing, evidence of adverse weather conditions contained in, 116
Weather changes, possible cause for Aztecs leaving Aztlan, 116

EARLY AMERICAN ORGANIZED SETTLEMENTS

Generally, 83

Archaeological artifacts, time of Asian migration based on, 83
Historical dates of settlements, 83
Hunting/food gathering, early practice of, 83
Meadowcroft artifacts, time of Asian migration based on, 83
Pittsburgh charcoal concentration, time of human existence based on, 83
Prehistoric Chilean communties, times when food gathering done in, 83
Water supply, organization of communities near, 83

EFFECT OF THE DISCOVERY OF AMERICA

Generally, 343, 345, 346

Christianity conversion, promotion of by Catholic church, 346
Churches, building of by Catholic movement, 346
Conquest of America, risks involved in, 345, 346
Conquistadors, low social status of, 345
Cultural clash, discovery of America causing, 343, 345
Dangers intailed in exploring work, 345, 346
Expansion of Spanish Empire, 345
Expedition financing, methods used to finance, 345
Expedition profits, splitting of with Spanish Crown, 345
Greed, coming to America as basis for, 345
High mortality rate among Spanish explorers, 345, 346
Hospitals, establishment of by Catholic church, 346
Missions established by Catholic church, 346
Motives of Spaniards for coming to America, 345

GENERAL INDEX

EMERGENCE OF THE AZTEC STATE

Generally, 156. 158

Absolute obedience, demand of by Aztecs, 156
Armed conflict, power gained by, 156
Classes in Aztec society, respective roles of, 158
Human sacrifice, practice of by Aztecs, 156
Materialist based Aztec world, observations about, 156
Mystic-militaristic system, establishment of, 156
Precarious existance, early Aztecs living in, 156
Religious beliefs, role in Aztec society, 156
Territorial gains, use of conflicts to gain, 156

END OF AZTEC EMPIRE

Generally, 43-49

Artillery pieces, number in Cortes' army, 43
Brigantines use, effect on outcome of battle, 43
Canoes, number in Cortes's army, 43
Capitulation of Aztec Empire to Cortes, date of, 43
Casualties of war, number of, 45
Capture of Cuauhtemoc, torture by Spaniards during capture, 46
Chalco people's assistance to Spaniards, nature of, 43
Cortes's army, inclusion of Indians in, 43
Cortes' illiness, death stench as basis for, 45
Cuauhtemoc, torture of by Spaniards, 46
Dead body stench, presence of, 45
European infectious diseases, defeat of Aztecs caused by, 43
Execution of Mexican Chieftains by Spaniards, 46
Fatalism, Aztecs' defeat based on, 45
Feet-burning by Spaniards, 46
Gold-seeking Spaniards, torture while seeking, 46
Gruesome Spanish torture, Aztecs's ability to withstand, 46
Horses, number in Cortes's army, 43
Inadequate leadership, Aztecs' defeat based on, 45
Mesoamerica culture, promotion of by Aztecs, 46
Mexico City, rebuilding of, 46
Modern weapons, Aztecs' defeat based on, 45
Outlying Aztec regions, conquest of by Spaniards, 46
Pestilence, dead-body stench as cause for, 45
Plentiful gold supply, Spaniard's mistaken beliefs about, 45, 46
Salt water drinking by Aztecs, necessity for, 45
Spanish superiority in numbers, effect in battle, 43
Squalid living conditions caused by war, 45, 46
Supernaturality of Spaniards, promotion of by infectious disease immunity, 45
Tenochtilan, destruction of by war, 46
Vessels, number in Cortes's forces, 45

GENERAL INDEX

END OF THE TOLTEC EMPIRE

Generally, 125

Crop failures, end of Toltec Empires based on, 125
Drought conditions, decline of Toltec Empires based on, 125
Factors contributing to end of Toltec Empire, 125
God of night/day, Tezcatlippca's role as, 125
Human sacrifices demanded by Tezcatlipoca, 125
Outside invasions, end of Toltec Empire based on, 125
Protector of sorcerers and witches, Tezcatlipoca's role as, 125
Quetzalcoatl, role played by in Toltec society, 125
Religious conflict, decline of Toltec Empire based on, 125
Time and duration of Toltec Empire, 125

ENGINEERING WONDERS OF THE AZTECS

Generally, 146

Aqueduct, supplying of fresh water by use of, 146
Artificial lagoon, creation of by Aztec engineers, 146
Flood-control dike, building of by Aztecs, 146
Floods, devastation effect of, 146
Lake Zumpango, elevated position of, 146
Natural outlet, absence for Lake Texcoco, 146
Salt level of lake, regulation of by aqueduct, 146

EUROPEAN VIEWS OF AMERICAN INDIANS

Generally, 85

Aristotelian theory of slave status, dispute concerning application, 85
Christianity conversion of Indians, efforts to accomplish, 85
Church dogma, origin of early Americans explained by, 85
"Dirty dogs," Spanish characterization of Indians as, 85
"Noble savages," Spanish characterization of Indians as, 85
Racist attitude toward Indians by Spaniards, 85

GENERAL INDEX

EUROPEAN VIEWS OF AZTEC CAPITAL

Generally, 148, 150

Aqueducs, observation of by Spaniards, 148
Canoes, provisions/merchandise carried by, 148
Castillo. comparison of Aztec capital with European cities, 148
Causeways, observation of by Spaniards, 148
Cortes' map of Aztec city, 150
Drawbridges, observation of by Spaniards, 148
Europeans, impression of Aztecs made by, 148, 150
Water supply, nature of, 148

EXPANSION OF THE AZTEC EMPIRE

Generally, 142, 144, 145

Administrative machinery, creation of, 144
Ahuitzol, extention of Aztec Empire by, 142
Axayacatl, expansion of Aztec rule under, 144
Court system, establishment of under Montezuma, 144
Cuauhtemoc ("fallen eagle") as last Aztec ruler, 144
Governors, selection of to rule provinces, 144
Hanging of Cuauhtemoc by Spaniards, 144
Lost military campaign, poisoning of military leader for causing, 142
Messenger service, establishment of, 144
Military academies, starting off by Montezuma, 144
Military garrisons, creation of, 144
Montezuma's armies, success of, 144
Montezuma's reign, character of, 144
Netzahualcoyotl, death of, 142
Looking directly at Montezuma, prohibitions against, 144
National Museum of Anthropology, location of basalt stone in, 142
Provinces, organization of Aztec Empire into, 142
Public administrators, forcing nobles to work as, 144
Religious leadership, establishment of by Montezuma, 144
Schools for nobility, selection of, 144
Tax collection procedures, establishment of, 144
Tizoc, expansion of Aztec Empire by, 142
Touching of Montezuma, prohibition against, 144
Weakness in Montezuma, decline of Aztec Empire bases on, 144

FANTASY IN THE WILDERNESS (ADVANCED AZTEC CONSTRUCTION WORKMANSHIP)

Generally, 56, 57

Advanced engineering techniques, use by Aztecs, 56
Advanced workmanship, presence in Aztec cities, 56
Anton, observation of Aztec art works by, 57
Beauty of Aztec cities, observation of by Spaniards, 56
Bridges, presence of in Aztec territory, 57
Canoes, use of by Aztecs, 56
Causeways, presence of in Aztec territory, 56, 57
del Castillo, observation of Aztec cities by, 57
Durer, observation of Aztec art work by, 57
European settlers, condescending attitude toward Aztecs, 57
Lake-cities, presence of in Aztec territory, 56
Lauvre Art Gallery, refusal to display Aztec art work in, 57
Tocqueville, condescending attitude by toward Aztecs, 57

FINAL OUTCOME RESULTING FROM WEST INDIES DISCOVERY

Generally, 19, 20

African slave trade, use of to cultivate crops, 20
Aztec Empire discovery, effect on Spanish colonial program, 20
Collapsing Spanish Empire, events changed by, 20
Enslavement of native by Spaniards, 19
European diseases, killing of Indians by, 20
Fevers, death to Spaniards caused by, 20
Gold, amounts discovered by Spaniards, 20
Gold supply in West Indies, insufficiency of, 19
Immunity to European diseases, lack of by Indians, 19, 20
Indian dress code, 19
Indian slaves, use of in mining operations, 19
Killing (wanton) of native by Spaniards, 19, 20
Modorra (drowsiness), death to Spaniards caused by, 20
Native of West Indies, stone age living by, 20
Reckless adventures of Spaniards, greed as basis for, 19, 20
Silver, discovery of by Spain Spaniards, 20
Slaughter of natives by Spaniards, number of slaughtered, 19, 20
Smallpox, eradication of Arawak tribe by, 20
Spanish richness increased by gold discovery, 20
Tobacco growing, effect on Spanish settlement programs, 20
Western Hemisphere, overwhelming of by Spaniards, 20

GENERAL INDEX

FIRST AMERICANS

Generally, 82, 83

Butchered animals, remains of, 83
Cheek bones, anthropologists' description of, 82
Facial features of first Americans, 82
Eye color of first Americans, 82
Hair texture of first Americans, 82
Land bridge, entry of first Americans over, 82
Nomadic tribesmen, southward migration by, 83
Paleo Indians, early arrival in America by, 82, 83
Skin color of people entering America, 82

FIRST SETTLEMENTS

Generally, 16, 17

Administrative abilities of Columbus, defects in, 16, 17
Arrest of Columbus, reason for, 17
de Leon, founding of Puerto Rico by, 17
de Esquivel, conquest of Jamica by, 17
Indigenous Indians, enslavement of by Spaniards, 17
Replacement of Columbus as Colonial Governor, 17
Royal trouble shooter, investigation of Columbus by, 17
Slave mines, existence of, 17
Velasquez, organization of first Cuban settlement by, 17
West Indies Governor, Columbus' son appointed as, 17

FIRST SPANISH EXPEDITION

Generally, 21, 22

Bartering in goods by natives, 22
Beans, presence on Guanaja Island, 22
Culture of Indians, observation of by Columbus, 22
Industry of Indians, observation of by Columbus, 22
Indian interpreters, retention of by Columbus, 22
Indian merchants, observation of by Columbus, 22
Mayan providence, native Indians coming from, 22
Mayan Yucatan civilization, missing of by Columbus, 22
Native trading vessels, travel route taken by, 22
Pre-Cortes incursion into Mexico by Spaniards, 22
Wealth of Indians, observation of by Columbus, 22

FOOD "FIT FOR A KING" (DIETARY PRACTICES OF THE AZTECS)

Generally, 269, 271

Aquatic life, eating of by Aztecs, 269
Avocados, consumption of by Aztecs, 269
Aztec banquet, type of dishes served at, 271
Aztec cooking, Mexican cooking based on, 269, 271
Chocolate drinks, content of, 271
Class-based eating practices, 271
Cooking oil, absence in Aztec cooking, 271
Crabs, eating of by Aztecs, 269
Duck meat, consumption of, 269
Exotic vegetables, consumption of by Aztecs, 269
Fish/fowl, consumption by Aztecs, 269
Frogs, eating of by Aztecs, 269
Hairless dogs, as main meat supply, 269
Honey, use in chocolate drinks, 271
Insects, eating of by Aztecs, 269
Methods of Aztec cooking, 269, 271
Mid-morning meal, foods eaten at, 271
Squashes, consumption by Aztecs, 269
Shrimp, eating of by Aztecs, 269
Snails, eating of by Aztecs, 269
Tadpoles, eating of by Aztecs, 269
Tamales, making of by Aztecs, 271
Tomatoes, consumption of by Aztecs, 269
Tortilla, historical origin of, 269
Tropical fruits, consumption of by Aztecs, 269
Turkey meat, consumption by Aztecs, 269
Vanilla, use in chocolate drinks, 272
Water-fly eggs, eating of by Aztecs, 271
White worms, eating of by Aztecs, 269

FUNCTIONS OF THE CIHUACOATL

Generally, 161, 162

Army commander, Cihuacoatl serving as, 162
Criminal judicial officer, Cihuacoatl serving as, 161
Financial officer, Cihuacoatl serving as, 162
Role in Aztec official system, 161, 162
"Snake woman," designation of Cihuacoatl as, 162

FUNCTION OF THE TLATOANI

Generally, 161

Accountants, use in Aztec bureaucracy, 161
Administrative bureaucracy, types of officials working in, 161
Administrative records, keeping of, 161
Europeans, destruction of Aztec records by, 161
Frequent wars, purposes for engaging in, 161
Genealogical studies, use made of, 161
Judges, use of in Aztec society, 161
Land assignment records, keeping of, 161
Legislative process, control of by Tlatoani, 161
"Lordship" government, nature of, 161
Map making by Aztecs, 161
Scribes, keeping of land records by, 161
Tax collection by Aztecs, 161

FUSION OF IDEAS

Generally, 290, 291

Aztec religion, overriding theme of, 290
God of night, function of, 290
Huitzilopochtli (god of war), human sacrifice demanded by, 290
Human sacrifice, Aztecs' belief regarding, 290
Priests, explaining of natural phenomena by, 290, 291
Religious functions, direction of by priests, 291
Sacrifice stone, reward for dying on, 290
Slave captives, use of for human sacrifice, 290
Supreme responsibility, Aztecs' belief pertaining to, 290

GENERAL INDEX

GEOGRAPHY'S IMPACT ON THE AZTECS

Generally, 65, 67

Agricultural crops, types grown in Mexico, 65
Agricultural suitable lands, percentage of in Mexico, 65
Arid Mexican lands, percentage of, 65
Chevalier, description of Mexican climate conditions by, 65
Desert regions, presence in Mexico, 65
Diverse geography areas, presence in Mexico, 65
Earthquakes, occurrence of in Mexico, 65
God-relationships, effect of geography on, 65
Raid forests, presence in Mexico, 65
Social/cultural life of Aztecs, geography's impact on, 65
Trading in Aztec world, effect of geography on, 65
Volcanic activity, occurrence of in Mexico, 65
Weather conditions, unpredictability of in Mexico, 65

GEOGRAPHICAL INFLUENCE THEORY

Generally, 77, 79

Aristotle, advocation of determinist theory by, 77
Cultural advancement, effect of climate conditions on, 77
Determinist theory, explanation of, 77
Hagen's climatic theory, effect on Aztecs, 79
Herodutus, advocation of determinist theory by, 77
Hippocrates, advocation of determinist theory by, 77
Mayan ceremonial centers, abandonment of, 77
Religious practices, effect of weather condition on, 79
Temperate climate, advantage to civilizations, 77
Trading activity, effect of climate conditions on, 79

GENERAL INDEX

IMPORTANT CONSIDERATIONS

Generally, 4, 5

IMPORTANT RELIGIOUS CONSIDERATIONS IN AZTEC SOCIETY

Generally, 202, 203

INDIAN CLOTHING AND PERSONAL ATTIRE

INDUSTRY AND CRAFTSMANSHIP IN THE AZTEC EMPIRE

INTERNAL CRISIS IN AZTEC EMPIRE

Generally, 153, 154

Caso, description of Aztec farming problems by, 154
Cook, suggestions concerning Aztec population control, 154
Human sacrifices by Aztecs, estimated number of, 154
Human sacrifices, drain on Aztec resources caused by, 154
Increased infant mortality, decline of Aztec Empire   based
on, 154
Tribute system, dissatisfaction with, 154

INTERNAL STRIFE IN TOLTEC EMPIRE

Generally, 125, 126

Ancient splendor of Toltec Empire, disappearance of, 126
Decline/end of Toltec Empire, 125, 126
Dieties, religious conflict between, 125
Military groups, conflict with religious leaders, 125
Theocratic leaders, conflict with military groups by, 125

JOURNEY BEGANS (TO AZTEC CAPITOL)

Generally, 29, 31

Authority of Cortes, challenge to, 29
Aztec gifts by Spaniards, failure to stop invasion by use
of, 29
Aztec religious symbols, destruction of by Spaniards, 29
Aztec territorial dissatisfaction, Cortes' knowledge of, 31
Civilian Council, establishment of, 31
Diplomatic tactics used by Cortes against Aztecs, 31
Execution of dissenters by Cortes, 29
Flogging of dissenters by Cortes, 29
Idols, destruction by Cortes, 29
Scuttling of ships by Cortes, prevention of crew escape by,
29
Subversive techniques used by Cortes against Aztecs, 31
Totomac warriors, Cortes's alliance with, 31

JUDGES AND COURT OFFICIALS

Generally, 197, 198

Judicial favors, prohibitions against, 197
Magistrates, limited jurisdiction of, 197
Members of courts, number of, 197
Misconduct of judges, penalties imposed for, 197
Nezahualpilli, dictation of the hanging of a judge by, 197, 198
Payment of judges, methods of payments, 197
Types of Aztec courts, 197, 198

JUDICIAL SYSTEM OF ANCIENT MEXICO

Generally, 181-201

Disobey laws, Aztecs' reluctance to do so, 182
Firewood gathering, legal restrictions placed on, 181
Nezahualcoyotl, making of Texcoco laws by, 181

LA NOCHE TRISTE (Night of sorrows)

Generally, 40, 42

Atrocties committed during battles, grusome nature of, 40, 42
Aztec causeways, military battles on, 40
Aztecs, continuing battles by, 40, 42
Cuitlahuac, choosing of as Montezuma's successor, 40
Death of Montezuma by stoning, 40
Discontinuation of battle, death of Aztec chief as basis for, 42
Equipment lost during battle, 40
Horse losses during battle, 40
Human sacrifice, use of Prisoners of war for, 42
Military losses suffered by Spaniards, 40, 42
Montezuma, appeal for calm by, 40
Spanish-Aztec battle, scope and extent of, 40, 42
Spanish casualties suffered during battle, 40, 42
Spanish prisoners of war, use   for human sacrifice, 42
Spanish superior battle tactics, effect of, 42
Valuable treasuries casted into lake by Spaniards, 40

GENERAL INDEX

LAST ELECTED AZTEC EMPEROR

Generally, 158, 159

Administrative office space, 159
Artisans, presence of near Emperor, 159
Attendants, presence of near Emperor, 159
Audience with Emperor, council permission required, 159
Aztec Empire, enlargement of by Montezuma 159
Aztec Prince, high lifestyle enjoyed by, 159
Bodyguards, presence in Aztec society, 158
Clerics, presence of in Aztec society, 159
Commoner looking directly as Montezuma II, death based on, 159
Coronation of Montezuma II, mass executions during, 158, 159
Election procedures used by the Aztecs, 159
Judges, rooms provided for, 159
Military officers, promotion of, 159
Montezuma II as last elected Emperor of the Aztecs, 159
Protocol requirements when meeting with Montezuma II, 159
Seden chair, use by Emperor as means of travel, 159
Tax increases, imposition on conquered states, 159

LEGAL SYSTEM IN TENOCHTITLAN (ANCIENT MEXICO)

Generally, 193, 195

Appeal court proceedings, 194
Arrest procedures, 195
Continuous session of the court, 194
Court messengers, use of, 195
Emperor/judge panel, existence of, 194
Emperor, judicial authority vested in, 194, 195
General court proceedings, 194, 195
Jurisdiction of various courts, 194, 195
Location of courtrooms, 194
Lower courts, composition of, 193
Senior officials, conduct of court proceedings by, 194

LITERARY INCONSISTANCY

Generally, 322

Archaeological discovery in Great Temple, 322
Chavero, expression of pro-Aztec attitude by, 322
Cortes, eradication of favorable Aztec views by, 322
Great Temple, discovery, historical significance of, 322
Inaccurate reporting about Aztecs, 322
Scientific information discovered in Great Temple, 322

MAIZE (CORN) AND ITS IMPORTANCE

Generally, 267, 269

Beans, growing of by Aztecs, 269
Cacao growing by the Aztecs, 269
Domestication of corn by Aztecs, estimated time of, 267
Human sacrifice, starting of planting season by, 269
Hybrid corn, discovery of in South America, 267
Land distribution, cultivation of corn based on, 267
Maize cakes, eating of by Aztecs, 269
Peppers, growing of by Aztecs, 269
Squash, growing of by Aztecs, 269
Superstitious farming, disadvantage of, 269
Weather conditions needed for corn growing, 267
Yams, growing of by Aztecs, 269

MARKET AT TLATELOLCO

Generally, 234

Bread sales at marketplace, 234
Castillo, detailing of market practices by, 234
Clavijero, description of commercial activities by, 234
Cortes, description of Aztec marketplace practices by, 234
Division of trading areas, 234
Domestic animal sales at marketplace, 234
Fowl sale at marketplace, 234
Human waste sales as fertilizer, 234
Low-price sales as marketplace, 234
Market supervisor, need to consult, 234
Number of items at trading post, 234
Number of people using market, 234
Number of vendors at marketplace, 234
Organization of marketplace, description by Motolinia, 234
Planting seed sales at marketplace, 234

MATRICULA DE TRIBUTOS (TAXING SYSTEM)

Generally, 247

Charcoal, form of taxation on, 247
Lime, form of taxation on, 247
Lumber, form of taxation on, 247
Sharecroppers, presence of in Aztec Empire, 247
Taxing groups, description of, 247

MAYA

Generally, 96, 98

Areas dominated by, 96
Astronomical calculations made by Mayans, 96
Calendar system, establishment of by Mayans, 96
Complex writing system employed by the Mayans, 96
Engineering techniques used by the Mayans, 96
Mathematical calculations, importance of in Mesoamerica, 96
Mayans, architecture, development state of, 96
Mayan language, continued speaking of, 96
Mortuary pyramids, construction of by Mayans, 96
Pyramids, used of for religious ceremonies, 96
Suburban residents, existence of in Mayan society, 98
Tikal, size/population of city, 96
Time, calculation of to infinity by Mayans, 96
Underground construction, extent engage in by Mayans, 96

MAYAN INFLUENCE IN MESOAMERICA

Generally, 99, 101

City-state organizations, decline of Mayans based on, 99
Culture, high degree development of by Mayans, 99
Decadence as contributing factor to Mayan decline, 99
Decline of Mayan civilization, results following, 99
Ecological abuse, effect on Mayan decline, 99
Foreign invasions, effect on Mayan decline, 99
Human sacrifices, effect on Mayan decline, 99
Inferior architecture, decline of Mayan civilization based
on, 99
Military preoccupation, decline of Mayans based on, 99
Over-population, effect on Mayan decline, 99·
Scientific knowledge Mayan's development of, 99
Survivors of Mayan Empire, distribution of, 99

MESOAMERICA

Generally, 54

Artistic beauty, attachment to by Indians, 54
Astronomy, knowledge about possessed by Indians, 54
Books, use by Mesoamerican Indians, 54
Fatalistic religious beliefs, practice of by Mesoamerican Indians, 54
Hieroglyphic symbols, use of by Indians, 54
Human sacrifice, practice of by Mesoamericans, 54
Kirchoof study of Mesoamerican society, 54
Maize (corn) use of by Mesoamericans, 54
Mathematics, knowledge of possessed by Mesoamericans, 54
Poetry, understanding of by Mesoamericans, 54
Religious games, participation in by Mesoamericans, 54
Solar calendars, employment of by Mesoamericans, 54

MESOAMERICAN INDIANS

Generally, 346

Astronomy, Mesoamerican's knowledge about, 346
City-state political organizations, use of by Mesoamericans, 346
Civilized state of Mesoamericans, 346
Educational system, existence of in Mesoamerica, 346
Legal system, existence of in Mesoamerica, 346
Literature, Mesoamericans' ability to write, 346
Mathematics, Mesoamericans' knowledge of, 346
Medicine, Mesoamericans' knowledge of, 346
Portilla, description of Mexican valley by, 346
Social system in Mesoamerica, 346
Time, use of calendar to measure, 346
Urban areas, Mesoamerican Indians living in, 346
Writing, use of by Mesoamericas, 346

MESOAMERICA PRECLASSIC PERIOD

Generally, 89, 91

Agricultural activity, types of crops grown, 89
Clay figurines, societal imprints left by, 89
Digging stick, use as an early American farming tool, 91
Forest burning, clearing of farmland by, 91
Hieroglyphic writing, development of by early Americans, 91
Lagoon of Xochimilco, valuable water supplied by, 91
Natural springs, water supply derived from, 91
Nomadic tribes, early existence of, 91
Poor farming conditions, food shortages caused by, 91
Pyramids, construction of by early Americans, 91
Rise and fall of Mesoamerican cultures, 89, 91
Rivers, water supplies derived from, 91
Temples, construction of by Mesoamericans, 91
Wall murals, painting of by Mesoamericans, 91

MESSENGERS OF DEATH

Generally, 21

Archers, number in Cortes' army, 21
Aztec Empire, Cortes' ignorance about, 21
Black servants, presence of in Cortes' invasion of Mexico, 21
Cannons, number in Cortes' invading army, 21
Cortes' invasion of Mexico, contents of entourage, 21
Cuban Indians, number in Cortes' invasion of Mexico, 21
Dogs, presence in Cortes' invasion of Mexico, 21
Gulf coast seaport, establishment of, 21
Horses, number in Cortes' invading army, 21
La Antiqua, moving of new settlement to, 21
Mayan interpreters, Cortes' use of, 21
Military strength of Cortes's invading army, 21
Musketeers, number in Cortes's army, 21
Vera Cruz, foundering of by Spaniard, 21

GENERAL INDEX

MEXICAN HIGHLANDS

Generally, 67

Cortes' unsuccessful attempt to climb volcanic mountain, 67
Geographical area covered by Sierra mountain, 67
Inactive volcano, presence of in Mexico, 67
Interpretation of volcanic eruptions by Aztecs, 67
Iztaccihuati (the lady in white), religious significance of, 67
Poppcatepeti (smoking mountain), religious significance of, 67
Sierra Madre mountains, importance of in Mexico, 67
Sulfur search for gunpowder source, mountain climbing to obtain, 67

MICHHOACAN SOJOURN

Generally, 121, 122

Mountain ranges, hazards presented by, 121, 122
Portable shrine carried by the Aztecs, 122
Tarascan Indians, resistance to Aztecs by, 121, 122
Uncivilized Aztecs, description of Aztecs as, 122

MIDDLE AND LOWER CLASSES

Generally, 165, 166

Debtors, inclusion of as lower class, 166
Disabled lower class, selling of children into slavery by, 166
Drudgery work performed by lower class, 165, 166
Exclusion of lower class from full participation in society, 165, 166
Lower class land ownership, absence of, 165
Middle class, groups included in, 165
Road building by lower class, 166
Slavery, selling of children into, 166
Temple/palace building by lower class, 166
Zorita, description of pre-Columbian life by. 165

MILITARY ORGANIZATION OF THE AZTEC ARMY

Generally, 255

Army recruits, shaving-head requirement, 255
Body ornaments, combat efficiency indicated by, 255
Cooks, presence of in Aztec army, 255
Crew-cut hair rules, 255
Engineers, presence of in Aztec army, 255
Healers, presence of in Aztec army, 255
Military officers, carrying feathered standards by, 255
Musicians, presence of in Aztec army, 255
Off-the-land living by the Aztec army, 255
Porters, presence of in Aztec army, 255
Purpose at Aztec wars, 255
Tribute exacted from adversaries, nature of, 255

MISCELLANEOUS AZTEC PENALTIES

Generally, 185, 187

Abortion, death penalty based on, 185
Common thief, lifetime of slavery based on, 185, 186
Disobedient children, selling into slavery based on, 185
Illegal corn harvesting, death penalty based on, 187
Kidnapping, slavery status based on, 185
Maize (corn) thief, death penalty imposed for, 187
Marketplace robbery, death penalty imposed for, 187
Poor/needy, planting of spare crops for, 187
Public fighting, slavery status based on, 185
Roadside planting of corn for poor, 187
Unpaid gambling debt, slavery status based on, 187
Violent stealing, death penalty imposed for, 185
Warehouse thieves, punishment meted to, 187

GENERAL INDEX

MORE IMAGINATIVE TALES

Generally, 318, 319

Appeasing gods, human sacrifice for purpose of, 319
Aztec obsession with human sacrifice, 319
Extravagant claims about Aztec misconduct, 318
Mass slaughter by the Aztecs, extravagant claims concerning, 318
Onderdonk, doubts about number of human sacrifices, 319
Prescott, estimated number of prisoners sacrifices, 318
Torquemada, estimated number of human sacrifices, 318

MUSIC AND DANCE IN THE AZTEC WORLD

Generally, 283, 285, 286

Aztec drums, description of, 285
Battle drums, use in Aztec battles, 285, 286
Bells, recent discovery of, 285
Brides, method of entry into wedding ceremony, 285
Drums, recent discovery of, 285
Flutes, recent discovery of, 285
Incense burning at end of wedding ceremony, 285
Mendieta, description of Aztec drums by, 285
Musical flute sounds, Marti's description of, 285
Professional entertainers, use to entertain the nobility, 285
Pure harmony, Aztec's familiarity with, 285
Rattlers, recent discovery of, 285
Religious ceremonies, song/dance during, 283, 285
Rubber-tipped sticks, use in drum beating, 285
Shell trumpets, recent discovery of, 285
Trumpets, number used in Aztec concerts, 286
Wedding ceremony, song/dance during, 283
Whistles, recent discovery of, 285

MYTH OF CREATION

Generally, 210, 212, 214

Birds, conversion of man into, 212
Cataclysmic forces, destruction of historical areas by, 212
Deity sacrifices, motion of sun resumed upon, 214
Five (5) ages in history of mankind, listing of, 212
Floods, destruction of world by, 212
Hurricane winds, destruction of historical areas by, 212
Monkeys, turning of man into, 212
Motionless sun, Aztec's belief regarding, 214
Ometecuhtli Omeihust (the Duality Rulers) creation myth concerning, 210, 212
Rain/celestial fire, destruction of earth by, 212

NATURE OF AZTEC LAW

Generally, 188, 190

Adultery, death penalty imposed for, 190
Aristocracy death penalty, drowning as means of execution, 190
Drowning, death penalty carried by, 190
Equal enforcement of Aztec law, 188
Execution of ruler's sons, involvement with women as basis for, 190
Laborer's public intoxication, punishment for, 190
Merchants, separate court for, 188
Public intoxication, death penalty imposed on noblemen, 190
Severity of punishment, class status as determining, 190
Upper class, separate court for, 188

GENERAL INDEX

NORTHERN/SOUTHERN PRE-COLUMBIAN CULTURIES

Generally, 52

OLMEC'S EARLIER CONTRIBUTIONS

Generally, 91, 93

GENERAL INDEX

PEOPLE IN THE SUN

Generally, 223, 225, 226, 229

African human sacrifices, purpose of, 226
Arrogant attitude of the Aztecs, 223
Aztecs' obsession with human sacrifices, 226
Carthage siege, human sacrifice during, 226
Chosen people, Aztec beliefs regarding, 223
Christian prisoners, sacrifice of by Romans, 226
Cult superiority, Aztec beliefs regarding, 225
Excessive tribute demands, 225
Homage to god, Aztec practice pertaining to, 225
New Year festival, human sacrifices during, 226
Old Testament, description of human sacrifices in, 225
Romans, mass human sacrifices practiced by, 226
Slaves, sacrifice while alive, 226
Sun movements, lack of knowledge about, 225
Syrian priests, human sacrifices performed by, 226
Texcoco residents, rejection of human sacrifices by, 225
War-aggressions, justification for, 223

PLIGHT OF AGRICULTURAL WORKERS

Generally, 166, 168

Aztec promotional system, advantage of, 166
Farmers and urban residents, differences between, 168
Merit promotions, existence in Aztec society, 168
Middle class, groups included in, 168
Nepotism, practice of in Aztec Empire, 168
Percentage of farmers in Aztec Empire, 166
Spanish destruction of Tenochtitlan, consequences of, 168
Special schools for upper class children, existence of, 168
Sufficiency of farm products in Aztec Empire, 166
Urban-dwelling farmers in Aztec Empire, 166

POST CLASSIC PERIOD

POTTERY/CERAMICS AND CRAFTSMANSHIP

PRACTICE OF MEDICINE IN AZTEC WORLD

Generally, 306, 308

Baths, use by Aztecs as a healing art, 306
Blood-letting, use by Aztecs as a healing art, 306
Dental treatment rendered by Aztex dentists, 306
Effectiveness of Aztec physicians, 306
Fevers, treatment administered to control, 306
Hallucinogen drugs, use by Aztecs, 308
Indian healers, practice of medicine by, 306
Materials used in teeth-cleaning procedures, 306
Plants/herbs/roots, use in healing processes, 306
Surgery, use by Aztecs in healing process, 306
Teeth extraction by Aztec dentists, 306
Types of hallucinogen drugs used by Aztecs, 308
Venereal diseases, thoughts of Aztecs about cause, 306

PRECLASSICAL CULTURES OF MESOAMERICA

Generally, 93, 94

Agriculture, limited use in preclassical period, 94
Ceremonial centers, construction of by preclassical
societies, 94
God, appearance of at Ticoman, 94
Hierolyphic writing, use of by preclassical societies, 94
Mathematical calculations, performance of during
preclassical period, 94
New farming techniques, use during preclassical period, 94
Olmec civilization, timeframe of existence, 93
Organized societies, existence of in preclassical period,
93, 94
Peaceful nature of early societies, 93, 94
Platform at Cuicuilco, historical significance of, 94
Pottery, manufacture of in preclassical period, 94
Pyramids, building of in preclassical period, 94
Superior cultures, appearance in preclassical period, 94
Urban centers, establishment of during preclassical period,
94
Volcanic lava, important monument buried under, 94
War, non-use of by certain Mesoamerican people, 93, 94

GENERAL INDEX

PRE-COLUMBIAN CIVILIZATIONS

Generally, 50, 52

PRE-COLUMBIANS GOVERNMENTS/RELIGIOUS

Generally, 57, 59

PYRAMIDS OF THE SUN AND MOON

Generally, 101, 103

Area covered by Pyramid, 101
Avenue right angle layout system, 103
Causeway Micaotli (Street of the Dead), length of, 103
Ceremonial center, location of, 103
Construction crew, size of, 101
Height of Pyramid, 101
Polychroatic painting, use in temple decoration, 103
Pyramid of the Sun, area covered by, 101
Pyramid steps, religious significance of, 103
Size of Pyramid, 101
Stairways, assorted decoration on, 103
Symmetry in original Pyramid construction, changes in, 103
Tile, use in Pyramid construction, 101
Unsuccessful restoration of Pyramid, 101, 103

RACIAL DISTRIBUTION IN MODERN MEXICO

Generally, 63, 65

Aztec language (Nahuatl), modern use of, 65
Caucasian group, percentage in modern Mexico, 63
Indian racial groups, percentage in modern Mexico, 65
Indigenous Indian language, percentage of Indians speaking, 65
Linguistic characteristics, racial classification based on, 63
Mayan language, number of people speaking, 65
Mestizo racial group, percentage in modern Mexico, 63
Mixtec language, number of people speaking, 65
Otomi language, number of people speaking, 65
Spanish language, percentage of people speaking, 65

RAMIREZ, CONDEX

Generally, 120, 121

Aztecs, time of arrival in central highlands, 120
Condex Ramirez, arrival time of groups based on, 120
Nahuas, time of arrival in Mexico, 120
Nahuas, time of departure from original homeland, 120
Pan American Highway (present), Aztec travel on or near, 121
Possible travel route of Aztecs, 120, 121

RELIGIOUS RITES

Generally, 219, 221

Children sacrifice by Aztecs, 221
Cooked human flesh, eating of by Aztec priests, 221
Corn dough, use in religious ceremony, 219
Corn flour, footprints of gods in, 219
Idol, sprankling of blood on, 221
Maiden sacrifice, 221
Trumpets, playing religious ceremonies, 219, 221
Types of people sacrificed, 221

RESULT OF COLUMBIAN EXCHANGE

Generally, 358, 359

Crosby, description of Columbian exchange by, 358, 359
Europe, introduction of metal from America into, 359
Gold, Spanish extraction of, 359
Humble, description of silver trade by, 359
Silver glut, effect on European markets, 359
Silver, Spanish extraction of from New World, 359

RETURN OF SPANISH INVADERS

Generally, 42, 43

Aztec army members, devastation of by smallpox, 42, 43
Aztec immune system weakness, spread of smallpox based on, 43
Battle supplies, furnishing of to Spaniards by Tlaxcalans, 42
Boat-building assistance by Tlaxcalans, value to Spaniards, 42
Hatred of Aztecs by Tlaxcalans, Spanish cultivation of, 42
Smallpox plague, devastation of Aztecs by, 42,

GENERAL INDEX

SCIENCE AND TECHNOLOGY IN THE AZTEC WORLD

Generally, 304, 306

Aztec mathematics, adoption of zero concept in, 304
Comparison between Spanish and Aztec armies, 304
Cortes, battle tactics used by, 304
Mayan hieroglyphics, descriptions contained in, 304
Mayan writings, subjects covered by, 304
Smallpox epidemic, defeat of Aztecs caused by, 304
Spanish horses, pathological fears caused by, 304
Wheel, limitation of use by Aztecs, 304

SCIENTIFIC VIEWS ON ORIGIN AN EARLY AMERICANS

Generally, 88

Agriculture, discovery of techniques by early Americans, 88
Asian origin an early Americans, theory concerning, 88
Beans, cultivation of by Indians, 88
Cassava, cultivation of by early Americans, 88
Chili peppers, cultivation of by early Americans, 88
Fire, use of by early Americans, 88
Hunting skills of early Americans, 88
Maize (corn), cultivation of by early Americans, 88
Neolithic age, advancement of early Americans, beyond, 88
Peanuts, cultivation of by early Americans, 88
Potatoes, cultivation of by early Americans, 88
Spears, use in hunting animals, 88
Squash, cultivation of by early Americans, 88
Stone-tipped lances, use of in hunting animals, 88
Weapons, type used by early Americans, 88

SEARCH FOR PAST IN MESOAMERICA

Generally, 59, 61

Age of Mesoamerica societies, scientific relevation about, 61
Archeological records, Mesoamericn historicl knowledge contained in, 59
Architecural skills, origin of in Mesoamerica, 61
Aztec society, exclusive concentration on, 59
Chroniclers, recording of Mesoamerican history by, 59
Ethnological studies, knowledge revealed by, 61
Inheritance of skills by Indians, 61
Mysteries of Mesoamerican society, revelation of, 61
Non-Aztec society, overlooking of my Europeans, 59
Religious Friars, recording of Mesoamerican history by, 59
Scientific investigations, knowledge about Mesoamerican gained by, 61

SEARCH FOR THE TRUTH

Generally, 316, 318

Aztec Mexican roles, misconceptions about, 316, 318
Blood-thirty priests, bad images of, 318
Cannibalism, image projected to Aztecs, 318
Death, preoccupation of Aztecs with, 318
European historians, description of ancient Indians by, 316
Mesoamerican civilization, historical descriptions of, 316, 318
Microcosm of ancient America, Aztec society as, 316
North American historians, description of ancient Indians by, 316
Skull racks, stories about, 318
Stuart, description of Aztecs by, 316

SEVERITY OF THE AZTEC LEGAL SYSTEM

Generally, 182, 183

Aztec life, predomination of laws over, 182
Common-law principles, use of in Aztec legal system, 182
Court decisions, release to public by judge, 182
Customs/traditions, Aztec laws based on, 182
Death penalty, use of in criminal cases, 183
Familiarity with legal system, necessity for, 182
Judges, impartial enforcement of laws by, 182
Judicial decisions, release to public by judges, 182
Knowledge of laws by Aztecs, necessity for, 182
Memorizing Aztec laws, necessity for, 182
Unchanged nature of Aztec laws, 182
Written legal code, absence of, 182

SHORT GLORY OF ITALIAN MIDDLE EAST TRADE

Generally, 8, 9

Asian trade by Italian merchants, 8
Black Sea, use of by Italian merchants, 8
Braun, description of Mediterranean decline by, 9
Commander, description of Mediterranean decline by, 9
Cotton cloth trade carried on by Italian merchants, 8
Egyptian trade carried on by Italian merchants, 8
Expansion of Ottoman Empire, effect in Italian trade, 8
Genoa merchants, trading in Middle East by, 8
Jewelry trade carried on by Italian merchants, 8
Muslin merchants, demanding of tolls by, 8
Ottoman Turk Army, interruption of European trade by, 8
Perfume trade carried on by Italian merchants, 8
Porcelain trade carried on by Italian merchants, 8
Portuguese trading centers, emergence of, 9
Silk trade carried on by Italian merchants, 8
Spanish trade centers, emergence of, 9
Sultan Mehemmed II, capture of Constantinoble by, 8
Syrian trade carried on by Italian merchants, 8
Venice merchants, trading with Middle East by, 8

SLAVERY IN AZTEC SOCIETY

Generally, 176, 177

Categories of slaves in Aztec society, 176
Children of slaves, freedom granted to on birth, 177
Criminal conviction, slavery based on, 176
Debtor status, slavery based on, 176
Emancipation of slaves, practice pertaining to, 176
Family type slavery, 176
Marriage of pregnant slave by owner, effect of, 176
Mistreatment of slaves, judicial punishment for, 176
Ownership of slave by slaves in Aztec society, 177
Personal property status of slaves, 178
Poverty, acceptance of slavery because of, 176
Pregnant slave, freedom bsed on marriage to owner, 176
Prisoner of war as slaves, 176
Prisoner's stay of execution, slavery based on, 176
Property-ownership by slaves, 178
Public debt, slavery based on, 176
Purchase of freedom by slave, 176
Recalcitrant slave, authorized punishment for, 177
Resale of slave, slave's consent required, 177
Restitution slavery, existence of in Aztec society, 176
Runaway slaves, devises used to prevent, 177
Selling of slaves by parents, 176
Slave contracts, contents of, 177
Slave market, existence of in Aztec society, 176
Slave sacrifice in Aztec society, 176
Voluntary slavery, existence of, 177
Wooden yokes, use to prevent slave escape, 177

SLAVE TRADE IN MEDIEVAL WORLD

Generally, 7

Egyptians, specialized use of slaves by, 7
Geno, excessive number of slaves in, 7
Gift of slaves, laws permitting, 7
Hart, observation of slave trade by, 7
Italian slave trade, presence of, 7
Northern Europe, use of slaves in, 7
Racial purity, doubt cast on by Hart, 7
Venice slave trade, extent of, 7

GENERAL INDEX

SOUTHERN PRESPECTIVE

Generally, 70, 72

Animal life in tropical forest, 72
Humid temperature in tropical forest, 70
Plant life, abundance of, 72
Rainfall, amount falling in tropical forest, 72
Tropical forest, presence of in Mexico, 70
Tropical low lands, presence of in Mexico, 70

SPANISH EMPIRE DEVELOPMENT

Generally, 343

Africa, Spanish attack on, 343
Expansive ambitions of Spanish Empire, 343
Italy, Spanish attack on, 343
Merchant class, control of Spain by, 343
Military technology, Spanish development of, 343
Perry, description of European domination policies by, 343
Religious pretext, Cruel wars conducted under, 343
Religious zeal, existence of in Spain, 343

SPANISH JUSTIFICATION FOR MISTREATMENT OF INDIANS

Generally, 354, 356

Christianity, mistreatment of Indians based on, 354, 356
Divine service, Spanish mistreatment of Indians based on, 354, 356
Gold-seeking, new world exploration based on, 356
Human sacrifice, Spanish opposition to, 356
Idolatrous worship, Spanish opposition to, 356
Spanish-Aztec cultures, clash between, 356

SPANISH RESPONSE

Generally, 11, 12

Albornoz, description of Reconquista by, 11
Crown on Aragon, extention of political control by, 11
English trade carried on by Portuguese/Spanish, 12
Unified Spanish government, expansion of commercial trade based on, 11

SPECULATION ON ORIGIN OF EARLY AMERICANS

Generally, 85-88

African/Olmec art, early presence of Mesoamerica, 87, 88
Amerindians as descendents of Babylonians, inference concerning, 87
Asian characteristics of Mesoamerican, recognization of by Humboldt, 87
Babylonians, Amerindians as descendants from, 87
"Bearded white men" theory, evidence of European contact based on, 87
Canoe, African origin of word, 87, 88
Chinese origin of early Americans, 87
Columbus' New World contact with Black traders, 87
Gladwin's Mediterranean contact theory, 87
Hrdilcka's Asian origin theory, 87
"Lost Atlantis" theory, Spense's thoughts about, 87
Lost Ten Tribes of Isreal, Kingsbrough's conclusions about, 87
Pacific Ocean travel by Mesoamericans, theory about, 87
Polynesian origin of Mesoamericans, theory about, 87
Prehistoric Hueyapan head, Black race characteristics of, 87
Smoking tobacco, African origin of, 88
Sweet potatoes, African origin of, 88
Uhle's theory about beginning of Indian culture, 87
von Humboldt, recognization of Asian characteristic by, 87
Wiener's shipwrecked theory, Indian's presence in America explained by, 87

SPICES AND MERCHANTILISM

Generally, 7, 8

Italian spice trade, extent of, 7
Kahn, visit to by Europeans, 7, 8
Marco Polo, service to Chinese ruler by, 7
Nocola, visit to far east by, 7
Polo, description of Far East by, 8
Polo's book, use by Columbus on first trip, 8
Salted beef, preservation by means of, 7
Smoked meat, preservation by means of, 7
Spices, use of in meat preservation, 7
Venetian merchants, visits to China by, 7

STRUGGLE FOR SUPREMACY BY AZTECS

Generally, 131, 132

Chichimecs settlements, location of, 131
Culhua, emergence of as dominating force, 131
Early settlement patterns, time of, 131
Fortification used by early Aztecs, 131
Lake Texcomo, emergence of Aztec nation near, 131
Peaceful period, arrival of Aztecs during, 131
Water supplies, adequacy of, 131

SUN STONE (AZTEC CALENDAR)

Generally, 296, 297

Archbishop, ordered burning of sun stone by, 296
Aztec cosmological views depicted on sun stone, 297
Characters depictd on sun stone, 297
Mathematics, advanced level depicted on sun stone, 297
Size of sun stone, 296
Weight of sun stone, 296

SWAMP RECLAMATION

Generally, 265, 267

Aerial radar survey, canal network revealed by, 265
Artificial islands, construction of by Aztecs, 265
Aztec underwater construction techniques, 265
Dikes, use to control floods, 265
Drainage ditches, use in swamp reclamation project, 265
Freidel, description of Mayan commercial activities by, 267
Land platforms, construction from lake mud, 265
Mayans, types of agriculture practiced by, 265
Schele, description of Mayan commercial activities by, 267

TALES OF WONDER AND MYSTERY

Generally, 341, 342

Art of war, Spanish acquiring from Visigoths, 342
Chinese city, tales about, 341
Golden palace, tales about, 341
Invaders of Spain, nations invading Spain, 342
Land ownership concept, Roman origin of, 342
Mare Tenebroum, tales about, 341
Medieval romanticism, Spaniards guided by, 341
Monster tales, effect on Aztec conquest, 341
Rose colored pear, tales about, 341
Spanish arrogance in conquest of Mexico, 341
Violent occupation of Spain, effect on Spanish mentality, 341

TEMPLE/PYRAMIDS

Generally, 299, 301

Building painting, geometric design of, 299
Cement, use by Aztecs in building construction, 299
Cycle for reconstructing pyramids, 299
Erosion, pyramids constructed to resist, 299
Hewn stones, use in temple/pyramid construction, 299
Outside stairs without bannisters, 299
Vertical wall construction by Aztecs, 299

TEMPLE OF SACRIFICES

Generally, 146, 148

Agriculture god, importance of, 146
Causeways, location of in walled city, 146
God of the air, dedication of temple to, 148
Intercity construction, buildings constructed in, 146, 148
Painting of buildings, color scheme, 148
Palace of Montezuma, sacred nature of, 148
Pyramid-temple, location of, 146, 148
Sacrifice stone, placing of, 148
Tenochtitlan, description of by Cortes, 148
War god, importance of, 148
Wooden racks, skulls of sacrifice victims displayed on, 148

TENOCHTITLAN (AZTEC CAPITOL)

Generally, 145, 146

GENERAL INDEX

TENOCHTITLAN ENTRY BY CORTES

Generally, 33-38

Arrest of Montezuma by Cortes, 36
Aztec defenses, study of by Spaniard, 36
Causeways, clogging of by greeting Aztec, 33
Comparison of gods by Montezuma, 35, 36
Cortes' mistress, unsuccessful interpretation attempt made by, 35
Courtyard, entry of Cortes and Montezuma into, 35
Divine emissaries from heaven, Aztec belief regarding, 35
"Feathered serpent, honor accorded to, 35
Food, furnishing of by Aztecs, 35
God of Quetzalcoatl, religious significance of, 35
"God like character of Cortes, Aztec belief regarding, 35, 36
Greeting residents, Cortes' entry into Aztec capitol impeaded by, 33, 35
Indian prophesy on return of god Quetzalcoatl, time for return, 35, 36
Indians, number of allied to Cortes, 33
Learning god, Quetzalcoatl as, 35
Lodging for Spaniards, furnishing of by Aztecs, 35
Lord Axayacatl's palace, Cores' entry into, 35
Montezuma's greeting entourage, manner of dress by, 33
Palace meeting between Cortes and Montezuma, 35
Patron of agriculture, god Quetzalcoatl as, 35
Patron of arts, god Quetzalcoatl as, 35
Patron of science god Quetzalcotl as, 35
Physical description god Quezalcoatl, 35
Puppet state of Montezuma, relegation to, 36, 37
Roads, clogging of by greeting residents, 33
Sierra Medra mountain march, exposure of Cortes during force march, 36
Spanish army, number Aztec capitol, 33
Spanish physical appearance, similarity with Quetzalcoatl, 35, 36
Theological justification of invasion by Cortes, 35
Untouchability of Montezuma, 35

TEOTIHUACAN

Generally, 101

Clay figurines, discovery of in former Teotihuacan, 101
Commercial Empire, significance of Teotihuacan as, 101
Cylindricl pots, discovery of in former Teotihuacan, 101
Location of Teotihuacan, 101
Obsidian mines, existence of, 101
Trading posts, existence of in Teotihuacan, 101
Pyramids, ceremonial use put to, 101
Urban center, development of in Teotihuacan, 101

GENERAL INDEX

TEOTIHUACAN INFLUENCE

Generally, 103-106

Apartments, land area covered by, 105
Aztecs, Teotihuacan influence exerted on, 106
Bernal, opinion about the beginning of Teotihuaca, 105
Eagles, painting of as religious symbols, 103
Elite class, composition of, 105
Estimated population of Teotihuacca, 105
Farming as principal occupation of Teotihuacan, 105
Fertility rites decorations on buildings, 105
Great Compound (marketplace), location of, 105
Grid-type street layout, 105
Indian art, religious significance of, 105
Jaguar, painting of as religious symbols, 103
Religious deities, painting of, 105
Snakes, painting of as religious symbols, 103
Teotihuacan architecture, effect on succeeding Indian
civilizations, 105, 106
Teotihuacan art, effect on succeeding Indian civilizations,
105
Teotihuacan commercial center, time of existence, 105
Teotihuacan housing units, description of, 105
Teotihuacan religion, effect on succeeding Indian
civilizations, 105, 106
Warriors, painting as religious symbols, 105
Windowless apartments, existence of in Teotihuacan, 105

GENERAL INDEX

TLAXCALAN EXPERIENCE

Generally, 31, 33

Appeasement of gods, human sacrifice used for, 33
Aztec ambassadors, role played by, 33
Bread, gift by Aztecs as token of friendship, 33
Cotton cloth, gift by Aztecs as token of friendship, 33
Defeat of Tlaxcalns by the Spaniards, 31
Deceitful Cortes greeting, slaughter of Aztecs at, 31, 33
Gold plates, gift by Aztecs as token of friendship, 33
Human sacrifice, ordering of by Montezuma, 33
Number of Indians slaughtered at deceitful meeting, 31
Spanish army cruality, extent of, 33
Spanish permission to enter city, false belief as basis for, 33
Tlaxcalan army, number contained in, 31
Turkeys, gift by Aztecs as token of friendship, 33
Unnecessary slaughter by Spaniards, 31, 33
Warriors, numbers in engagements, 31, 33
Wine, gift to Spaniards as token of friendship, 33

TOLTEC EMPIRE

Generally, 122, 124

Ce Acatl Topiltzin (a/k/a Quetzalcoatl), expansion of Toltec borders by, 122
Collapse of Toltec Empire, entry of Aztecs upon, 122
Efficient land cultivation by Toltecs, 122
Human religious sacrifice engaged in by Toltecs, 122
Mesoamerica, types of influence exerted by Toltecs, 122
Mexcoatl, ruling of Toltec by, 122
Rise of Tolec Empire, time of, 122
Tula as sacred capitol of Toltec, 122

GENERAL INDEX

TRADE AND COMMERCE IN ANCIENT MEXICO

Generally, 232

Administrative bureaucracy, existence of in ancient Mexico, 232
Aztec centers of commerce, importance of, 232
City infrastructure, development of by Aztecs, 232
Clavijero, description of Aztec trade practice by, 232
Cotton trade carried on by the Aztecs, 232
Fish trade carried on by the Aztecs, 232
Immigrants, number coming to Aztec capitol, 232
Maize (corn) trade carried on by Aztecs, 232
Negotiating trade skills of the Aztecs, 232
Stone/lime trade carried on by the Aztecs, 232
Trade system, establishment of by Aztecs, 232
Wood trade carried on by the Aztecs, 232

TRANSFORMATION OF A GOD

Generally, 288, 290

Beliefs of other peoples, acceptance of by Aztecs, 288
Bloody religion, establishment of by Aztecs, 288
Cataclysmic forces, Aztecs' beliefs regarding, 288
Custodial god, direction of efforts by, 290
Deities of other peoples, acceptance of by Aztecs, 288
Fatalistic view of life held by Aztecs, 288
Huitzilopochli (sun-god), demanding of human sacrifices by, 290

TRIBUNE OF THE EIGHTY (80) DAYS' SPEAKING

Generally, 195, 197

Advisory role of tribune, 197
Composition of tribunal, 197
Debates before the tribunal, 195
Decision-making authority of the tribunal, 197
Jurisdiction of the tribunal, 197
Military court, jurisdiction of, 197
Nobility court, jurisdiction of, 197

WAR AND TRIBUTARY (TAX) SYSTEM

Generally, 251, 253

Aztec army raid, purpose of, 251
Battle dress of Aztec warriors, 253
Draft age of Aztec men, 251
Massing of warriors by priests, 253
Military draft age of men, 251
Pre-battle religious ceremonies, nature of, 253
Priests, military planning by, 253
Raw materials, use of military raids to obtain, 251
Self-mutilation, pre-battle types engaged in, 253
Soldier compensation, method of payment, 253
Tribal elders, military planning by, 253

WAR AS INSTRUMENT OF STATE

Generally, 250, 251

Absentee landlords, noblemen as, 250
Confederation members, role in Aztec schemes, 250
Food storage preserves, absence of, 251
Governmental organization, military theocracy as nature of, 250
Hassig, description of Aztec control by, 251
Insufficient transportation system in Aztec Empire, 251
Land control, warlike measurers used for, 250
Military theocracy, Aztec Empire as, 250

WISE MEN

Generally, 291, 293

Astronomers, wise men acting as, 293
Chronology of time, wise men's expertise in, 293
Counselors, wise men acting as, 291
Honesty, teaching of by wise men, 291
Interpreters, wise men acting as, 291
Intuitive truth, beliefs of Aztecs regarding, 291
Kindness, teaching of by wise men, 291
Logic, use by wise men to solve problems, 291
Mirror, use by wise men as teaching technique, 291
Origin of man, beliefs regarding, 291
Philosophers, wise men act as, 291
Psychologists, wise men acting as, 291
Public morals, protection of by wise men, 293
Teachers, wise men action as, 291
Tlamatinime (wise men), regard afforded to, 291
Ubiquitous characteristics of Ometeotl, 293

WORK OF SAHAGUN

Generally, 332, 335

Art, books about Aztecs covering, 332
Authentic nature of Shagun's historical data, 332
Botany, book about Aztecs covering, 332
Codex Matritens, Spanish version of, 332
Laurentian Library of Florence, historical documents
contained in, 332
Literature, books about Aztecs covering, 332
Medicine, books about Aztec medicine covering, 332
Royal Academy, historical data located in, 332
Sahagun's method of compiling historical data, 332
Spanish Church, suppression of historical data by, 332
Spanish government, destruction of historical data by, 332
Zoology, books about Aztecs covering, 332